PHONE CALLS
FROM *THE FUTURE*

FUTURE HISTORY & ANCIENT HISTORY
FROM THE PEOPLE WHO WERE THERE

THROUGH

ROBERT SHAPIRO

OTHER BOOKS BY ROBERT SHAPIRO

EXPLORER RACE SERIES

SHAMANIC SECRETS SERIES

All print books also available as ebooks plus two on ebooks only
Explorer Race Combined Books 1 & 2 and Nice Little Stories

To order print books, visit LightTechnology.com, Amazon.com, or your favorite bookstore.
eBooks are available from Amazon, Apple iTunes, Google Play, Barnes & Noble, and Kobo.

PHONE CALLS
FROM *THE* FUTURE

FUTURE HISTORY & ANCIENT HISTORY
FROM THE PEOPLE WHO WERE THERE

THROUGH

ROBERT SHAPIRO

Light Technology PUBLISHING

For information about special discounts for bulk purchases, please contact Light Technology Publishing Special Sales at 1-800-450-0985 or publishing@LightTechnology.com.

ISBN-13: 978-1-62233-096-6
ebook ISBN: 978-1-62233-818-4

Light Technology Publishing, LLC
Phone: 1-800-450-0985
1-928-526-1345
Fax: 928-714-1132
PO Box 3540
Flagstaff, AZ 86003
LightTechnology.com

CONTENTS

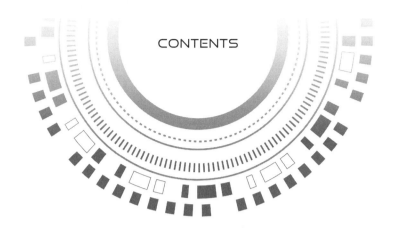

PART TWO:
ANCIENT HISTORY

CHAPTER TWENTY-ONE: TEOTIHUACÁN: A STIMULATING INVITATION..............................271

Historian and Future Teotihuacán Visitor • October 10, 2019

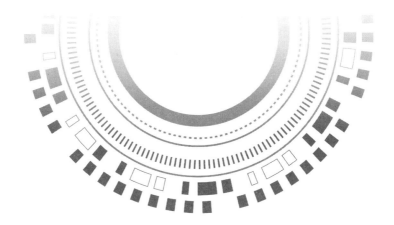

FOREWORD

Isis

This is Isis. The purpose of this book is to bring to your awareness who is involved, what is going on, and where things are going on. The purpose is ultimately to show you how much alike you are to beings from other places and other times and to show you other ways of surviving, living, coming, and going.

Most of you won't resonate with the entire book, but many of you will resonate with some portions — sometimes big portions, sometimes small portions. You'll be reading something and it will feel like whoever wrote it is writing directly to you about your life right now.

The purpose of the book is to let you know that you are important. And ultimately, it is like a personal note to you and every other you who reads it.

Goodlife.

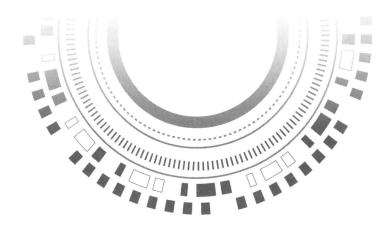

INTRODUCTION

Zoosh

AUGUST 3, 2022

All right, this is Zoosh. You all have an opportunity to create the world you want, and it's going to be up to you to decide. What world do you want? Do you want a world of people saying, "Oh dear, is this going to happen?" or do you want the world that is largely painted in this book?

You will find a lot of good possibilities. Granted, they're not all perfect for Earth, but you can use them as stimulation for your imagination and create the world you want for yourself, your family, your friends, your loved ones, and everyone else on Earth to the best of your ability. You don't have to do magic. You just need to be able to use your imagination or picture it. It doesn't have to be in words. You don't have to say "Well, I'd like this," and then you can't think of anything.

Imagine a wonderful place that you would like to be — not temporarily but permanently. What if life was so wonderful that people would want to live for more than 100 years, maybe 200 years? Don't put any limits on what you imagine. Remember that the original creation of all kinds of wonderful inventions you're enjoying these days, not the least of which is different forms of transportation, all started with somebody's imagination.

Imagination precedes creation. And you can create. I give you permission. Give yourself permission to create a world you would love to live in.

Goodlife.

PART
ONE:
FUTURE
HISTORY

MINING ON THE MOON

Doc

MAY 15, 2019

Greetings.

Greetings.

Some people on Earth are striving to do something that has been the subject of science fiction for years: create a community on the Moon. People are working on it now in my time. There is also an individual who wants to colonize Mars, but realistically speaking, the Moon can be used first as a training ground. From there, perhaps they can try to get to Mars.

I want to talk about this a little bit because it will be done. I am not going to discuss what has been done in the past or what's happening in your time other than to mention that there is no question that mining is happening on the Moon and that most of the people who are doing the mining now are not Earth people. I will

3

Image 1.1. NASA photo of the Moon's Giordano Bruno crater

acknowledge that. But the reason I'm coming through to speak about this is because it is going to happen in your future, and there is money behind it.

People can see that the Moon could become a place where things can be mined. Partly, the reason people can see this is that astronauts have had experiences that have allowed them to notice others — extraterrestrials — mining the Moon. This has been discussed a bit in the past, but I want to mention it because now there is a choice to do so. At one time, we were part of the community of Earth people that will develop on the Moon. We were initially there to mine and explore what deposits on the Moon could be exploited or fulfill Earth's needs. After a while, it became a place to simply interact with extraterrestrials in a safe and mutually beneficial way. I feel that might be an interesting thing to explore.

I can see that there isn't a pressing "need to know" on Earth, but I assure you that it is just a matter of time before various people make the effort to create a community to bring about mining on the Moon. People will not have to shuffle around in huge astronaut outfits, because there is much progress being made to create a fully sealed environment, which might be the beginning of using almost no equipment.

There will be oxygen created from plants and so on, but you will have a nearly sealed environment that will allow you to mine areas that have already been investigated. That is the purpose of many trips to the Moon, by either machines or humans. There are places right now where Earth people would like to pursue such mining.

Pleasant Encounters

In our time, when we were Earth people (we are not anymore), mining by various groups continued for five, six, or seven years. Even during the mining, there were interchanges with extraterrestrials that were, for the most part, friendly. This is an opportunity for you to have such interchanges without having to be concerned about the public's reaction. I am not saying all the public would be frightened by encounters with extraterrestrials were they to land on Earth now in the open, but some people would be frightened. On the Moon, things would be different. I feel this is something you might enjoy exploring.

Yes, absolutely. How far in the future are you now from where we are?

About 40,000 years of your now time.

Okay.

But this doesn't mean that we are comparing our now existence to your then existence, okay.

Were you personally one of those who went to the Moon in a past life?

Yes, that is why I am talking. I was there. I was an Earth person but not one of the mining or geological people. I was there because the ongoing communications with extraterrestrials were a struggle. Sometimes the extraterrestrials could communicate successfully, but other times the Earth people did not know how to respond. I was sort of a combination of an anthropologist and a social worker. That was accepted, and I was able to communicate with the ETs in ways they were comfortable with, which means basically telepathically.

I was also able to discover how to adapt to getting along with them and doing things that would not offend or harm them while at the same time instructing them on how to interact with human beings in ways that would not offend or harm humans. In other words, it was just like meeting a group of people you have never met before: You have your ways, and they have their ways. You must learn how to get along together. That was my job.

Fascinating job! Were you chosen because you were sensitive?

I was hired by the mining company because the extraterrestrial contacts, while benefiting the mining company, had other aspects to them. The workers were getting excited and distracted, and sometimes they would have accidents because they weren't paying attention. By having a social worker-anthropologist there (and of course I had some staff), we were able to tell them, "Okay, we will communicate with them for a while and get things sorted out. You just do your work, and we will instruct you on what to do and how to do it." It was sort of a diplomatic function. That is what we did.

New Frontiers

Initially, we started working for the mining company. Then after it became clearer that the Moon bases for mining could become something more, the mining aspect continued, but other bases were developed. The ETs showed the mining company how to synthesize certain elements from materials on the Moon in a way that was not as expensive as bringing up materials to the Moon.

In short, a separate colony was created for the study of interactions between Earth human beings and extraterrestrials. That was something I moved on to after setting people up in the mining colony. Then after about six or seven years, the people I had organized there were able to spread out to other mining encampments, and I moved on to the diplomatic exchange area. This was still supported by business, and it was where people could learn how to do things in different ways that were supportive and enlightening.

Ultimately, this led to Moon tours (granted, in a limited way). Only a few could come up at a time, but it was a fun thing for them. They would usually go to the mining areas, but occasionally they came to what I'm going to call the diplomatic area — if they were completely comfortable interacting with beings that did not look like them. They didn't look extremely different, but they looked somewhat different. Some of them were, at the very least, humanoids, so they had to be comfortable with that.

That is all I'm going to say for today. This is just the beginning, and we will continue next time, if that is all right.

Absolutely. I am thrilled that you came, and I have many questions.

Good. Then we will continue for as long as your questions last.

Okay, yes!

Good night.

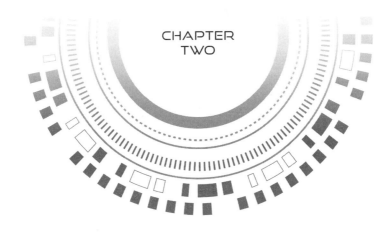

CHAPTER
TWO

LIFE ON THE MOON

Doc, a Human from a Moon-Mining Base

MAY 17, 2019

All right, well, we will resume. What would you like to talk about today?

Okay, what year were you born in this life?

Is that important?

Sure, I want to know when you went to the Moon.

No, because you are really asking when it happens, and I cannot tell you that.

All right. What kind of vehicle did you use to get there?

Just conventional vehicles like you have now, such as rockets.

A rocket, so not a shuttle. How many of you went on the first trip?

Do you mean in the circle of my profession, or how many people in general went with the mining colonies and all of that?

On your first trip, how many went to do the mining?

Image 2.1. View of Earth from the Moon

Oh, the first time was really a bit of an exploration and there were maybe a dozen of us, but that was not the most comfortable trip; it was kind of cramped. Not everyone got off the vehicle. Some people stayed with the vehicle because at that time maintenance was important.

Okay, how long were you there?

Just a few days. It was just to see whether the information that had been picked up, for the most part remotely, was going to prove beneficial for the mining work to begin. We just went to a few places and landed in a likely spot, not exactly where the mining would begin but close to it. From there, we took a vehicle, a rather slow-moving, ponderous vehicle, to the place and then to another place as an alternative, in case we didn't find what we wanted. That was it, and then we returned.

We did a dig to pick up samples to analyze. I'm speaking as a miner here, but that really wasn't my job. Since I was with the group, we all sort of pitched in and did a little digging. In my case, of course, with my interest in anthropology and sociology, I was hoping to find something that would suggest a previous civilization had been there. I was disappointed. The experts on minerals, however, were quite happy with what they found. We stayed for no longer than forty-eight hours and then went back.

How long was it before you went again?

It was about a year before I went again.

Had they sent up habitats and things in the meantime?

Not so much habitats — they sent up the means to create an enclosed environment. To call them habitats would be a stretch of the imagination. They were very rustic. The people who went up to do the initial digging were really roughing it. It wasn't the sort of place you would want to call home and hang your hat.

I was on Earth a year before I returned. Immediately when we got back the first time (they didn't need a long time to analyze the findings), they sent up another crew and those were the people who were roughing it. They regularly went back and forth because they found what they wanted and needed; then they brought it back to Earth. By the time I returned, things were more livable.

What were they excited about finding? What is it they were looking for?

No, I can't say. I will give you the reason, which is that the materials that were found were used in something you haven't invented yet.

Oh [chuckles], well, all right, then. Can you say who you worked for? Was it a government or a private industry?

Private industry.

Does it exist now?

It is in its infancy.

The Usefulness of Sleeping Pods

So you went back after a year. How long was it before you actually saw and interacted with an extraterrestrial on the Moon?

It wasn't the second time that I went back. It was the third or fourth time. That was a good thing because the purpose of my being there was to help the mining crew adapt and also put procedures in place so that if something was found that had to do with a previous civilization, it would be filtered out and set aside. These procedures were put in place. But mostly what I did was help set up a social system that would make living in such a remote area (to put it mildly) tolerable for the people doing the mining.

One thing that made it more tolerable was sleeping pods. Some of these sleeping pods already exist on your planet.[1] You have these (you may not have heard of this) pod-like places where you can sleep, where, for example, business people in a city for a short time who don't want to spend a lot of money for a room can sleep. This isn't so much in your part of the world, but in some parts of the world these kinds of pods exist where people can sleep in a small space.

That kind of thing was set up so that people could have privacy. They would also have the means to remember loved ones and communicate in a way with friends and family. Also, the corporation made things available so that the job (which paid very well, I might add) would look more attractive even though you still would be roughing it in a lot of ways. Obviously, you would have a company

---

1.   A capsule hotel, also known as a pod hotel, is a type of hotel developed in Japan that features a large number of small bed-sized rooms known as capsules.

store where you could buy a few things. There was not too much available; it wasn't like going to Walmart. There needed to be communication from workers to Earth to suggest that this was a great job even though it was kind of rough. The miners were glad they only worked there for three or six months and looked forward to going home. After a while things got better, and people said, "Hey, this is really pretty good. It's not so bad anymore."

At that point, they even had things like movies, because eventually it had to be set up so that people would want to come. Of course, over time everything became more automated. Digging initially was done using basic mining equipment, but once it got more automated, the job prospects looked better. The corporation did not have to continue raising the pay to astronomical levels to attract people. In fact, at one point the pay did not go up for quite a while. It just remained really good pay.

So let me have an idea of the scope of this operation. How many were in the first group of miners?

No, Melody, that's really not important. Do you mind if I call you by your name?

No, go right ahead. What is your name?

It's not really important, but if it makes a difference to you, there were about forty people in the first group of miners.

Were these pods that they lived in set up above ground or underground?

They basically camped out. They slept on the ground.

They had to have oxygen at all times so that they could breathe?

Yes, of course. It was basically miserable, and that's why the pay had to be really high. People were informed before they went up there that it would be rough. They did not accept just anyone. A lot of people thought it would be an adventure and that it would be fun, but it was not. You had to be very strong, very rugged; you had to be in the best of health. It wasn't unusual to accept people who were just out of the military and in very good shape.

How did they eat, and how did they get food?

Everything had to come from Earth.

I know, but how can you eat in a pressure suit? How did that work?

There was, of course, a canopy over the entire area, a sealed system so that they could move around to work and eat and so on.

Oh, okay, yes.

The system was filled with air, and no dust could get into the places where sleeping and eating would be going on. In the mining area, where there was a lot of dust, they would wear special gear and their helmets would filter the dust.

I see. So how were the living conditions when you went back a year after the first trip?

Better than before, but it was not wonderful. By that time, they did not have pods yet, but they had tents. They were a little better than pup tents or small tents that you use to camp with. Oh, I'm using the wrong word. They were portable shelters.

Getting Along

Exactly what did you do to help people adapt?

I helped them find ways to get along with each other. When you have a lot of people doing a lot of very hard work in extreme circumstances, it is not easy to get along with everyone all the time. It is not as if they were working for themselves. They were working for pay. There were bosses, so they had to always be getting along with each other. They could not get mad at each other, because there would be no place to go to blow off steam. They were essentially in a capsule unit, so things had to be set up to help them. Someone decided that a gymnasium with punching bags and other equipment would be a good thing for people to blow off steam.

You did counseling also?

I counseled as needed. The second time I went up, I had two other people with me, and they were well-versed in our specialty. There did not need to be counseling all the time. It wasn't a big mining group. Most of the people working there took pride in how strong and rugged they were to be living under those conditions. As a matter of fact, when things improved, these "old timers" kind of made fun of the newer ones for not having been through the rough times. You understand that.

Yes, absolutely. So how long were you there on your second trip?

I was there about three months. Then I came back to Earth for two years to recruit more people while the other two stayed on the Moon, because things were going all right. Then I went back up for six months to make recommendations for setting up the pods and entertainment facilities.

Then you went home and came back again?

I went home and came back very quickly. The turnaround was something like three days. That's because they had started seeing ETs approaching. People were seeing ships all the time. Some people got jumpy, and that's why they needed counseling.

Meeting the Andromedans

ETs approached and the ships landed. ETs got out and were friendly. They walked over to where we were. Even though they were friendly, some people were upset. The people I left there communicated with me that they felt it would be helpful if I returned because everyone knew me and felt good about me. They called me Doc, and they needed Doc back because Doc could help in this situation.

My people on the Moon were able to create communication of a sort with the ETs, but the mining crew was still nervous. They needed support, so I went back. I had just enough time to take a shower, change my clothes, and get a couple of good meals. [Laughs.] But ETs being there made it kind of an adventure, so they didn't have to bring me back kicking and screaming [laughs].

[Laughs.] Which ETs were they?

At that time, they didn't tell us who they were. They looked like humanoids, and looking back on it, they might have been from Andromeda since they were very tall. But their heads were not as big as you would expect and not in proportion with their bodies but smaller. I think that's part of the reason the crew was so upset and frightened, because these beings were so tall. Even though they were strong men, they were frightened — not surprising when confronted by something like that.

The ETs make gestures, they had arms and legs and feet. I'm going to make a gesture in the air here, but you can't see me: Imagine putting your hand in front of you with your elbow bent and moving your hand down slightly. Just up and down slightly, which is apparently universal. This is a gesture perhaps even made in your time — to suggest that someone quiet down.

Oh yes!

So that was the only gesture made that was recognizable by the people from Earth, and they took it to mean things would be okay. They sort of relaxed.

How tall were these ETs — 8 feet or more?

Something like that, yes.

Okay, what was the first thing you did when you got there?

Well, I tried to set up a formalized means of communication. The ETs wanted to come in, and of course the corporation did not want that, because the corporation didn't understand that the ETs could come in without creating a hole in, I'm going to call it, the bubble. That's what people were calling it.

The corporation didn't understand that the ETs could step through the bubble without (in any way) creating damage to it. I was able to come up with a basic sign language, until I heard one of them communicating. That was quite a surprise.

ET Interactions

You heard it telepathically?

Yes, and that had not happened before. I remember smiling at them, and they smiled even though I don't think their faces could smile at that time. I think their face muscles were there, but they were not exercised. I could see their eyes were smiling. Then I thought, "Oh, okay," and I asked them in my mind, "Are you communicating in my language?" They shook their heads no. They were communicating in their language, and I heard them in mine and vice versa. This was the beginning of real contact. Within a few days, I was able to communicate to the company that I felt this was going to turn into something wonderful for the people of Earth and for the company. The ETs knew where a much richer deposit of the minerals that we were mining was located.

The company was getting about 20 percent of the minerals they wanted, and the rest of it was not what they were looking for. The

ETs said they knew where there was a better deposit that it would produce 80 percent of the minerals we were mining. I told the company this, and of course they were very excited. That's when they began to trust the ETs. The company and I weren't sure what to do, but that's when things changed.

Another bubble was created within five or six months (as quickly as you can do things like that) at the second mining site. Of course, the company was absolutely thrilled. The vein proved to be even better because it was producing — in a range from 83 to 85 percent on a regular basis — the mineral they were looking for, and there were even a few bonus minerals they did not expect. The bonus minerals turned out to have value on Earth.

How many Andromedans were there in the beginning?

In the beginning it was just one and after a while sometimes two, but apparently they did not want to overwhelm us. It was usually one, sometimes with a second one, who sort of hung back. I began to think of that person hanging back as some type of security. He did not carry any weapons that I could see but was always the same one. The one I was communicating with was also always the same. I began to think of that person as somebody who was in a field similar to mine.

Did you know that you could do telepathy?

No.

The ETs had no interest in the mineral your company was mining?

Right, it wasn't anything they were interested in at all. They were just being helpful.

What brought the ETs there? Were they mining other minerals, or was it something else?

No, they just happened to be passing by and noticed what we were doing. These beings landed and said they knew about another place to mine and maybe we would like it. That launched, from my point of view, a wonderful thing. Once the company started bringing up those rich deposits, I asked them whether we could have a small bubble just for interactions with the ETs. Then maybe they could give us other ideas that would be helpful for the people of Earth and of course for the company. The company said, "Yes, let's do this." So that is what led to all of this.

We are going to have to stop; it's been a pretty long today. I will see you next week, all right?

Marvelous. Can we just call you Doc? Is that okay?

Doc is fine!

Okay, then I will ask for you next Tuesday, because I have lots of questions.

All right. I have lots of answers.

CHAPTER THREE

FUTURE FROM THE MOON

The Head of the Company

MAY 21, 2019

Hello, there will be a slight delay because Doc is busy, so I think I will speak and get used to the process. I'm one of the people who worked with Doc [chuckles]. I like that name. Can you hear me all right?

Yes, you are doing great.

You have questions about the mission. First, I will tell you a little bit about myself. Before Doc's people went to the Moon, some of us in the mining business talked about the potential for mining on the Moon. We had read and heard about what we might expect. We even had a former astronaut (I think you say) come and give us a talk about what we might expect. Among other things, it was brought up that beings from other places, not of this Earth (who may or may not look like us), would probably either be there or would stop to interact with us because they were (mostly) friendly and always interested in who was coming and going.

Image 3.1. NASA composite image using 15 images and three color filters
to aid in interpreting the surface soil composition

Most of the board members were not happy about that, but I liked it a lot. I thought this was an opportunity to meet people, go places, do things, and discover other ways of being. I have to admit the idea sprung into my head at the time: "What if they give us information we might need to know, such as cures for diseases?" I started thinking, "Maybe we could start a pharmaceutical branch." You must think this way when you are a businessperson, you know. This intrigued me, and I said to the board (they usually listened when I spoke) that I felt it might be a very good idea, and they all perked up (the former astronaut was still there).

One of them said, "You mean you think they would give us things and maybe not want much from us?"

I said, "Really, what could they want from us?" But I think they didn't get my joke. So I said, "I think we should get some medical people on board." Eventually the idea with Doc and Doc's crew came up, and that's how it happened.

I worked with the person who would come to be known as Doc, but when he was on Earth, Doc didn't like that name and preferred to be referred to by his real name. He was a little stiff, so to speak. But seeing how hard people worked on the Moon and that they were willing to suffer, to sleep on the ground, you know (I mean literally sleep on the dirt, the surface was sort of fluffy but with stones below), he melted a bit. When they started calling him Doc, he figured he would just take it in stride, and after a while, he grew to like it.

I mention that because I want you to understand that we are just human beings like you, Earth people, and I'm speaking from that time. We are just like you, and nothing has changed. The experience turned into a good thing. While I personally didn't go there, I was always interested in Doc's adventures. When he came back, he told me all about it. Now, I feel Doc in the wings, so to speak, so I'm going to say goodbye. Enjoy your life as it comes!

Thank you for talking to us, thank you.

A GREAT ADVENTURE

Doc

All right, Doc here. I am sorry for being late. I was helping the channel who had an injury this morning and helped himself, but he needed a little extra help. I think he will be all right.

Oh, all right, I didn't know that. He didn't say anything about it.

No, he's like that. What shall we talk about today?

This fellow who just talked, was he the head of the company you worked for?

Yes, he was the head of the company and had a good attitude

about it. We became good friends even though he was as far up the company ladder as you can go. He liked what I was doing and had a good sense of humor. He was the one who originally encouraged me to accept the name Doc and recognized that the workers wouldn't give me a nice nickname if they didn't like me, so I should be comfortable with them and call them by their nicknames.

They had totally accepted me and I realized that this was an honor and a privilege, because the workers might not have accepted me and then given me an unpleasant nickname instead. I stepped back a bit and realized I had been somewhat starchy; then I got over it. The Moon adventure was one of the greatest things I had ever done, and I think it improved my life. I looked at my whole life after that and realized I had been kind of a stick in the mud and could spread out into more things. So I did. It really proved to be a growth experience for me that led to a better life.

How old were you when you first went up?

Thirty-seven.

How many years did you interact with that project on the Moon?

Oh, I think almost sixteen years. It was almost a life's work, except I wasn't done in my profession when I stopped going to the Moon, but I never forgot it. It was a great adventure and really was the beginning of something wonderful for Earth. I think for a while the information spread slowly to some parts of Earth because some people weren't quite ready to believe that the Earth humans (the workers on the Moon) could so readily accept the ETs. But, of course, in the beginning they didn't.

Once they realized the ETs were friendly and sang songs, they said, "Oh, they are like us!" At first they didn't understand the songs and thought the beings were mumbling, but they were actually singing. The miners were like that too. They sang songs and kind of mumbled to themselves. That was when they realized how much alike they all were. There were differences of course, but the ETs' culture had many similarities with the Earth humans'. Then the miners thought, "Oh, this is okay." It led to something special when everybody realized that the others were singing. The singing was a big breakthrough, leading to the miners accepting the interchanges.

There was a time when we got together, when three of the ETs were in their ship and then left it (the ship just remained there floating above the ground) and they came through what we call the bubble. It was completely safe, but some workers got upset. After a while, the men realized that somehow the ETs could step through the bubble. It was safe because this was some kind of interdimensional thing. The ETs created (I am not a scientist) sort of a temporary vacuum when they went through the bubble, so it was safe. They would come in and the men would sing their favorite songs. Sometimes they sang songs from different parts of the country; other times they sang songs they had created on the Moon. When the men stopped, the ETs sang their songs. It made a nice connection between them. You know, music makes such a difference.

Yes. How many Earth people were there when the three ETs arrived?

Well, of course some of them were at work but there were about seventeen of them who were not working or sleeping. seventeen were available for the song fest.

How long after the humans first got there did they have this song fest with the ETs?

About three years. One moment. I hear a noise. I must put the phone down. All right, the noise just means someone is getting the help they need.

Yes, it's a siren.

It is something I noticed. I was a doc [laughs], not a medical doc but still it is something I noticed. There were no sirens on the Moon. We had vehicles with flashing lights. Sometimes the lights meant one thing, sometimes another. There was a medical crew, and their lights flashed red. The workers' lights flashed yellow, I think, and so on. They didn't wear them; it was just the vehicles.

Were the three ETs the Andromedans you mentioned before? Or by this time had you branched out to meet other civilizations?

Well, I know what you are trying to say, but of course we didn't branch out. It all depended on who was going by and whether they stopped to chat. It wasn't as if we were reaching out to them; they were just passing by, and they were Zeta Reticulans.

Mining the Moon for Medicine

When we talked last time, I thought what you were mining was something that would be used in manufacturing a device or electronics, but when the man who ran the company spoke, it sounded as if you were getting into pharmaceutical mining. Did that ever happen?

We weren't doing anything pharmaceutical. The company's founder was probably thinking about it at the time, but the pharmaceutical branch didn't happen during my tenure there. The company's founder didn't come to the Moon to interact with the ETs. But when the ETs helped us or shared information, it would get back to Earth, and the founder and his medical people decided whether it was something that could be packaged.

Usually it was just advice and couldn't really be packaged. It went into an information database, and when they had enough advice, they consulted with others already in the pharmaceutical or medical business. In time, I think it resulted in a book — a simplified version people could use for home cures and so on. A lot of it had to do with, "Press here on this part of your body" or "Press there on that part of your body." I think some of that already existed in a form of healing therapy called acupressure. But these were things that did not exist at that time in the acupressure system, so it turned out to be the next logical step.

There was only one pharmaceutical that was developed out of the information. It was a variation of, what is called in your time, aspirin. Instead of having an acidic affect, it had the opposite effect, producing relief for both pain and anxiety. People could take it if they were having, for example, an ulcer. The pain and anxiousness would go away. The drug would actually calm the ulcer and help heal it. That wonderful drug quickly became something you could just purchase.

For a short time only, it was something a doctor had to write a piece of paper for. The demand was so great, because there was a lot of nervousness on the planet at that time. It became widely accepted and licensed so that everyone could buy it. I think it helped to calm people's nerves all over the planet. The company didn't try to take credit for it. We smiled and said, "This is a good thing. Maybe we will be remembered for this." You know you always want to be remembered in a good way.

Was the product mined like a rare earth sent to Earth in ounces or pounds, or was it something they had to send back in huge amounts, like tons?

They didn't send back tons. At the initial place, they were digging a lot but only got a little. When the ET said, "Dig over there where there is a much richer vein," it was easier to separate, and more was sent back to Earth. I know you are asking for the volume that went back. I don't think I could call it tons. It was more like pounds.

But they had to separate it out. Did they have to do any refining with equipment?

No, nothing like that. It was a matter of separating it, and it was obvious what we were mining looked different from the color of Moon soil (calling it soil doesn't seem quite right). Moon soil looks really different from the dirt or soil we have on Earth. But the "other matter" (I will call it) was clearly distinguishable, and to get it was more like sifting.

Selective Telepathy

Okay. Let's get back to your telepathic abilities. You hadn't been there very long when the Andromedans spoke with you telepathically. Did that ability increase as you used it, and is that how you communicated with the ETs from then on?

Well, it doesn't really have to increase. Once you learn how to do it; it is like flipping a switch. You don't get better at it; it just opens a door. That would be a better analogy. It opens the door, and once you have that door open, you can always go through it. I did not, however, use it with my crew or the miners, because I didn't want to add that to their lives. After all, this kind of thing is more my specialty, but after a while, some of the ETs made telepathic contact the same way with my crew. They each had the experience uniquely, one at a time.

Occasionally we used it among ourselves, when it was necessary to communicate quickly. Most of the time we spoke out loud, because people who don't do it might notice it going on. If people in my crew started looking at each other and nodding (a natural thing to do), the miners would realize what we were doing, so we didn't do that. We knew it would distance us from the miners, which we couldn't do, because we needed to serve them. We did it as little as possible, only when it was just us and even then not too much, so we wouldn't get used to it.

Right, it would make you seem different.

It was difficult enough for doctors, therapists, and psychologists to be accepted by the miners and others. So we thought, "This is a wonderful thing for us, but we won't use it too much." Of course, we used it all the time with the ETs, and the men accepted that. To them it was like, "Oh, you're talking to them in that funny way," and then they laughed. From a distance, they could tell when we were communicating with the ETs, because there was no sound except a mumbling that came from us or them. The miners would look at us, laugh, shake their heads, and go on with their duties.

Gestures Unique to Earth

How long was it from the time you got there and put up that second bubble before you could interact with the ETs?

Oh, are you talking about the bubble over the mining operation? When the ETs came forward, there was a tube, long but rounded on both ends like a cylinder. It was a bright light version, and they stepped through; then it went away. I think we called it the bubble because it looked like a long bubble a child would make with soap bubbles. Have you seen those? It looked like that.

You said after the ETs showed you how to get 80 to 90 percent of the product from a new vein, the company provided a bubble for you to interact with the ETs.

Oh, that wasn't the same thing. That was a separate bubble, and we are talking about a bubble over the entire mining operation.

Right, and then you said there was a separate one where you could interact with the ETs.

Yes, that's right. It was a small one, maybe at its widest 64 meters (about 210 feet), or something like that.

Tell me some stories about what happened with you and the ETs. What were some of the interesting things you learned when talking with them?

It was always interesting, even if they didn't tell us anything. Just observing them and how they acted was interesting, such as how humans might scratch the top of their heads or pull on their beards when nervous, that kind of stuff. I noticed the ETs were never nervous. They never made gestures like that. I remember once talking with the ETs and they said they saw me put my fingers up to the side of my face and my thumb in that sort of thoughtful gesture (you know the thinker kind of thing). They asked, "What are you doing?"

I said, "Human beings do this either when they are nervous or when they are trying to concentrate on a point or how to say something."

They said, "Oh?" They had heard of gestures human beings made, but they thought these were like signals or signs, such as holding up fingers or putting your thumb out to go hitchhiking. They didn't know gestures were either to relieve personal tension or focus more deeply on something they were thinking about. It was very interesting to them. They didn't have anything like that in their culture, nor had they ever interacted with any other human culture that had that. They had interacted with human cultures many times, and none did that.

Of course this made me wonder, "Is this something that only developed on Earth?" That really got my attention, because in the psychological and especially the anthropological community, things like that are very exciting. I wrote something about it in one of the journals, and people got excited about it and really interested, because by that time in that particular journal, it was known that we were interacting with ETs. I might add this wasn't a journal for the general public. It was a private journal within this company and a few other companies. So that's why I'm calling it a journal and not a magazine. There was great excitement in that field. The idea that something everyone does on the planet and seems to do naturally is unique to Earth human beings and was very exciting.

There are other human beings, many others; but we haven't met any of those yet.

But the ETs had. The ETs had visited many places where there were humans and never saw that. They talked with other ET friends who came and went. They looked it up in the materials they had about human races, and it doesn't exist anywhere except on Earth. That was even more exciting for us, so of course I put that in my journal, and everyone was excited. People started making pictures of what "this" means and what "that" means and creating a book, because they realized this didn't exist anywhere else: "We have to make sure we get it down and that we know what these gestures mean."

An example gesture is when you go up to the corner of your eye because and you had to touch it for just a moment. After that, you continue to make that gesture, all kinds of little gestures people do that mean something to them at that moment. But they also frequently communicate meaning to other people, such as, "I want to get out of here as fast as possible." In short, there is a great deal of sign language that everyone takes for granted on Earth, but it doesn't exist anywhere else. So that's exciting!

Yes, yes, it is. Well, so who else did you meet? You mentioned Andromedans and Zetas. What other civilizations came by to visit you?

A Diverse Range of ETs

Well, so who else did you meet? You mentioned Andromedans and Zetas. What other civilizations came by to visit you?

Well, they didn't always tell us where they were from and we didn't ask because that would have been impolite. If you are doing anthropology on Earth, you don't go into a community and say, "Who are you?" because when you go into those communities you are the one who is asked this. At some point, they will tell you if they accept you, even for a little while. They will say, "This is our knowledge" or "This is our wisdom," but very rarely will they give out their names. You know, this is the general idea of movies and TV in your time, "Oh, we are 'this,'" or "We are 'that,'" but people don't do that, and very often the names provided for these groups weren't names they gave themselves. Others gave them those names. I don't know whether you know that, but it is a well-known anthropological fact. So we didn't ask, because, after all, they had been coming and going from that area for hundreds of millions of years for all we knew. I do not specifically mean those beings but their cultures, and they could have asked us who we were, not the other way around.

Based on how they looked, how many different groups would you say you had contact with?

Three or four groups contacted us, judging by their appearances. You can't just say they were all different groups, because that's like saying, "Does everyone on your planet Earth look exactly the same?" All human beings basically look the same, but there are different colors, and sometimes there are facial and other differences. We shouldn't assume they all looked alike. There were four basic types, but we didn't have any reason to think everyone on their planet looked the same.

I know. I've heard some Andromedans are 2 feet tall and some are 10 feet tall.

Well, then you understand.

Yes. Were these ETs mining on different areas of the Moon or just passing by?

They were usually just passing by. The ET miners on the other part of the Moon were a ways off, and we were aware of them. Sometimes one or more of them wandered in our general direction, but we just waved at each other and that was that. They were friendly enough. They didn't interfere with us, and we didn't interfere with them.

Oh, you didn't communicate, share information, or anything?

Well, they were busy working, and we were working too. You don't stop your work to do that. Work is not about chatting with passersby.

Would they pass by walking, driving, or what?

Usually they were just walking, but you know the Moon is a much smaller place than Earth. You can be over the hill much sooner than you would be on Earth.

Right. Were you on the light side or the dark side of the Moon?

Oh, do you mean were we on the side seen from Earth or on the other side?

Yes.

We were sort of in between.

At the edges.

At the edges, yes.

You seem to be sort of a diplomat with the ETs.

I had to be. I had no choice.

That was in addition to your duties, though.

Yes, and we made it very clear to the ETs that if they wanted to stop and chat, we were working at that time and couldn't chat. So we just waved at them, and they waved back. They understood that, because we taught them the gesture. Waving meant happy to see you, busy now. We gave them a friendly wave and pointed at our work. They understood the gestures and were interested in them. We think they might have wanted to tell other ETs about the gestures, but I don't know whether they ever did.

Did you give them a copy of the book that was made?

No, the book was for Earth people.

I know, but it would have helped you communicate with them, right?

I'll tell you what, when you have another life and go to the Moon, you can do that. [Laughs.] No, it's not like that. I'm making jokes with you. When you are in an anthropological community and discover people living there in a civilization, happy doing what they are doing, are you going to give them a book to educate them? I don't think so. You're going to learn from them. My job is to learn from them, not to tell them who we are with materials they never asked for. It is important, because on Earth, I think you'll find people do that; they want you to study their culture and be like them. You think that happens on Earth now. Has anyone ever come up to you and said, "Have you discovered this?" and then tried to talk you into something and wanted you to be like them so that you could be friends? Don't you know about that?

Oh, yes, there are religious groups like that.

Yes, that's right. There are religious groups but also groups who want other people to be like them in other countries. When you say, "Why didn't you give them the book?" it makes complete sense in that moment. But now I've explained it to you. I am explaining it to you for the purpose of you leaving it in there, because it's very important to put these little subtle things out there.

In time, it's the subtle points that will be remembered in all the material you put out. All those subtle points will come into a single book long after your time on the planet, and that will help shape the true singular culture of Earth human beings. That book will be about how to get along with everybody.

Well, wonderful, good!

Let's stop for today, and we can continue tomorrow, okay?

Okay.

All right. Good night.

Thank you.

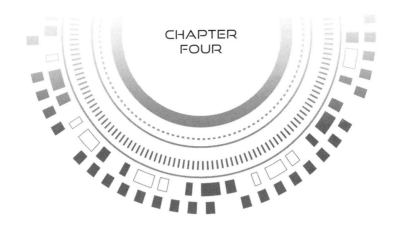

DOC'S IDENTITY

Doc

MAY 22, 2019

All right, here we go.

All right, I have some questions. Are you a male?

No.

Oh, you're a female!

Well, that's a good guess.

The head of your company referred to you as a male, probably to protect your identity. I had no idea they sent up a female with the mining crew.

Well, sometimes that's considered to be a plus.

Have you had any problems with the tough guys?

Oh, there have been a few wisecracks, but they're all good-natured, so I was just good-natured back. In the beginning, I was a little stiff with them. I felt they needed to respect me and call me Doctor, but they insisted on calling me Doc. One of the people I had

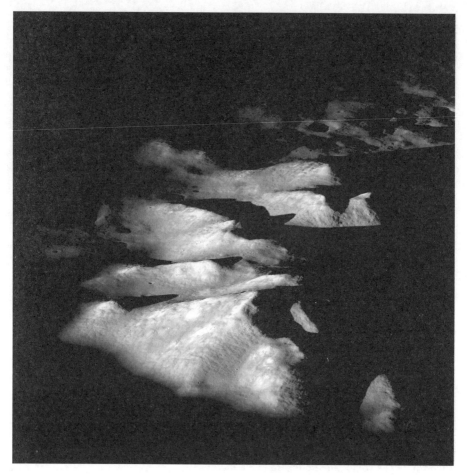

Image 4.1. NASA photo of shadowy mountains on the Moon

with me said, "Lighten up. They don't mean any harm; they are just kidding with you." So I accepted "Doc," and over time we got along.

When other people came up, the original miners looked out for me. If anyone in the new crew gave me a hard time, one of the originals would pull them aside and explain a few things. That worked out pretty well.

Are you American?

I am not going to say.

Brotherhood and Sisterhood with ETs

Okay, so you went up in a rocket. Did they do the thing they did in 1969 — where you go up in a rocket and there is an orbital vehicle and then there's a lander? Is that how it worked? Or did they have something a little more modern when you went up?

Well, it was pretty much the conventional way. Many companies are doing things like that now, and they will continue until someone figures out how to do it electrically. For now, it takes thrust to get away from Earth's gravitational pull. It will take thrust for quite a while (we think), until there are enough liaisons with the extraterrestrials and they feel Earth people can be trusted. That is why it's going to take a while. Once trust takes hold and is proven to be deserved — meaning things are working out in all directions — vehicles will be loaned to Earth just like they have been loaned to other places. People will learn how to construct the vehicles, and they will have their own. This takes time.

What is the attitude of people on Earth now toward ETs? Are they still being told ETs don't exist?

Well, you know a lot of it is based on religion, and I really don't know that much. I'm just looking at the records. Some religions accept it and feel it is real. There is also hope that branches of other religions (largely unspoken, according to our records) will connect to a deity through ETs. There will be places where ETs come from as well as a feeling of brotherhood and sisterhood. In some communities, there is hope that it will be a good thing even though religions consider it taboo. That's going to gradually change, because there is a groundswell among serious practitioners of various religions who feel this could be a good thing. That's all I can say. Keep in mind that my knowledge is scant compared to others. You understand? I am just a person who doesn't have that much knowledge about it.

Are you speaking from your life there, when you went to the Moon?

No, when you asked me the question about Earth and Earth people, I couldn't speak of that. I haven't the slightest idea. I had to go to my "now life," when I say I'm looking at the records.

I see. Can you say what civilization or planet you live on now?

It's not one you've heard of.

Okay, so your company was the first one to go up there. After a couple of years, were there other mining companies from Earth?

Well, we heard there was a group doing explorations, but it seems the company had a deal granting it exclusive access for a time. Now, I think, that's beginning to change. Perhaps time ran out on that deal, I don't know. We heard there is another group operating, but it's not going to be a big operation. According to what I've heard, it is pretty small and not expected to get much bigger. That's all I know.

Do you think the deal was that they would share the material they brought back with other companies?

I can only speculate, but it seems to me that would be the obvious thing.

Ties That Bind

By the time you left after — I think you said sixteen years — were there any others from Earth on the Moon besides that one exploratory mining group?

By that time, there was another group, but it wasn't for mining. Someone was trying to create a sort of place to come for vacation. The people who came up would be roughing it even with the best available comforts. Everyone at this time had to rough it on the Moon. Life there is difficult. But there are people who like that kind of adventure, so the company was trying to create interest in that. From what I know, they were successful.

Yes, like a tourist attraction. In all the years you were there, was the basic work you were doing with the miners as a psychological consultant or therapist?

Yes, I acted as a therapist to support them. After all, these people were far away from their homes and families. Even though there was some means of communication, there were no hugs involved, so it was hard for the miners. Some of them, the ones I call the old-timers, were originally chosen because they didn't have many family connections. They weren't married, and they didn't have any dependents. The company wasn't sure whether anyone would survive. All the company could really offer was high pay. They couldn't offer vacation time, because the people were on the Moon, and that wouldn't do them any good. So the job paid a lot of money. The first ones (the old-timers) who came didn't have any ties that bound them to Earth, but the ones who came later did. That's why the old-timers returned to Earth sometimes and then went back: they didn't have any ties that bound them there. When they came back, they were ranked at another level, always getting the highest pay level for miners.

They figured when they returned to Earth that they would be able to live well, and as far as I know, they did. There wasn't really any negative impact healthwise, but I think there would have been psychological damage if there hadn't been a therapeutic unit. Of course, there was also a medical unit, but that wasn't my thing. I think most of the old-timers stuck around until after I had left, because I don't recall any of them leaving while I was there.

The old-timers kidded me at the time, saying, "Hey, you're abandoning us," and stuff like that. I think they stuck around quite a while. About five years after I came back to Earth, the old-timers started to trickle back down to Earth too. We stayed in touch, as you tend to do when you go through something like that together.

Oh yes, it was so deep and dramatic. How did they handle medical emergencies? Was there a hospital facility for emergencies and operations?

Yes, the medical unit was as well equipped as it could possibly be. It was the sort of thing you might find on a large ship — not a commercial one, but a large military ship able to handle just about anything. The medical unit had a bubble within the bigger bubble. It was like a vehicle in which there was something underneath, something above, and something all around. To get in and out of the unit, you had to go through several doors where there was air.

Air locks.

That's it; you had to go through air locks to get into the unit and get out. It was a fine piece of equipment.

Now what about you and the ties that bind — you didn't have any?

No, that's why I was picked.

When you went back to Earth, did you get married or anything?

[Laughs.] Nosy, eh? Well, yes.

Good. Well, I am nosy, yes, because it's hard to do this when there are some things you can't reveal. To make the story interesting, I try to get as much detail as I can.

[Laughs.] Just joking, okay!

[Laughs.] Okay.

Diplomacy with ETs

So you were experienced in working with the miners and were pretty much the diplomat for the Moon with the ETs.

Well, I know what you're saying, but it wasn't official. It was just that I was the most thoroughly educated and experienced with anthropology, and the other people on the team were all psychologists. Well, a few of them had some anthropology under their belts, but I had more. I also had contacts with remote people on Earth. Of course, there are not many remote people left on Earth even in your time, I think, but there are still a few. Interacting with such people, looking back on it now, I can see that it was great preparation for being able to accept the ETs as they were without any attempt to make them like me. I accepted them exactly as they were. Though, until the telepathy started, we had pretty thin communication. The hand-gesture thing didn't work other than they caught on to what waving meant.

All the other hand gestures and expressions everyone recognizes on Earth (happy, sad, and all), they didn't know about. Not that they didn't get happy or sad, but their expressions for happy and sad were not the same ones that we have on Earth. That's the thing about anthropology: You go in assuming everything will be completely different, and then you learn that things it seems everyone knows are actually not known there. You have to assume you are dealing with beings who are not anything like you except in appearance.

Yes, I can see that, because I have trouble in the opposite way. When I talk to ETs, I assume they are like us, and I get into trouble sometimes.

Yes, and they are not usually like us. If you are talking to ones who are diplomatic, they are probably tolerant of such things, but if they are not diplomatic, they don't know what you're talking about. If you are unlucky, they sort of hang up the phone [laughs].

[Laughs.] I haven't had that happen to me yet.

Telepathic Communication

Okay, so in your interactions with ETs, did they ever share knowledge with you that you could use? Did things get friendlier as the years went by?

Keep in mind these were not the same ones that came and went all the time.

Oh, were they always different?

It was rare to see the same people.

Ah, so you had to start all over every time, wow.

Yes, once I had been taught telepathy by the one being, I used it to build bridges right away. Most of the ETs used telepathy, so that made it easier. Before that, it was a struggle. As for the one who taught me telepathy, it was just that one encounter, and I didn't see that being again. I'm very grateful to that being for helping me.

The ETs didn't talk to me about psychological issues. They looked at the miners and understood that our unit was one thing, the medical unit was another, and the miners were roughing it. Sometimes they were compassionate and shared things with the medical unit, but it was obscure, because people in the medical unit were not telepathic.

The ETs sometimes told me something that I was supposed to share with the medical unit, and usually it was a formula of some sort. They carefully instructed me how to write something down, and if I didn't get it right, they said, "No, it goes this way." It was a chemistry thing. They shared something with me for the medical unit, a chemical formula or a mathematical formula, something like that. They checked to see that I got it exactly right, and when I did, they asked me to give it to the medical unit, who knew what to do with it.

Wonderful. Did the medical unit ever tell you what it was for?

They didn't know, but they could understand some of it. They sent it to the home office on Earth, but the home office didn't share what it was exactly; the only feedback they ever gave was that they were very excited. It had something to do with the transformation of pathogens from toxic to benign. It was for all pathogens, so they were really excited. They didn't understand it yet, but they thought it might apply to cures, or at least treatments, for various diseases.

By the time you went home, you didn't hear any more about it?

No, why would I? Keep in mind that although I had been there, my specialty was psychology and anthropology. Why would the company share anything with me about chemistry? They thanked me for sending the formula, and that was it.

I guess I'm just curious.

I completely understand the fact that you are curious. I was curious too, but it wasn't my field. I hoped the company would turn it into something that would help people. One of the reasons I was chosen to do this work on the Moon is that I was very healthy. All the people chosen had to be very healthy and naturally resistant to disease. Do you understand?

Yes, of course.

I never found out. It's possible it percolated into the community in some form. I never had to go to the doctor.

Contact Was Hit or Miss

Did the ETs have a method for which they had a ship in orbit? Did they send down a small ship to see the humans there, or do you think they came for another purpose?

No, I didn't see anything like a big ship that sends out small ships. I think the biggest thing that ever came — and this is an estimate — was maybe 35 or 40 feet wide from the widest portion. Another vehicle might've been around 18 to 22 feet tall. So they weren't very big. They were just passing by, and if they felt interested, they stopped. Sometimes we saw them go to another place on the Moon, where I think there was another mine, established long before we got there. I told you about that, right?

Oh, the ETs you said who waved sometimes.

Yes, the ones who were friendly but kept their distance. Sometimes their ships went there, and they didn't come see us at all.

What did those beings look like? Do you know what culture they were part of?

They didn't look exactly like us, but they were human-ish. They had two arms, two legs, a body, and their heads were, well, I am not quite sure. They had something around their heads. Perhaps they needed some kind of breathing apparatus, so I couldn't get a clear picture of their heads. Other than that, they looked human but perhaps taller.

You never interacted with them other than waving?

Waving was it, and I think that was probably because we were with different companies. They probably knew we were a private company, and I assumed they were also.

Just from a different planet, that's all.

They were probably told not to come any closer, because it would be normal to talk about what you were doing. That's why I assumed it was a private business venture; otherwise, natural curiosity would have had them come over and ask, "Hey, how are you doing?"

Or ask, "What are you doing?" Yes, absolutely. How often would it happen that someone from another planet landed to talk? Was it once a month or once a year?

In the beginning, it was rare, but it happened. I know you're asking how often it happened once it started. We saw others occasionally. No one made a special trip to see us. If they happened to be in the neighborhood and were interested, they stopped by to see what was going on. It was kind of hit and miss, not on the second Tuesday of every month or something like that.

On average, would you say you received visitors once a week or once a month?

Averages are not accurate, because something can happen fifteen times a year all on the same day, and the average would come out to be one point something per month.

[Laughs.] Okay. Is there some way that you can communicate about how often you interacted with these beings?

Well, sometimes it was once or twice a month, and other times three months went by and we didn't see anyone. It was completely irregular. I cannot create a regular schedule for you for an irregular event.

[Laughs.] Okay, that's fine.

The ET Child

Of all the beings you communicated with, who impressed you or interested you the most, other than the one who taught you telepathy?

Well, I didn't know where the being was from, but there was one who meant a lot to me. I'm not 100 percent certain (but at least 90 percent) that this person was a child. I was intrigued because this small person with other bigger people was very curious and outgoing, similar to an Earth child, but they were not Earth beings. They were humanoids or human-type beings, because their head shapes were not very different.

The one I'm calling a child was hard to describe, but I really felt love from that being. I think it was its nature to be loving toward everyone. It was hard for me not to hug that little one when it left, because I really wanted to. The child must have known that, because I knew I wasn't supposed to touch them unless they made the first move. That's how it is in anthropology.

The ETs started walking away to go back to their vehicle and suddenly the little one (the one I'm calling a child) turned around and spread its arms very wide, almost like a hug from a distance. Then I did that too, and we had a wonderful moment of love. I didn't experience love like that again until I had my own children on Earth. Then I was 99 percent sure that being was a child. But it didn't click until I had my own children. That's the one I remember best and most fondly.

Rules of Engagement

What was the context of the communication with the adults?

Oh, just the usual, "Who are you, and what are you doing here?" They happened to be going by, so when they asked, we told them. With ETs, we really didn't hold back anything other than private company information, and it was recognized early on that they were not competitors.

If they ask you, "Who are you, and what are you doing," why can't you do the same?

In anthropology, you don't do that. They need to volunteer the information. I received the same question from my staff all the time. I told them to be receptive and interested if the beings talked about themselves but not to ask questions. You see, in normal Earth communication, asking a question is perfectly natural. Sometimes you get an answer, and sometimes you don't. Anthropology is more respectful. A question you ask could cause others pain. I know that sounds strange to you, but it is well established in anthropology on Earth. You will have to look up information about anthropology and read more about it if you want to understand. Anthropologists on Earth have asked questions, and sometimes it has been perfectly all right and other times it has been a complete disaster. That's what I have learned.

Yes, but you're using rules from Earth and applying them to dealing with people from other planets, who may not have the same reactions. Isn't that possible?

Yes. You are saying to take a chance. What's the harm? But what if there is harm? Then what? Can you make it all better? Can you make them forget the harm? No, the harm is done, and who knows what it would do on their home planet. It could totally ruin their lives. Do you want to do that just because you are curious? Is it okay to get what you want even if it harms other people? That isn't okay with me.

Give me an example of the harm that you have experienced or read about when some-one asked a native person a question, because I am not familiar with this.

I will give you one example, but I recommend that you personally read about it because a lot of people on Earth know about this already. When I was a greenhorn, I went on an exploration with someone, and a teacher said, "Now, don't say anything. Just watch and learn, and we will discuss it later." At some point, there were young people, and I was a young person too. We were all in our twenties. They asked questions and laughed but not in ways I understood. I could tell they were asking questions, though, because they looked at me curiously and said something in their language. I didn't know their language at the time, but eventually, I learned it.

When one person laughed, I asked, "What is your name?" It didn't make any difference when I said, "What is your name?" Isn't that a simple thing on Earth? If I asked you what your name is, you would say so-and-so, right? Only the sounds I made did not equal "what is your name?" in their language. It meant something completely different. I don't know what it meant, but my teacher said that was the end, and I was booted out of that class. The teacher told me years later that they still weren't sure what I said or what it meant, but it really hurt the person's feelings and the mission to that group of people. My group had to leave. My simple question, "What is your name?" was a disaster.

Were you trying to say it in their language?

No, I said it in my language. I expressed curiosity with the sounds I made in my language, but in their language, they meant things that were very bad to them. Then I saw on their faces that it was like someone slapped them, and they sort of caved in. All the other people ran away. I wasn't that far away from my teacher, who was looking daggers at me, and I was out of the program that minute.

That's a tough lesson and a tough way to learn a lesson.

It wasn't tough for me, but it was for them. They were harmed in a way that could never be fixed. What do you think of that?

Well, it's not good.

Well, there you go. You asked for an example, and I gave you one. In my experience on Earth, most people had some knowledge of these things but not very young people, and you personally are very young at heart. In that way, by being young at heart, you don't quite have that thing. Of course, you're an experienced adult, but when you are enthusiastic, you are young at heart, which allows you to do this work and be curious.

You are curious as a child and have the ability to speak as an adult. The curiosity comes from a happy, loving, childlike space in you. That's why you're good at what you do and why it feels as such a burden when you have to do work at the office, because that's adult work. The child in you says, "Aw, do we have to?" Yes, you recognize that feeling.

Yes, you see, I am a walk-in. I have only been here a couple of years, and they say I've never been on Earth before and don't know where I'm from. I'm sort of the current tenant in this body.

I am talking about your physical body, which has always been the way your body is. I understand what you mean by "walking in," and I am not saying that you brought that in.

Oh, that was the nature of the original personality, okay.

Yes, and that's in the body, so if anyone else walks in, it will be like that for them too.

Okay, well thank you for all this personal information. I understand now why you couldn't ask questions. Someone without that previous experience on Earth might've asked the child's name.

Yes, and that's why I was very strict with my staff. I told them about that experience, and their response was, "Ouch!" They understood very well that it was a disaster. Instead of asking questions, they were receptive, just as I was. Of course, with the miners, because we were all from Earth, I could ask them questions. It was only with the ETs that I didn't.

Right, and you communicated with them telepathically.

Universal Translator

Do you know some of them have universal translators, where they speak in their language and you hear it in yours? Did you experience that?

I see you don't understand how a universal translator works. I will explain it to you, okay? A universal translator works telepathically!

[Laughs.] Oh, I see. I thought it was a device.

It is a device for some, but it functions telepathically, so it is an aid. The universal translator is being developed on Earth right now. It can be done, and that is why they are trying to get all these languages together. It is not keyed into becoming telepathic. It is just to translate one language into another language, and it's coming along. But they still haven't figured out that it needs to be telepathic. They will have to accept telepathy at some point. Then they will realize, "Oh, that's a lot easier."

Are you saying this device enables people who are not telepathic to be telepathic?

No, we did not have such devices.

But I have heard so many different ETs talk about it. They have said, "Oh, we have a universal translator."

Yes, they have a universal translator, and the purpose of their device (I can't speak for every culture) from what I know is to detect what language you are speaking. The device has all the stuff programmed in it, and if it doesn't detect the language, they can communicate strictly telepathically without the use of the device. But if, for some reason, the ETs do not do telepathy, you would need to find a person to communicate with the ET using the device. It wasn't obvious to me that they were, like, pushing a button, and it wasn't similar to a walkie-talkie.

As far as I know, the device for those who say they have a universal translator is sort of like putting something between this process. People can be telepathic on Earth, because you can talk to your dog or cat without a translator. The thing about talking out loud is that you stay completely focused on what you are communicating to your dog or cat, and you say words and then notice how their eyes look. Sometimes dogs will make noises that people call "whining." If it is whining, that's one thing, but if it's just little noises that happen all the time, then that is the dog trying to communicate with you.

I have seen that in my cat, yes.

Yes, sometimes animals are communicating with you and hoping that you "get it" on some level. Maybe you do, but it may not be conscious. The cat (in your case) could easily communicate telepathically with you. But if you were going to try that, what you could do is whisper what you want to say to the cat, and this keeps you focused. When you are telepathic, you have to stay 100 percent focused on what you are saying or receiving, otherwise your mind goes 1,000 miles an hour. If you're going to be telepathic, you have to be totally focused. You don't have to open your mouth and talk, but for a human being, it helps to keep us totally focused. You hear what the animal says in your head, and it just comes through in your language, whatever it is, including your lingo.

You might have jargon in your culture, and the other being is saying something in a different jargon of its culture, but the meaning comes through. You can work it out after a while: "This" means "this" to us, and "that" means "that" to them. It is translated in the natural telepathic function of the human being. You are made from the material of the dirt, of the earth, and the planet Earth is telepathic.

Planet Earth has substances called earth and rock and so on, which is all telepathic. All nonhumans, for example, trees, are telepathic with each other. It is the universal way to communicate, and this is based on my experience then as well as now. But, of course, I am no deity laying down the law. I am not suggesting that these are words from on high. According to my experience, knowledge, and wisdom I can call on here in my now place on my now planet, we don't know everything about everything. We have some wisdom accumulated over time, so this is what I believe based on all I can assimilate at the time.

We believe telepathy is a universal thing; it is for our entire universe. But I don't know everything, so maybe it isn't. However, based on what we know, it seems universal. But don't quote me on it.

When you came back to Earth with this telepathic ability, were you able to find people on Earth who also could communicate that way?

Well, I didn't drop my professional standards when I came back to Earth. People who are psychologists and anthropologists have practices and professional standards, so I didn't walk around asking,

"Oh, can you hear me?" All children on Earth, as far as I know, are naturally telepathic. Part of the reason they cry when they are young is really that they are telepathically saying, "Why can't you hear me?" When I had children and they were telepathic with me, I was telepathic right back at them.

Were they able to keep that as they grew up?

Yes.

Oh, that's wonderful. What more can you tell me about this? It is pretty interesting.

Well, I will tell you what, since you're going to have a little time before your next session, if anything occurs to you, such as questions you could have asked, just keep them in mind so that we can continue.

Okay, let's see what comes up then, and I will try to think of things that will add to the story without being too curious.

Well, I understand that you can't be too curious in your work. You can probe a little bit, and if I can't go there, I'll just tell you. You understand the reason I can't tell you something is that you are like a journalist even though this is not a newspaper. You want to get information out that will help your people on Earth.

Yes!

I wouldn't want to restrict you from doing that. The reason I pause at times is because I am checking to see what I can tell you. If it's something that might develop in the future, whether it's good or bad, I will know in seconds whether I can talk about that. If I can't talk about something, it's because it has a bearing on the future.

Yes, well, I understand why you can't.

This is for the reader, then.

Yes, it is. Like you said in the beginning, you couldn't tell us what they were mining for because we haven't invented the gadget yet. Okay, would you like to say a closing statement or save that for next time?

I don't want to say a closing statement yet, because I feel we will continue. Perhaps at some point, unless you are no longer interested, this can become its own book, or it will put a big footprint in the middle of another book [laughs].

Okay. Good night.

Good night.

LIFE ON THE MOON

Doc

JULY 12, 2019

The Moon is really big news right now all over planet Earth, because it's around the fiftieth anniversary of the first moonwalk by our astronauts. NASA has plans to go back to the Moon, commercially, as well as other countries. A report I am reading in the New York Times *("The Moon Is a Hazardous Place to Live," July 8, 2019) says, "When the Apollo astronauts walked the Moon, the dust clung to their spacesuits, scratched their visors and made their eyes water and their throats sore. Lunar dust, which is composed of shards of silica, is fine like a powder but it cuts like glass." They say that's the dirt on the Moon. How do you handle it?*

We have goggles that fit very well, and people wear special suits. They are like jumpsuits. Those who are in direct contact, meaning the miners, have a completely enclosed suit with an air system. Keep in mind that the equipment (they are not digging with shovels) they use allows them to remain in a sealed cab. Therefore, they are not in any way exposed to the glass, as you call it. On Earth, you have volcanic glass, which is similar, but this is pretty well pounded up. There is some misunderstanding in your time as to how it got to be there. This is because much of it is essentially slag from previous

Image 5.1. NASA photo of a young unnamed crater on the Moon

mining and digs. It is also the result of objects hitting the Moon in the past.

You probably don't know this, but in ancient times, the Moon was very smooth. It had a glassy surface. Other people, we don't know who, were there. We were able to find the records that they left, but we couldn't understand their language. There were enough illustrations that we could see that the Moon had been very smooth, but it was not naturally smooth. The Moon was natural, but there was something on its surface that made it highly reflective, much more than it is now.

You mentioned the ground glass on the surface. That helps to explain why the Moon is as reflective as it is in your time. So apparently people came and put a thin layer of something down that made the Moon highly reflective, and we don't know who or why. It might be interesting to find out why, but I can't give you any more than that. So that's how our people are protected from the dust. As you said, it is not exactly dust or dirt. But we call it that because on Earth we are used to "dirt."

I have seen the immediate tailings from very deep digs, and the interesting thing is that even in the deepest digs, there is a glass-like material on the surface of the Moon. We are not entirely sure, but it might go down to the center of the Moon. It would be interesting to know, but we don't.

As Light as Aluminum but as Strong as Steel

When the people mine, you said they are in a "cab-like enclosed vehicle." Do they have something like a machine out in front that digs and brings up the desired mineral or substance?

Yes, it's just like mining procedures in the past (your time), which are the foundation of the mining systems they use here. The only big difference is that the mechanisms are made of a lighter and stronger material, not plastic or anything like that. It is a metal alloy as light as aluminum but as strong as steel. I don't know what it is, because that's not my job. But I have picked up a part of it that was about 7 or 8 feet long, and it looked like a box-shaped hollow tube. I picked it up to get it out of my way and was amazed at how light it was.

Is that a result of how gravity is on the Moon? I think it is 1/6 that of Earth. Or was it just superlight no matter what?

No, it has to do with the alloying of the materials to bring it to the Moon. You can understand that lighter materials are easier to bring to the Moon.

Right, right. But how do you deal with gravity? Do you bounce around?

No, we wear unattractive-looking shoes.

What do they do? Do they magnetically grip the ground or something?

No, they are just heavy.

Oh, okay. I am reading a paper that says, "The Moon is like a desert but it's really more like an ocean because it has a very undulating surface like swells." Is it difficult to walk on the Moon?

No, I have never found it to be difficult. I suppose if you come across a crater, you will want to walk around it. But if you must walk through it, you usually can, and I have been told it's no big deal. Do you still say that, "no big deal"?

We do, yes. They also mentioned an intense contrast between light and dark, which can play tricks on your eyes. Have you had that happen?

Yes, it's very bright. Like I say, the material is much more reflective than I realized. It is not unlike what has been described as snow blindness. Perhaps you have seen the goggles that people wear in areas where there is a great deal of snow or glaciers. The goggles are more like a face mask, but they feel like the old-fashioned goggles that pilots might have worn years before your time. You can adjust the mask to allow only light that you absolutely need. The mask creates a filter as well as a temporary slit you can look through. That surprised me. I was told by others that I would be surprised, and they were right.

Moonquakes and Meteors

The article I'm reading says that the Moon is tectonically active with a lot of moonquakes. Have you noticed any?

I haven't noticed very much, but I have felt a couple of things. The miners here think it has to do with other peoples' mining ventures. But we don't know that for a fact. Our geologists are not doing basic research. They are here to help the company, because we are all employees. So unless the company says it is interested and you can check it out, which they have not done, then I really can't say. I have felt a couple of tremors but nothing major. I experienced an earthquake on Earth that was rated about a 5.2 but nothing that strong on the Moon.

On Earth, we have day and night every 24 hours. A Moon day lasts around twenty-eight Earth days, or 655 hours. Where you sleep, do you have to control the lighting and set up day and night for your body no matter what's outside, like on a space station?

Oh, I see what you mean — like people on Earth who live very far north.

Yes. Is it true that day changes to night only every twenty-eight days?

That's not very unusual; it exists on Earth in places.

Well, I've been to Alaska where there is daylight at midnight. In your sleeping quarters, you need to make it dark at night, right?

Of course.

Okay, what about radiation? This article says there is really strong radiation on the Moon. Do your suits protect you from that?

Yes. On the Moon's surface, the suits will protect people for up to four hours. But to be on the safe side, we encourage people, if they are just in their suits (people are usually in insulated vehicles), to be on the surface for no longer than an hour and a half. This is erring on the side of caution, you might say.

Yes, because they say the cosmic rays can cause dementia, memory deficit, anxiety, depression, and all kinds of stuff.

Well, you know that's part of the concern on Earth, about the ozone layer and all of that, but I think you will solve it.

What about meteors — do you have meteors slamming into the Moon?

No, and the assumption of the people working there (I don't know exactly what they did) was that meteors would hit the Moon all the time. But apparently they don't; it's very rare. It happens but not any more than it does on Earth. When they hit, they don't burn up through the atmosphere as they do for Earth; when they hit, you feel it. If the meteor started out 5 feet across, by the time it hits the Moon, it is still 5 feet across.

In comparison, if something hits Earth and it's 5 feet across when it enters the atmosphere, by the time it actually hits Earth, it might be only 6 inches. I don't know exactly how it works, but everything burns up in Earth's atmosphere except for some scraps of dense metal.

So the Moon doesn't have an atmosphere?

Not that I've noticed.

Do you know whether it ever did?

I don't know about that — just a moment. I was waving to our friendly-at-a-distance "other" miners. We see them sometimes. They wave at us, and we wave back.

So you are talking now from your life on the Moon?

I have to do that, because where I am in my now time in my now place, I can't even talk about digging. Digging would be harming.

Yes, right.

Safety First

This paper says that the lava tubes carved by ancient volcanic activity could be turned into spacious living quarters. Do you have these underground?

Where did you get this information? I don't know anything about lava tubes.

Okay, then — is there volcanic activity there?

No.

Oh, all right, so much for that. As I said, the information comes from a New York Times *article. What about robots — do you use robots in your mining and building?*

You know, we use equipment that operates autonomously at times. But very often what we are doing is delicate, because our people are mining small veins. The mining staff believes it is better to use machines directed by a human being who is highly experienced. The combination of a highly experienced human being who can know and a machine that can detect is the best option. A machine might detect something by its color, shape, or odor, but it may be mistaken. It is possible for a machine to make a mistake, and in mining, that could be catastrophic. So if there is a percentage of possible failure, meaning maybe the machine has it wrong, we don't leave that up to maybe. That's where skilled professionals come in. That's probably the best way to work with machinery everywhere. Our mining company takes no chances, and we think that is for the best.

Absolutely. Some of this information talks about plans right now to build what they call a gateway space station close to the Moon. Did they build something like that?

They built something at the halfway point. I don't know whether it's a gateway. But building at the halfway point makes a lot of sense.

Oh, is it similar to the space stations we have now?

Well, it's nothing like you have now, because what's on board is essentially scientific. It was initially for commercial operators and, of course, had medical facilities. But it didn't have any place for R and R (rest and relaxation). It was strictly for resupplying or repairs that might be urgently needed (it was rare, but it has happened).

You wouldn't want your vehicle to break down on your way to Earth, especially when carrying a heavy load. The load doesn't feel heavy at first, but it does once you are in Earth's atmosphere. If there is a problem, it is possible to stop at around the halfway point, which people here tend to call the halfway house. I think it's a joke.

Just stop at the halfway house and fill up with whatever you need! There are a lot of jokes here. People try to keep it light because they are thousands of miles from home.

Right, right. So you go up in a rocket and come back in something like a piloted shuttle? Is that how it works?

Something like that, yes. You come back in a shuttle because the shuttles go regularly with materials. There are shuttles of different sizes to transport even small amounts of materials. I have not been aware of shuttles specifically for personnel to go back and forth. If their shift has ended and they are ready to go back to Earth, they can ride on a shuttle carrying materials back to Earth. Even if they have to stay on the Moon for a couple of extra days after their shift has ended, that's okay. People are willing to wait even though they want to get home as soon as possible. There are no commercial flights.

Not yet. Can you say if, by the time you are there, we have a base on Mars? Any kind of human habitation on Mars — do we have that?

I don't know much about Mars. Why would I know about Mars?

Well, it would be in the news, wouldn't it?

If you want to talk about the Moon, that's fine, because my job is on the Moon.

Okay. I was just trying to sneak in a little future history.

Please do not do that, because you will find that when you're working with doctors, some don't like to joke around. I know you're not my patient, and I don't mean to be too strict with you, but sometimes I must.

I could probably use your services if you're a psychologist and a counselor.

I do not claim to have that expertise.

That's what you do there, isn't it? You're a counselor?

Yes, but I am also an MD.

Oh, I didn't know that. You talk so much about anthropology. I didn't know you are an MD.

It is considered necessary if you are going to be on the Moon, in case medical staff is unavailable. That is a skill I also have, but I don't have to use it much. A lot of the people, including the miners themselves, are well-trained in what you would call first-aid. That is because there are not very many people here, just the number there needs to be. Even though there is somewhat of a base on the Moon, it is not what I would call a thriving community. It is not the sort of place you would want to visit on vacation.

Yes, you said that's why the company paid the miners and other workers so much in the beginning, because it was so difficult.

Yes, and they pay them a little less now, because the really tough parts have been accomplished. The original people got paid plenty. The people who go up there now (meaning the time we are referring too) get paid pretty well but not as much as the original guys, as they call themselves.

Women among the Miners

Are they all men, or are there any women among the miners?

There are no women among the miners. This is not a sexist thing; it is simply because it is deemed hazardous. Men get lonely and sometimes they might get overly friendly if there were a woman present. A woman might be here if she is someone they can't do without.

And that's you.

Yes, and some people on my staff. There is a certain amount of kidding but no touching allowed. The company does not want people to get jealous, because that causes problems. Even for people who might have formed a relationship, 100 percent discretion is required.

This article says that the lunar south pole has craters holding ice that could produce water. How do you handle getting water there?

It's all delivered; every bit of it comes from Earth. It's not my job, so I really don't know the details, but the exploration of such things (and this is second- or third-hand information) was considered too valuable by scientists to try to convert it to water. In other words, it's apparently not water as it is on Earth. The thought was that it could be done, but why do it when they could bring up water?

If they tried to use that water on the Moon, they would have to set up a small distillation plant so that water is essentially re-distilled. A lot of water is simply brought up here. There is a lot of effort that goes into discouraging people from working up a sweat. People do not go jogging on the Moon.

[Laughs.] Yes, I see. The less water you have to use, the better.

The miners have to be in good shape, and they have to work hard. They sweat, but they are encouraged not to. You have to take into account every last bit so that you can support your people. So it's not like they are encouraged to go jogging. Not that you could go jogging on the Moon but there's always someone who would want to try.

[Laughs.] Right. I don't remember because it has been a couple of weeks, but didn't you say that a company was exploring the idea of setting up a place for tourism?

There's talk about that, but the mining companies in no way wish to participate in it because of the liabilities if people get injured. You would basically have to create a bubble, and it would be very expensive. So this is not something our company is involved in, but I hear talk about it.

That brings up the question: Are there several mining companies from Earth mining on the Moon now?

In our time, yes.

Are there also some extraterrestrials mining?

Yes, those are the ones we wave at and they wave back. They are friendly, but they keep their distance, and we think that is a good idea.

Human-Like ETs

I don't think I have asked you to describe the other miners. Are they Zeta Reticulans, Pleiadians, or strange-looking?

I have personally met two ETs who are not humanoids. One might be related to Zeta Reticulans, but the beings didn't introduce themselves. They don't have huge eyes or anything like that. Their eyes are about the same size as ours and are slanted differently. Their heads are shaped in a different way, but they are definitely humanoids, if you know what I mean.

Excuse me, I'm not getting my words right, here. It's not easy to describe. But they are very pleasant, and they communicate telepathically, which is something I like to do. If they happen to be passing by, they might stop if they feel welcomed. But as a general rule, they don't stop, because this is a company and people are working. It's not as if they can just stop by for a little barbecue or something.

But during your off-time you could communicate with them.

Individually, yes, but my off hours are not off hours for everybody else.

Have you seen any who look like humans?

I have seen one, but that was someone waving in the distance. The only reason I knew the being was extraterrestrial is because the being was with the other people that wave at us. It's hard to describe this, because it's a physical thing, isn't it? You can tell when people are together that they are friends and that they are used to being together, so I assumed they weren't from Earth.

For one thing, they all were wearing equipment that was totally unlike what our people wear. It was much less equipment but apparently very effective — and how we would love to have it! They waved at several of us who were there. Of course we were really fascinated because they were clearly not from Earth. They were wearing suits with a very thin film, as far as I could tell, over their hands and faces, but there wasn't any external breathing apparatus apparent. We don't know how they do that, but how we would love to know so that we could do that too!

Wow, maybe we could talk to one of them through Robert and ask.

Perhaps another today. What's the timing like, because he has to get out of here.

It's time right now, so we will stop. Do you want to talk again about other things?

Of course, we can continue. Sorry for this being brief.

No, I knew he had limited time. Okay, thank you very much. We will talk again. Goodbye.

Yes, good night.

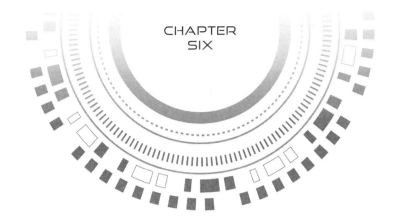

WATER ON THE MOON

Doc

JULY 12, 2019

What is the prevailing opinion in your time: Could people ever move to the Moon and live there full-time even though there is no water?

No, people do not live there, but they might visit. Even in the times we have been discussing, some people might've been on the Moon for a while, but it is not the kind of place you would retire to or hang your hat by the door. It's rough, and at the very best it's rustic, so to speak, so no.

Okay. How do you stake out your territory? Is it like gold mining in the old West, where the first one there stakes out a claim?

No. It's much more easygoing than that. There isn't anything like that. Besides, when we got there, there were already "other" people there. I don't know what it would've been like if we got there first, but we didn't. Generally speaking, people are helpful as long as you are not digging where they are digging. We don't get in anyone's way. There is a tendency to be helpful. So, no, there are no claims as you know it.

Image 6.1. A composite image using data from NASA's Moon Mineralogy Mapper. The blue shows areas of confirmed water ice on the lunar surface.

Have the countries on Earth divided up the Moon's surface?

No. It's not political like that.

Are you concerned about environmental damage?

Not very, the environments on Earth involve a great many things working in harmony with each other: water, wind, many different life forms, and so on. Other than the miners here, we have not personally perceived any other native life forms, so environmental issues don't really come up.

Mining Techniques

Okay, your Moon mining must have needed some infrastructure. Who did that? Did robots come up, did you use 3D printers, or did the humans do it as they went?

All materials were brought up in vehicles and put together as needed by human beings. There is not a lot of robotic stuff involved, because such machines are highly technical and vulnerable to dust. Dust is all-pervasive, and we didn't see any point in paving the place because at any given moment we might have been digging here, there, or everywhere. So robots would have been a mistake; human beings have done it all.

With the mining, is it like a vein and you have to follow where it goes?

Yes, exactly. Equipment was brought up to basically dig a hole. We know where to dig because of the assistance from others. Then it was exactly what you said. You follow the vein or, if more than one, you follow both veins or make a note that there is another vein there to follow.

Fortunately the "other" miners in our area are not interested at all in what we are interested in, and we are not interested in what they are interested in. But we keep an eye out for what they are interested in. I remember one of our people came across something one time and said, "Aren't the other people interested in this?" and they realized, "Oh yeah, that's right," so we managed to get a message to them, and they were very grateful. But the others, the ETs, were the first ones that helped us before we were able to help them.

They helped you find whatever you were digging?

When we first got there, if you remember, we thought we had found an area that was promising. But as we worked, they kept pointing to another area. Finally, someone went out there with not much in the way of machinery (they took a borehole or something like that), and they found the vein almost immediately. The reaction was, "Oh, that's what all the pointing was about!"

The Question of DNA Mutation

Did you have to move what you call "the bubble living space" to that new vein, or was it close enough that you could go there with just a vehicle?

It was not necessary to move the bubble living space.

Okay, now something interesting happened on the space station — the circadian rhythm of the people there went from the 24-hour period of Earth to 24.9 hours that Mars has. Has anything like that happened to you and your people on the Moon?

Do you mean, have we adopted a different life rhythm since we have been here?

Yes.

No, and this is what I think the reasons are: For one thing, we can usually see Earth (unlike on a space station where they may be conducting experiments all the time). Also, there are quite a few people here and not everyone is a scientist. It is a cross section of humanity. We are on 24-hour time.

Another thing that happened was when NASA Astronaut Scott Kelly stayed on the space station for 340 days. He had a 7 percent DNA mutation. Have you noticed anything like that with your people — the miners or the scientists?

We haven't noticed it, but there hasn't been much testing, which is easier to do in our time. We just pay attention to their mood: How are they acting? Are they happy, working hard, or grumbling? We are not studying them in an experimental situation. We attempt to provide a product needed on Earth. But we are not involved in scientific experiments as basic research.

Wouldn't you be interested to know whether your DNA has mutated?

What makes you think it has?

Well, why would DNA mutate on the space station and not on the Moon, which is farther away from Earth?

Exactly, we are farther away than the space station.

Maybe it has to do with weightlessness instead of distance.

The best guess is that it has to do with weightlessness and a lack of being able to do the things that the person would normally do on Earth. Is astronaut Kelly married?

Yes, I think so.

His spouse would have had an Earth life surrounded with all that he does there. But when he's in the space station, also known as a capsule, life is totally and completely unnatural. So certain portions of his functioning might shut down a bit or adapt to something that amounts to a prison. He is not being guarded or held behind bars, but he still cannot go anywhere or do anything. He is basically stuck.

When people are in these kind of situations certain parts of them shut down and other parts may become more active.

Ninety-Day Rotations

What about you. You said you were on the Moon for over seventeen years. Did you go up and stay there and then come home every couple of months, like a rotation?

Because of the ships coming and going so regularly, I went home often. I think if I had been there any longer than a ninety-day stretch, it would've been really hard. One time, I think I was there for longer than the ninety days and found it too long. You learn by being one of the first there. We took up the idea of rotating the workers. Some employees preferred to stay there for longer lengths of time. But for me, personally, it was too much. People could opt to stay there for six or seven months at a stretch if they wanted to.

One of my jobs was to keep an eye on people to see if they started behaving oddly. If they were not behaving oddly (and no one mentioned that so-and-so is acting strange), then they were allowed to stay longer. Of course, when they stayed longer, they made more money — a part of the motivation that we understood. Other than that, a ninety-day rotation was considered perfectly acceptable.

After ninety days, you went back to Earth for ten days or two weeks. If you were not feeling well, you stayed on Earth for maybe thirty days because obviously they did not want you to go back to the Moon, say, if you caught a cold and might give it to everybody.

I see. So ninety days on the Moon and two weeks back on Earth was normal, then?

Something like that, yes, but it wasn't rigid.

Did that work for the miners too?

That's who I am talking about, the miners. When I'm talking about the workers, I'm always talking about the miners.

Okay, so it was you who did ninety days on and two weeks off.

Yes, I tried to explain that, but maybe you didn't understand. When I first came up, I thought I could stay longer. But after ninety days, I started to notice that I was getting uncomfortable. Being in the profession that I am, I realized I needed to be back in Earth's environment. I went back down to Earth, and within a few days, I felt fine. That's how I got the ninety-day idea that became current practice.

Did you go up with the first miners, or had they been there awhile by the time you went up?

I went up with them.

Oh, so you were there during the very rough times when they had to create everything.

Yeah, that's why I get so much respect from the old crowd. Here's something you must understand. The company was worried that people would go crazy. They figured it would be absolutely essential for someone who had a broad perspective on different cultures to be there, because not everybody who works there comes from the same culture. I had that knowledge and I also had the psychological skills. It felt good to have someone along who could help if people started to go nuts. In other words, the general feeling was that we didn't know what could happen, so we had better send someone along who could help with any issues that arise. That's why I went with them and got a lot of respect.

Can you say how old you were then?

I don't think I'll say that.

Well, you were pretty young, weren't you?

Pretty young, yes. When you are younger, you don't really think you're invulnerable, but there is a sense of vitality that simply isn't present when you are older. You understand?

Doc's Difficulties

What was the most difficult thing in the early days for you?

I think there were a couple of things. One was not having other people around like me. I was sort of a counselor, and normally counselors work in proximity with other counselors. Not having this was problematic, because I would've liked to have others to consult with. By consulting, I mean face-to-face. If you are not face-to-face, you miss a lot in communication. The other thing I missed was the food.

What did you eat up there?

It was a kind of space food not much different from what astronauts have to deal with. I'm saying "have to deal with," because that's really it. There are no cupcakes on the space station. It's a joke. I'm not saying I needed cupcakes. I am just saying that the simplicity, lack of variety, and general lack of pleasantness got to me. There was no sitting down to have a nice meal, none of that. You are basically eating out of tubes. No glass of wine, nothing like that. I'm not saying that I needed that, but you might go out to eat on Earth and have a nice meal — none of that on the Moon.

Well, did that improve over the years?

Not by much. It's not a place to go for vacation. You know you are working when you are there. You expect to be roughing it, and that's why they pay you well. They can do that because the elements that are being brought back are sold for a very high price. The company shoulders tremendous expense to get these products back. Since they are basically nonexistent on Earth, with only minute traces available, they can charge whatever they want. The company needs money, because it has an awful lot of overhead.

Yeah, but it seems with all the money they are spending that they could send some decent food.

You are mistaken, and the reason is that you are thinking in terms of camping out some place. Camping out on the Moon is not the same as camping out on Earth.

Okay, but couldn't they have sent frozen meals or something?

No.

Because they didn't have room on the spaceships, or why not?

Because it is not possible to eat like that in such a place. If you want to understand it better, look it up and see what the astronauts eat and how they eat it (this is public information). It is not much different for us. When you eat on Earth, you chew and breathe with your mouth open a lot. There is an exchange of air and so on. When you are on the Moon, it is completely hostile to human life. So you don't live on the Moon like you do on Earth.

Even inside the bubble living space?

Even inside the bubble.

Medical and Counseling Crew

How many miners are there in your crew?

The crew flexes between thirty and sixty, never more.

How many of you are medical and counseling people?

Once we were established, it was me and sometimes three or four staff members, as few as thirty or as many as sixty.

Okay, so a spectrum of thirty to sixty. What were some of your most difficult counseling experiences? Can you give a couple of examples?

It's always the same thing — people missing Earth for one reason or another. When it interferes with their work, meaning they are distracted, they are sent home. They have to train quite a bit to come to the Moon to do the job, and for a lot of people, it doesn't work out. There's not as much training as for astronauts, but there's still a lot involved. Not everyone can do it. They can do the job, but not everyone can function on the Moon, living Moon life, so to speak.

Some people just can't do it, so that's another expense for the company with all that training. They screen people as much as possible to find out about their personalities, psychology, and confidence. But this is an extreme situation, and there is currently no data about it. Every moment is extreme. Some people can embrace that, throw themselves into their work, and spend as little time as possible thinking. If you are thinking, you're going to be missing home. Everything you are thinking about is what you are missing, especially if they have loved ones at home and things they like to do.

There is nothing on the Moon to compensate. Some people can't take it, so we send them back. They are not punished by the company; they are just basically released: "Okay, thanks for trying, but you are released." They don't get a bad write up for their next job. It's something like "served as well as possible."

Job Requirements

How long do they train on Earth before they can go up?

Usually five or six months. They have to learn not only the specific job they are going to do but also the basics of everyone else's job. If someone is suddenly sent home or is not well and has to take a day or two off, then others can slide right in and do the job. This training takes time. It's not like on Earth when someone can't do the job, you can call a temp agency to send someone else over. In any event, it takes time to get from Earth to the Moon. There are some jobs that are more delicate or more demanding than others, so you need people to basically keep the system running. That's why people train not only for their specific jobs but also (at least a little bit and frequently more than a little bit) for other people's jobs. This is to keep the system going and keep the company in business.

What percentage of those who came up had to return because they couldn't do it?

In the beginning, many returned. But the ships did not come and go as often. The ships brought up materials, but they did not take back the product right away. Still, it was maybe 17 percent fallout (people who had to be sent back). But over time it was possible to get clearer on what might be available and who could do the job.

Also, people were promised that after ninety days on the Moon, they would be able to come back to Earth for rest and relaxation. The company paid them the same amount when they were on Earth, or they could opt for an all-expenses paid vacation. For the people who had wives and kids, they could get an all-expense paid vacation. Some people didn't, but that just gives you an idea of how the company takes care of its people the best it can. This was attractive to younger miners and also some older expert miners who were thinking about retirement. There are a lot of attractive perks (you might say) to the job, if you are willing to do the tough part. The tough part is being on the Moon and doing the work.

Communication with Earth

Did they come up with a psychological profile for those who would be more apt to be on the Moon?

Yes, they had this from the beginning. They had an ideal standard still used on Earth for companies whose people are working in remote and extreme circumstances, maybe in the blasting hot desert or in a swamp. You can't expect just anybody to do this kind of job, because it takes a certain toughness. Plus, a lot of consultation with NASA and various businesses working in space helped.

Was there communication from the Moon to Earth? Could the miners contact their families while they were there?

Yes, there was something like that. But it was a bit slow — something like texting or emailing but not video.

Oh, no video. That would have been too expensive?

The company felt it would've been a big expense, so they did not do that.

Did they feel it would be too traumatic for the miners to see their families or something like that?

No, it was an expense they didn't want. Like I said, it was not a picnic up there. You are not going to camp. The reason I'm using those terms is because that is the way we spoke then. People sort of embraced each other with comments like that. You came up there to do the job and were paid very well to do it, so there was a lot of implied toughness. You're up on the Moon, and not everyone can say that. Aside from the toughness, there was a certain amount of support. It was not easy, and I had sympathy for the miners, because they were doing the tough stuff. I wasn't out there with a shovel and pick. I wasn't exposed to what they were exposed to. It was pretty rough.

Common Languages

What about languages? If they came from all over Earth, did they speak different languages?

Yes, they did, but there were certain common languages. Sometimes there was a sort of lingo that people picked up, because everyone had to learn the terminology of mining. So the terminology of mining became the foundational element of the lingo the miners used. I'm not really able to impart any of that, other than a certain amount of slang.

So most of your counseling was to help them adjust to the situation. Would you say that?

Yes, I helped them adjust to the situation and supported them with the idea that if it was too overwhelming for them, they didn't have to be there. It was not like during their off hours, they could go some place to hang out and have a beer and talk. And the work was exhausting. There were machines, but the work was exhausting anyway. When their shifts ended, they went back to the rough quarters where they resided. When not working, they were basically just eating or sleeping. That was it, no playtime, nothing. It takes a tough person to be able to do that. But you would be surprised how many people are willing to do that if they are paid very well.

Keep in mind that they didn't need a college education for the job. So think about it, in your time people probably need to move ahead and make a lot of money, yes or no?

Yes.

Well, to be a miner you don't have to do that. You just have to be willing to work in very tough conditions. If you're willing to do that, it's fine. You won't be talking much or palling around with the other guys. You're going to be working, eating, and sleeping. That's basically your life. You don't go there for fun. Granted, when people arrived for the first time, they sometimes stood and looked back at Earth, because it was an amazing sight. They looked at the Moon because it's an extraordinary experience when you first get there. But that gets old.

Medical Emergencies

You said that you are an MD. Did you handle any medical emergencies up there?

There were occasional medical emergencies. I patched up people and sent them home. There was a lot of safety equipment; the company went way out of its way to make conditions as safe as possible. The company felt that the miners were their number one asset on the Moon, so they protected them to the best of their ability. People didn't get too many injuries.

How could they get hurt, then?

You could get a cut, bruise, bump, and so on. If it looked like it was going to get infected, I did what I could. People didn't lose fingers or toes or anything like that, but if they needed further care, they were sent back on the next ship.

Were there any things that got easier and more comfortable for you over the course of seventeen years?

What made things better was humor. When you are in a tough situation like that and you can say one or two words, it makes you laugh. For example, "no picnic." The reason I picked that is because it was the first joke people used. People continued to use it because it was true, and it was also funny. After a while, you pick up certain things that are a joke and people say regularly, but up there it was funny. Funny things are an element of Earth, and laughing out loud is an element of Earth. This is really a wonderful thing. Sometimes we laughed out loud, but we would have to be in the bubble to do that.

Did you spend most of your time in the bubble, or were there times when you went outside?

Most of my time was in the bubble. But I went outside the bubble when someone needed help. I didn't go into the mine, because if they needed help, they came out. But I went to the surface where they were.

Oh, I didn't understand that there was actually a deep mine. I thought you were working with these little veins on the surface.

It was all underground.

Oh, so even underground, they were in these vehicles with the digging attachments.

Yes, of course. It was like a coal mine. If you can find pictures of people in a coal mine, it is really quite similar.

Because you talked about these veins, I thought they were on the surface. How far down did they go? How many feet?

You know, I don't really have those figures, but I can give you a general idea. It was usually no farther than a quarter of a mile down. That's not so unusual for mines. On Earth, you have mines like that, don't you?

Yeah, but I didn't realize they were mining down a quarter of a mile.

I said it was usually no farther down than a quarter of a mile. But sometimes it was that deep, so it took a lot of equipment.

They had lights down there, right?

Yes, of course.

Mining like that could lead to claustrophobia and all kinds of things.

Most of the people had been tested for that.

Did anything else change for the better during the time that you were there?

Not really. I don't know how to answer your question. What happens is that you get used to in any situation after a while. When you get used to it, then it seems better, because you don't have the unrealistic expectations of it getting better than what it really is. You just get used to it, so then that is better.

What about your personal life? After seventeen years, you retired, I gather?

Yes.

Was there more wear and tear on you or did you age more or did you have any problems that you wouldn't have had if you had stayed on Earth?

Well, it's hard to say. What would've been intended for me spiritually in terms of how long my soul would be in my body and all of that, I couldn't say. I can tell you how old I was when I died on Earth.

How old?

Fifty-eight.

Well, that's pretty young. Was your life shortened by being on the Moon?

It is possible, but I do not know that for sure.

Yes, but you went back to Earth and had children, so that's wonderful.

Yes, that is wonderful.

Expect the Unexpected

Well, okay, I am out of questions. If I ask Zoosh how that glass got on the Moon, are you able to listen to what he says?

Why is that important to you?

Well, because it's so unusual.

I don't feel the need to have that told to me.

Okay, no problem. You just mentioned that you were curious when you told me about it.

Curious, not desperate.

Okay, so what haven't I asked you or should have asked you? What else would you like to say?

I will say this: If you are looking for an adventure of something you would never forget, you might want to consider becoming a miner on the Moon or consider space travel as an occupation, which I feel in your time will probably be a potential occupation. But know that it will affect your life sometimes in wonderful ways and unexpected ways. If you go into something like that, then expect the unexpected. Good night.

Thank you very much. Thank you.

THE ORIGINS OF THE MOON

Zoosh

JULY 19, 2019

Welcome, Zoosh. What do you do with your time when you are not around Robert?

It is difficult to answer that for someone who is in sequential time. This is why spirits will often say, "I am," because we are wherever we need to be.

Okay, listen, here's what I want, and I want a whole bunch more but I don't know whether you will want to talk about it. There seems to be a layer of glass on the Moon to make it more reflective. Can you tell me who put it there and the circumstances surrounding it?

A layer of glass — are you talking about something that resembles volcanic glass?

I don't know. We are doing a book called Phone Calls from the Future, *and we were talking to a female doctor who is part of a mining operation on the Moon. The astronauts who were up there fifty years ago and this doctor all mentioned a substance on the surface that is not really dirt but more like ground-up glass. You can't breathe it because it would kill you.*

I see.

Image 7.1. Image of the Moon comprised of more than 200,000 shots pieced together by two astrophotographers with color saturation increased.
For more information on the making of this image and to access the highly detailed 174 megapixel picture:
reddit.com/r/space/comments/wtl9fj/two_years_ago_i_teamed_up_with_a_fellow_redditor

The Moon Was a Planet

So where did it come from, and how did it get there?

You understand that the Moon, and moons in general, didn't start out as a moon. They are usually portions of something else. In the case of your planet's Moon, I think it originally started out as a small planet, but over time, it lost its atmosphere and shrunk. The people in the distant past who were interested in the planet were expecting what you now know as your Moon to be a small planet.

When they found it, it was not yet a moon of Earth, and it was way too small for them. But they created something slightly below the surface that would function for them.

Their base, unlike your flesh, blood, cells, tissues, and so on, was mineral, not molecular. Since their base was mineral, they did not eat, so they did not have to eliminate. To live, however, they needed to have surfaces (either the actual surface or, in this case, slightly below the surface) that would sustain their life form. So they put it up there. Keep in mind that, as I said, it was not the Moon at that time. It was just a small planet slightly bigger than it is now.

They realized very early on that it wasn't big enough for them, but by that time they had already established a form of glass that was more like crystal with which they had encased the Moon (and I'm calling it Moon for lack of a better term). Their residence there was not very long, but they did change its orbit. The change in the orbit, while it moved around your Sun, was at the time when Earth was going through one of its changes.

The meeting of Earth and the Moon did not take place immediately. The time of the absence of these beings doesn't relate, because it is interdimensional, but for the sake of simplicity (to understand it in sequential time), it would've been about 40,000 years.

To create a crystalline effect around what you now know as the Moon, they took that planet's atmosphere, brought it down into the planet, and used it to stimulate the crystal around the planet. I want to say "crystal glaze" but that sounds like glass, so "crystal layer" is more accurate. As I mentioned, they did not stay. Their absence was about 40,000 years, and there no longer was any atmosphere to prevent passing objects from hitting it. For 40,000 years [in sequential time], objects hit it and eventually just smashed all of that crystal into the glass you are now talking about.

How did it get in such a peculiar orbit? It is as if it were designed to be where it is because the two orbits are synchronized, and we never see the back. How did that happen?

Keep in mind that at that time, the Moon was a small planet and Earth was otherwise occupied — meaning not in that dimension at that time. I think that has been channeled about before. If you look, you will find out that Earth, for a while, was no longer here.

Of course, what I'm calling Earth also might have been some place else. You will have to look it up.

Yes, I know. You are saying it's before the planet from Sirius came here.

That's right. As a result, the orbit of what you now know as the Moon was in the neighborhood of what you now know as Earth. But Earth is so much bigger than what you now know as the Moon that it did exactly what other planets do. Other planets have lots of moons that have been captured by their gravitational field and rotation. So that's really what happened. Earth was much bigger than the Moon, and the former planet became Earth's Moon.

Was the Moon one of the planets that was in the orbit of what is now the asteroid belt?

No. It was in an actual orbit of its own. It was a planet. It was just small.

Oh. I didn't know we were missing anything in an orbit.

It's what scientists nowadays would call a planetoid, but that's just terminology. It's actually a planet.

Meteor Strikes

There's one other thing that I have read about on the internet, I don't know whether it's true or not. There seems to be one huge crater with an incredibly large amount of metal. Did something smash into it that didn't quite go down to the mantle?

I don't know what the authors of that article mean by "incredibly large," but many of the objects flying through space were something at one point in time. Most meteors that hit Earth were incredible masses of metal. So if they are talking about something that has actually been discovered, it's certainly possible. Just think of all the craters on the Moon: Something has hit it, and what doesn't shatter on impact becomes the densest part. Of course it wouldn't have burned through any atmosphere of the Moon. It would have been just whizzing along and disposing pieces of itself as it went. To make this as brief as possible, the chances of something like that being a large mass of metal is certainly possible. I don't think the hint that it is a machine is accurate, though.

Yes. I never thought of that before. It's obvious that the meteors we get here are mostly iron, nickel, and other minerals. That is what survived the trip through the atmosphere. Everything else burns up in Earth's atmosphere. Is that what you are saying?

Yes, on Earth meteors burn up. So if there is a mass of metal on the Moon, it's possible that the object they are talking about that hit the Moon might have gone through various atmospheres on its way. But there probably wasn't an atmosphere on the Moon at that time. It is possible, but I don't think so.

Right, okay, so all the wild stuff they talk about of the Moon being hollow and manufactured, we can put all that aside, because it was just a small planet.

That's right.

Okay, thank you very much.

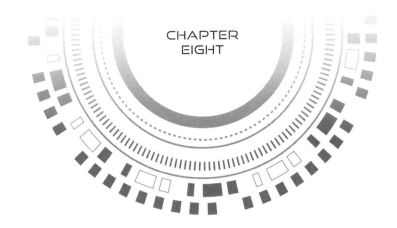

STOP DIGGING TOXIC MATTER ON EARTH AND LIVE 7OO YEARS

Mars Visitor from Andromeda

AUGUST 12, 2019

Are you someone who went to Mars in our near future? When did you go there?

An Andromedan: Do you mean according to your calendar?

Yes.

It was 2056.

Okay, that's near. Why were you there?

Well, at that time, we had a small outpost there, and I went to restock supplies, so it wasn't particularly adventurous or interesting.

Who had an outpost there?

Oh, I see. Who am I and where am I from, right?

Yes, all that good stuff.

We are from the Andromeda galaxy, and we had a small outpost on Mars that was involved in observing the outer planets of your solar system. The outpost had no interest in Earth whatsoever.

They were observing the outer planets. This did not involve telescopes. It involved flights from time to time to check on the other planets. Almost all of them needed sources of heat to be habitable. Most of the people lived underground, but occasionally there were sources of heat near the surface, and people lived near that source of warmth. An example might be hot waters or perhaps warmth from underneath the surface, which might have had to do with volcanism. It's hard to say. I am not a scientist. But most of them lived under the surface, and our people took an interest in supporting such populations.

Can you say which planets have these populations?

Well, all the planets beyond Mars.

What dimension were they in? Do you know?

Do you mean would you see them if they were standing there?

Correct.

Two out of three, you would see if you were standing there.

Which ones?

That's all you get.

[Laughs.] Somebody's talking to you already?

Yes, I have someone whispering in my ear, you might say.

Okay, so you came from Andromeda with supplies, food, clothes, and fuel — stuff like that?

Yes, the necessities of life.

You were assisting these people, then?

In a sense we were assisting the people who were assisting the people on the planets, but if you are talking about our planet's interest in supporting such civilizations, then yes. We assisted such civilizations, and you might reasonably ask what good this did you on Earth. Well, the people on your planet (granted not a lot, but some) have interest in colonizing the surface of Mars.

Yes.

We think that there won't be much of an objection to that. But if you do your usual stuff, digging and corrupting the surface (punching holes in it and digging), then you will not be supported,

Image 8.1. Colorized photo of the Mars surface
taken by NASA's Curiosity Mars rover

because you won't have to go much further than (I'm going to use your measurements) 8 or 10 inches into the dust. What will come up will be toxic.

If you are going to build anything on the surface, you will have to put your supportive life form structures on the surface only and not punch any holes, just to be safe. Your people do not necessarily all act as a single group, if I understand correctly. They don't have a single authority or motivation for accomplishing goals in a united way at this time. As a result, the chances of you corrupting the surface are strong, and if that happens, you will not survive.

Civilizations on Mars

What is so toxic?

Beneath the surface is a slight layer from previous civilizations, but once you get 8 or 10 inches below, you get to the original surface. The original surface has considerable amounts of the materials. I am not a scientist, so that is all I can say. I don't really have the words. The materials are toxic to your delicate form of life. You are a delicate form of life, you understand — not much between you and the outer world. Plus, you have to breathe, taking in the outer world all the time and eating and so on. You are constantly taking in the outer world. You are vulnerable to just about anything. Even the smallest amount of that material getting into the air you breathe spells doom. As long as you as a civilization manage to build on the surface, you will be all right. Don't dig and don't mine; it would be your death.

How did the civilization that was on Mars before handle that?

For the most part, they built on the surface. But over time, interactions with other civilizations — some of whom did not know about that — made them decide to dig down just a little ways to get to something they needed. They thought they could fill it up right away so that everything would be okay. When they did that, the life on the surface (not human beings) became ill. They could not survive as a civilization, and most of them managed to get away or were rescued. The buildings gradually decomposed and became the surface matter.

But it is my understanding that there were humans on Mars a long time ago.

Yes, this is possibly true, but that's not the civilization I am referring to.

Okay, well, I think the human one was quite a long time ago, when there was water there.

There wasn't any water when I was there. At least I didn't see any. It wasn't my job to observe; I was strictly a delivery person: Take the stuff there, drop it off, then go on to the next place.

What was the next place?

I was delivering supplies to various places. Most of them had to do with our planet. After a while, we became friends, and they sometimes asked (since we were going in that general direction), "Would you mind dropping this off?" Things like that. I'm going to use your humor if that's all right.

Absolutely.

We collected things, you might say. There were a few other places where we dropped off supplies since we were going that way.

I have talked to Andromedans and they come in all sizes. How tall are you?

I am about 9 feet tall.

Ah, you're one of the tall ones. Is this your regular job, or do you just volunteer sometimes?

It is my regular job, and I like doing it. It is uncomplicated, and I like that. Also, I like a certain amount of travel, and I don't have much in the way of family on my home planet. I have a few friends and one family member, but that family member is involved in other things. We don't get much chance to interact. There is not much holding me on my home planet. I go there and enjoy home planet things, but traveling here and there is really appealing.

How long have you been doing that?

A moment — calculating in your time, about ninety-five years or something like that.

Can you say how old you are in our time?

I am about one-quarter of the way through my life.

Okay, so how long do you live?

A moment — generally about four to four and a half times as long as the oldest human beings on your planet might live.

So 400 to 450 years. Do you have a crew or group that goes with you, or do you go alone?

Oh no, no alone stuff, we go with a crew. We have a good-sized vehicle large enough to carry lots of different supplies. Some of these require special handling, as you might expect, and there are plants and other types of beings. Most of it is packaged. The size of the crew varies; sometimes there are only nine, but there might be as many as nineteen — not usually that many. On average, there might be fifteen for the crew.

That sounds like fun. Can you stop and sightsee if you want?

It's a job, so that's not encouraged. The simple answer to your question is no.

Okay, so in 2056 there aren't any humans from Earth on Mars, or are there?

Well, there are none that I've noticed. Keep in mind that I go to a specific place on Mars. We don't go around the planet and inspect everything. It's not impossible that on some other part of Mars there are human beings I don't know about. We just go straight to our people and then on to the next place.

Travel by Attraction

The people on your outpost — you said they fly to outer planets to observe them directly because they don't use telescopes or anything.

Yes, they have ships and go to the outer planets to observe. They land if assistance is requested. Usually those civilizations — and this is mostly in the past — maintain their lifestyle, whatever it might be, quite well on their own. We are just available if they need help or supplies from other places. If they don't have a regular way to get these, our ships will go help.

Are they observing the people on the planet? Is it like sociology or anthropology?

No. They are not putting them under a microscope. They are literally just helping out — good neighbors, you might say.

This solar system's outer planets are quite a ways away from Andromeda — a little too far for just being good neighbors.

Well, it's only quite a ways if you are using a means of space travel like propulsion. We do not do that; we have vehicles that get where they need to go quickly without using propulsion.

What would you call it — electromagnetic?

Attraction.

Oh yes, attraction. Many beings have talked about that before. On your ship, are you a captain or a navigator?

There are no captains because we do not have a hierarchical system. Everyone does a job, and that's fine. I am just another person on the crew, nothing special.

Okay, I don't know what else to ask.

In your time on your planet (I am looking at it to the extent that I can because it is so seriously corrupted), there is already a lot of hole-punching. Since I have some knowledge about this, I think most of the diseases on your planet are because of you corrupting its surface, including to build your structures. I don't know if you know this. Perhaps that is why I'm here, because you want people from the future to help you in your present. Isn't that the purpose of your project?

Yes.

If you go digging down into your planet (especially in places that don't have much plant life growing but are not covered with water, as well as other places) 9 feet, or in some places as little as 16 inches, you will always bring up material and matter that might have been useful to a past (nonhuman) civilization but is toxic to your present civilization. Sometimes it appears to be matter from plants or trees, perhaps some residual matter — pollen, you might say.

For a lot of people, this creates problems for which there is no apparent cure. Things are available for some of the symptoms but not all of them. I recommend, as much as possible, ceasing to dig into you planet. For any place where digging has happened, cover it over as best you can and don't dig anymore. If you can do that as a unified project with everyone on the planet, we would be glad to help. I think civilizations from other places would also be glad to help, but you will have to welcome us first.

We won't come if you're going to treat us in a hostile fashion as you do with each other. We understand that you are not a sub-form, or lower form, of life, and by "lower," I do not mean the way you might classify animals, insects, and so forth. If you are life forms that harm each other and yourselves, then this is hostile and unwelcoming to us. I am not saying that you are like that, but apparently you are not allowed to remember your accumulated wisdom as total beings. This, I do not understand. It is a severe handicap that apparently all of you have, so you cannot be blamed for this. Still, perhaps there is some way you can recover the knowledge and wisdom that you all have in your total being, but I do not know how.

If there is a way to recover that knowledge and wisdom, I hope you will at least desire it. If you all desire it, then perhaps it will be presented to you in some form. This is how we have learned on our planet. If we need to know something, we all become aware of it. If one was involved in normal communication processes, then people would go there and let them know what was needed. So everyone would desire it, not constantly because life goes on, but the desire would be there.

As a result, we have teachers or others visit and teach us how to do whatever we need to do for ourselves. This temporarily provides us with what we desire and need until we can do it for ourselves. From my travels here and there, this seems to be the pattern all over, at least in the places I have seen. If you can do that, I think it is the means to reclaim your good health.

In my experience with other forms of human beings who look like you, their actual lifespan can be a minimum of 300 years. I have not known them to live longer than 1,200 years, and apparently (I am not a scientist) they function like you and look like you. They have mouths, ears, and all of that, so they take in the world around them. If you can do these things, desiring them as a global community, and can live in some way that is better for all of you, then I think the teachers will come help you with your needs. Perhaps that is why I am here for your project.

Well, I really appreciate it.

Perhaps I'm here to let you know this thing.

Well, what I'd like to do now is let Zoosh talk more about what is in the holes and what we can do about it. Would that be okay?

Yes, of course. Good night.

Thank you very much.

HUMANS CAN LIVE 700 YEARS

Grandfather

I'm Grandfather. I'm sorry, but Zoosh is not available.

Okay, what do you know about this toxic material that we are digging up, causing all kinds of diseases that supposedly were gone from the planet?

This is the situation: Your physical body has the capacity without any changes at all (no surgery and nothing removed) to live 700 years, the way you are born right now. You do not, because of toxins on your surface and in your atmosphere as well as some incorporated into building materials, such as sand, crushed stone, and so on. This toxic material is from long ago when the surface of the planet was not a host to any type of life except perhaps non-motion. Non-motion means a form of life that does not move.

To put it in the simplest possible way, a non-motion life form means not an air breather or sea breather. The toxic matter you are asking about covers the widest range of molecular matter that you can imagine. I feel it is beyond anything you can possibly manage at this time. You cannot somehow magically put it all back where it was. It's not possible now.

The only thing that you can do is ask it to change into a safer version of itself. That is what has been taught through this channel for years now, because your civilization has been exposed to this material for thousands of years. If you go back thousands of years, human beings were not even living as long as you live today. You live as long as you do now because there have been some efforts in recent years to combat these diseases. However, these efforts can only do so much. I should let you ask a question.

Well, what I want to know is how did the toxic material get there in the first place?

There is really no point in going into that. Do you mean how did the material on the surface of the planet get there in the first place? Is that what you're saying?

No. How did the toxic material get there? You talked about a civilization that didn't move, and it doesn't sound as if they were plants. I don't know what they were.

They were stone. Stone is alive.

Okay, so it was stone. Was that stone — which turned to sand or gravel or something over the course of time — the toxic material we are talking about?

I realize you are trying to say, "Tell us what it is so that we can deal with that thing." Correct?

Well, things — because there are probably more than one.

It's everything like the pollen from trees and plants that have not been around for hundreds and thousands of years, which your bodies are not adept at dealing with. It is simply matter. You know it was a strange idea even just a few hundred years ago: The idea of going into a cemetery, digging things up, and putting structures there was something people would never do. People came to believe that there were ghosts there, but the original reason they never did that was the belief that there were things there, rotted bodies for starters, that would not be safe to be exposed to. But in your now time, that does not seem to stop construction over ancient sites and graveyards. All those old stories including ghosts and whatnot are not stopping anybody. Why? Because there is money to be made.

In some simple cases, it is ignorance, because you don't remember or understand all this. When you come here, you don't remember who you were. When you are a baby, you remember all of it. You can get to a point where you can be telepathic. Babies are born with all knowledge of their entire being. It has been this way for the past forty to sixty years. Babies are born with all their lives — their whole being, spirit, and everything — total knowledge, including that they can communicate telepathically.

It would be like communicating with an adult. You would be able to say to a beautiful baby, "I am having this issue: I went outside and started sneezing, and I'm wondering what I can do about it." The baby will immediately tell you what you can do about it. He or she will look at you and smile with love in his or her eyes, and suddenly you will know. The knowledge would come to you in your language and even in the form of your language. If you are a scientist, it will come to you in scientific language. If you are not a scientist, it will come to you so that you can understand what has been said.

The simplest and quickest way for you to get all the knowledge you need now is to learn how to become telepathic. I will teach you right now. This is something to practice, and I recommend it be done with young people first because they are more likely to be open to the possibilities. Young people, listen up, and by "young," I mean teenagers or even younger, but elders can do it too.

TELEPATHIC TRAINING

Notice the sound of your friends' voices when they talk. Some go up, high pitch, and then go down, and some talk with one tone throughout. Other people talk very quietly or very slowly. Just notice their voices. This is a fun thing to do with each other. Do this one-to-one to start with when you're not together. You can be at home. If you live in one part of town and they in another, or maybe someplace far away, it will still work. This might work better with friends, but it is okay to do with family too. You don't have to do this at a certain time, but you can if you want. Just start talking to the person quietly. Just say the name and that you want to talk now.

Imagine what the person would say back to you in his or her voice so that you hear the person's voice in your head. Then he or she will hear your voice the way you speak. When you do this long enough, eventually one or the other of you is going to have a conversation. You can phone each other and ask about it. You might pick up something, but in the beginning it won't be much. Eventually some of you will be able to pick up bits and pieces of what the other person was saying.

Wisdom from Babies

That's my first instruction. I will give you more another time. I am not saying adults can't do this, but I feel it's best suited to younger people and recommend it most for them. When you get good at it, or when you get really good at it, I will give you more instructions at some point so that you will be able to communicate with babies. Babies are born with all kinds of knowledge. You can talk to them. To babies, usually up to three months old, you can say, "You know someone I know is having this problem — what would you recommend?" Something like that, or you can ask how something can be fixed in the easiest way. Whatever you talk about, you will get back information that you can pass on to others. That's what I recommend. It is the simplest and fastest way that you can be sure that things will get better.

For those of you living as well as possible and surviving on this planet now (because it is not easy), know that you all have many things in common. One of those things is that you wanted to go some place exciting. You will notice that regardless of your language, the idea of excitement is very appealing, especially to younger people. The older you get, the less interesting this idea becomes. Desire for something new and fun is something you all had at one time when you were younger, or even have right now. Remember you all have much more in common than not. Being united doesn't have to be hard. It is only hard because of what you have learned in your experience or, more likely, have read or heard from others. So in short, try to get over that. Good night and goodlife.

Thank you.

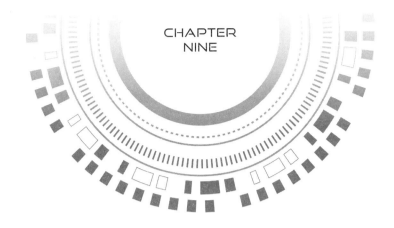

CHILDREN AND DOGS ON MARS

Zoosh

AUGUST 16, 2019

All right, this is Zoosh.

Hey, welcome. When Robert and I were talking last time, I said in **Phone Calls from the Future** *I wanted past history and future history. He said, "Oh, you can't do future history because you will change it." But we have half a dozen sessions with Doc about mining on the Moon. That's not going to change history, is it?*

We don't think so, because it is taking place on another planetary body. It doesn't actually have anything directly to do with the physical future of people on Earth.

Okay, I'd like to ask for a human being from the future living now who was one of the first who went to Mars for whatever purpose. Is there any problem with that?

Yes, because that is so close. There are people among you now who are really striving not just to go to Mars but to be on Mars. You can try and see what happens. I'm putting the phone down.

CHILDREN ON MARS

Human Child from Future Mars

Hello.

Hi, welcome.

Thank you. I am a child, and I was a very young baby on Earth when we moved to Mars, as you call it. I think the name was changed at some point by those who were living in the new colony on Mars, because they did not like what Mars connoted for people on Earth. It essentially refers to strife. So while people on Earth still called it Mars, the colonists changed the name to something that sounded more like a garden; I don't remember what the name was. I can picture in my mind all the photos that my mother showed me of a garden in a book that came from Earth.

I was a very young baby when I went to Mars with my parents, so I don't remember Earth. Mother and Daddy were concerned that I would spend my life on a planet and not know where I came from. So they were always showing me pictures of Earth, and they were very nice. We returned to Earth once when I was much older, but it wasn't like the pictures; things had changed. I went right back to Mars, but it was nice to have seen Earth, where I was born. Anyway, I am a child in my now time in the future, so I will talk like that if you don't mind.

Okay, so did you go as part of the colony?

By the time my parents took me to Mars, the colony had already been established for quite a while. Of course, children were not allowed until everything on Mars was very established, safe, and secure. It took quite a while before the colonists wanted to have families there. The scientific community had reasonable concerns about colonists giving birth on Mars or even children living on Mars until everything was understood as absolutely possible. The concerns were totally reasonable because one of the first babies born on Mars did not survive. The other babies were rushed back to Earth as fast as possible, where they did survive. With a start like that, it took a while for young babies or children to be welcomed.

When the colony was established and the scientists felt things were safe and secure enough for babies and children to live in the colony, new colonists came with their babies and children. That's how I got there.

Can you talk about growing up there? What kind of habitat did you live in? Was it above ground or underground?

We lived on the surface. There was, at first, a tendency to dig down into the planet. This is normal on Earth, but not long after the digging started, it stopped because people got sick. The anthropologists and the scientists assumed (and they were right) that the organisms and particles in the soil, which was a sandy material similar to a desert area, were probably to blame, and they decided digging should be avoided as much as possible. After that, there was much more caution.

Waste on Mars

How did they build on the surface? Did they have to build on platforms?

Yes, they put down some things in areas that would support low-rise buildings. Everything that would normally be underground in your times was just below the bottom of the buildings. Nothing was discharged purposely into the soil, and there was no digging. Of course at first there were spills and other problems that needed to be solved and avoided in the future.

The trouble with starting a colony on another planet is the remoteness. The common things you take for granted on Earth will probably not be available on Mars, because they are very different. When there were spills in the time of the first building and settling of the colony, of this or that material mixed with the surface area, the effects at that time were largely unknown, and it became problematic.

Generally, if there was a spill, it would be isolated as much and as quickly as possible. Sometimes they would build a structure over where the spill was so that there wouldn't be as much of a chance of anything or anyone coming into contact with the spilled substance. This gives you an idea of what they had to do and what they had to work with in the beginning. They had some materials, but sometimes these would have to be used in creative ways to cover up and contain spills and so on.

Also, human beings, with their physical bodies, consume food and produce waste, so that must be considered as well, in addition to the number of people in the colony. Pardon me for the way I talk. I am at the level of what you would call a school student.

Okay, what is an example of something problematic that was spilled?

Waste matter.

Oh, I see. Okay, not chemicals or anything.

No.

Okay. When you were there, how many humans were there? Tens, hundreds, or thousands?

Approximately 1,500.

Did more arrive as you got older?

I must go now and someone else will come in.

Well, thank you very much.

MORALE BOOSTER

Dog

You want to talk to the colonists from Mars, is that it?

Yes, someone who came from Earth and has lived as a human.

Is that critical?

Well, go ahead, so who are you?

I have lived on Earth, but I am not a human. I was a dog.

Oh, all right.

I was on one of the first expeditions with the people who went to establish a foothold on Mars. One of the humans insisted on bringing a dog, and that was me. The scientists accepted this because it was a part of life on Earth and maybe someday there would be pets with the colonists on Mars. They were willing to see how it would go with a dog in the beginnings of the colony. There was a lot of support for me to go because people love their pets and their pets love them.

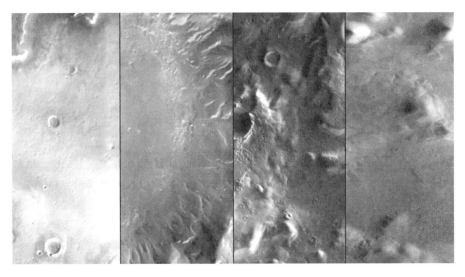

Image 9.1. Four images of morning frost on Mars via NASA

I'm also a dog in my now life. You wanted a being who was on Mars. I know you wanted a human being, but I'm the one available now.

Okay, well, welcome. Please tell me some of your experiences there.

I felt that my job on Mars was to keep people from becoming too frightened. For some people who were there, the idea of being on Mars, on another planet, was an exciting adventure. It was also possible for them to return to Earth if they wanted. Some people thought they would give it a try. Other people thought they would go to Mars and never go back to Earth, for various reasons. But after a while, many people began missing things on Earth, which is understandable. Then there were others who did not miss the things on Earth or felt that these were things they could do without. The first people to go there were not the sort of people who seemed (to me) to be appropriate, meaning self-sufficient people who know how to make things work with what is available. The self-sufficient type of people seem to be the ideal people to go to Mars.

Of course I might think that, because that was the thinking of the human I was living with, first on Earth and then on Mars, and it is her thinking that I have now. But that was not really accepted, because many types of people with specialties were needed to build the colony, solve problems, and understand how to live on a new planet. All the people with specialties had jobs to do, and all the jobs were necessary. The only person I can recall who was self-sufficient and could make things work with what was available was the human being who took me. That was her specialty: making things work with what was available. I couldn't understand at the time why everyone wasn't like her. People usually specialized in one thing.

It must have been assumed that everyone who specialized in one thing or another would always be compatible with the others who first went up to Mars. But you know human beings are not always compatible. Sometimes they got mad at each other and whole projects were delayed until they could agree on what should be done. I thought it was a little funny, when it wasn't a matter of life and death — meaning it wasn't related to having enough food, water, air, and things like that.

My job, I decided, was to try to keep people from being too frightened. The person who brought me told me to go around as much as I could and remind human beings that it can be fun starting a new colony on Mars. I tried to be as fun as possible. I think on your planet many dogs are of that noble calling, to help human beings not be so frightened and to show them how fun things can be.

Yes, so did you actually get out on the surface dirt, or did you have to stay in the buildings or covered areas?

Oh, no, I was on the dirt except when I went into the buildings. The people walked on the dirt too, except when they went into buildings to do things. Is it that way for you on Earth? Don't you step up into buildings?

Yes, but Earth's surface isn't toxic like Mars's surface is. Could you scratch into the outside surface or dig?

No, I did not dig or scratch. My master, the lady who brought me, said, "Do not dig." The reason I was allowed to come is that I followed her instructions; I was well-trained.

Yes, but you were also smart. What did the lady you came with do?

In my experience, just so you know, all dogs are smart. We know a lot more than you think.

I've talked to the souls of dogs before for a book we published called Animal Souls Speak. *What was the person who brought you there to do? What was her specialty?*

She was what I think you would call a mechanical engineer. She used to like to say that she knows what goes where and why. She laughed as if it was a joke, but it was actually her job. She was that sort of person before we left Earth, always knowing what goes where and why. I remember my dog father who grew up with her on Earth telling me that they used to go out in remote areas and she took the minimum amount of stuff with her. She made a shelter wherever it was safe. In the woods, she made a safe shelter, but sometimes she went to remote areas where there was junk. So she chose things from the junk to make a shelter. She knew how to do things like that because, of course, life was difficult on Earth. I lived on Earth for a few years before starting a new life on Mars.

When the people first settled on Mars, many felt both nervous and excited because there were a lot of new things to experience and problems to solve. It was a new planet. There was a lot of work to do, and they were more devoted to what they were doing because establishing the colony was important to their survival. That's why they were on Mars, and all their specialties were needed. Toward the middle of my time on Mars, people were not as nervous, because it was familiar. The people had made some friends and understood better how to live. Toward the end of my lifetime, it was more like a city and people were feeling better about being on Mars. They had more fun than when they first arrived.

There wasn't any crime because it was such a small colony. In a small colony, when anyone does anything bad, everyone knows. There were police, so if you committed a crime, you were arrested and sent back to Earth. Looking back on it in my now time, perhaps the punishment was more severe than it would have been if they were on Earth because of the effort involved in bringing them there.

Spirit of Adventure

What do you think the colonists felt? Was it that they wanted to get away from Earth and start anew, or did they just want an adventure?

I think a lot of them just wanted to do something completely new and different. They had a spirit of adventure, and it was exciting, even though they knew it would be hard at first. The whole idea of excitement was very popular at that time. I think also there was a strong belief among them all that if it didn't work out, they could always go back to Earth. Surprisingly, over the time I was there, only about 5 percent of them actually chose to go back to Earth. They could do it because ships came and went carrying supplies and whatnot. Anyone could go back if they missed friends or companions or just did not like living on Mars.

Some of the other colonists tried to talk them out of it if they wanted to go back just because they missed their friends, family, or other things on Earth. But if they really did not like living on Mars, the colonists understood. The colonists liked having people stay because they developed friends and a community, depending on each other. But life on Mars was not for everyone, and the colonists who liked it there and wanted to stay understood that.

A lot of people wanted to return to Earth in the beginning, because things were still being understood about how to live and solve problems. But after a while, many decided to stay on Mars because they were familiar with it. Things were working out better, and they liked their lives there. My feeling is that those who went back to Earth were happy about it. The rule was that once you were on Mars and then chose to go back to Earth, you couldn't come back to Mars again unless going back and forth was part of your job. In the beginning, some people had the job to go around and ask what was needed or what could be adapted and built to create what was needed. Then they went back to Earth to get whatever supplies and components they needed to bring back so that the colony would be successful. So there were a few people who came and went all the time.

What did they come and go in? Did they use rockets or some type of spacecraft?

They used a type of rocket.

How did they get the rocket off Mars?

They used the rockets and saved fuel, and fuel was brought from Earth.

So there was a spaceport on Mars where the rockets could blast off?

All you really needed was a flat place where the rocket could land and be totally stable. The rocket could take off from any flat place.

Oh, okay. So did they grow food there, or did they have to bring all their food from Earth?

That was one of the initial things believed to be absolutely essential. I think in the beginning, as far as I know, they used hydroponics. This was successful, and they continued to use it. This way, they could grow fruits and vegetables in an isolated, safe, and controlled environment. There was talk toward the end that they were going to bring soil from Earth on the rockets to Mars, but that was controversial. I don't think they ever did that. They chose the safe route and used hydroponics because it worked very well.

What about water? At this point in my now time, we don't know if there is water on Mars.

There is a little bit there, but from what I understand, most of the water was brought from Earth on the rockets. The water was used, and then what could be reused was filtered. They needed a distillery in place that could run all the time. Then our water would be all right, and water was always being brought to us from Earth, so we always had as much as we needed. The distillery had to be very sturdy and reliable to constantly maintain it.

Can you take a look to see whether that colony stayed there and expanded or they all came back to Earth in the end? Do you know what happened to them?

I don't know. You can ask others but probably not today.

Okay, so there weren't any luxuries. It was probably like living on a spacecraft, right?

It was like living in a remote area where nothing could be taken for granted, so it was more like an outpost.

Yes, well what about you; did you get enough to eat? Was there any meat there for any of you?

Yes, of course the people wanted to eat meat.

Oh, they brought it, then?

Yes, of course. Keep in mind that in your now time, astronauts want to eat meat. The supply ships bring plenty of it and other foods, all packaged and stored safely for the long journey. They don't have farms. [Laughs.] I know you know this. I'm just trying to make a joke.

[Laughs.] Right, that's wonderful, thank you. Are you a male dog or a female dog?

I am now a female dog, but back then when I was on Mars, I was a male dog. I was the only dog on Mars for the whole time I was alive. I don't know if they allowed other dogs after me, because I think they looked at it as an experiment at first, but human beings like to have dogs as companions. They were not sure whether it was a good idea to have more pets for the people on Mars or even if it would be safe for dogs to be born there, but when I was there, the colonists interacted with me in a friendly way.

Animal Support

It was my job to help humans who were frightened and show them how things can be fun. Plus, the human I was with felt that it was a good idea for me to be there because things were so new in the beginning. There was only one person who was not comfortable with having a dog in the colony; all the others were happy I was there.

How did they govern themselves? You said they had police, so did they have something like an elected council? How did they make decisions?

I don't know that. It was run like a business. It wasn't a country of its own and not a city-state, as you would say. It was a business, so it would've been run like a business because it was a commercial venture. It wasn't something done because Earth wanted to colonize Mars.

What was the business? Did people have to pay to go there?

I'm not allowed to say. Everyone who went there was an employee.

Employees? And you cannot say what they did?

I cannot say anything, because the business exists on your planet now.

Well, I can't imagine what that would be because they can't mine and they can't dig in the dirt. Well then, how did you feel when you went into spirit?

I felt that I would miss the lady, and she said she would miss me too. That's it. What I felt was love.

I shall say something to finish: Now, on Earth, you have problems. You have problems because you humans are somehow incomplete. On other planets, I believe you do not have these problems, because you are complete. I do not know what is missing from you on Earth, but something is. Beloved pets help you to be more complete. Pets can be close to you, comfort you, have fun with you, and help you to have fun. I think sometimes it is difficult for human beings to be happy, but with pets it is easier. I think having pets helps some of you to find that thing that is missing, and it is often love. Goodbye.

Thank you very much for coming. Goodlife.

PART
TWO:

ANCIENT
HISTORY

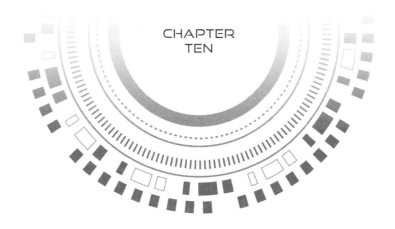

SPIRITS OF THE BILOBA TREE CREATED YETI (BIGFOOT) PEOPLE

Being Created by the Spirit of the Biloba Tree

JANUARY 16, 2019

We are here for the book.

Thank you.

Welcome.

The brief civilization we had on your planet may be something you are interested in. We lived around (what you call by your calendar) 1400 BC on your planet. Mostly we were underground, but sometimes we came close to the surface. We had a liaison there; this is why we came for a short time, because the beings that we were connected with were in our genetic past, considerably into our past. They still had our genetics in a stream of their abilities, meaning a stream of consciousness, but it wasn't really that. It was more like something that you could use if you needed it: a physical application of something that might be brought about by need or desire. You wouldn't think about it usually.

This group of beings in our genetic past is known by other names in your time now. Sometimes they are called the yeti or, for some strange reason, abominable snowman or, my favorite, Bigfoot even though their feet are not entirely that big compared to some people's feet. We are not those beings, but they have a strain of our DNA, and we were on the planet because we wanted to find out more about them, exploring our ancestry in a way. We live in our now time well in the future from your time. But we went back in time to 1400 BC on your planet because that's the time when it was safe for those beings, when they could walk around and go places and do things, and there wasn't much interference or much danger.

Those beings are very good at interacting with all forms of life. The only form of life they had any problem with was human beings, which were at least somewhat technical, having tools and so on. The more one gets involved in tools, meaning external objects to bring about one's needs, the more there is a tendency to forget one's creative capabilities. These beings were well tuned to that, and they got along with all the life forms, including some that don't exist on Earth anymore. But the last vestiges of the yeti are still around. Our people were there on Earth five or six months based on your time. During that time, we were totally involved and interacted with these beings that you now know by those various names.

We found out that this strain of DNA or RNA, or whatever you want to call it, that existed between us was a complete surprise to our science people. We discovered from our genetics that we were beings from their past. This came as a complete surprise to us; we discovered this halfway through our stay on Earth. So our people wanted to know from them how it was that they were there on Earth at that time. We are from very far away on another planet but still in this constellation. And they very slowly explained, giving us time to digest it over the next three months, speaking to us every day.

To condense what they said, they (yeti/Bigfoot) were from very far in the future from your Earth point of view. But from our point of view of time, they were about seventeen generations in our future. They were looking back at their past at one point and discovered that there was a strain of their ancestry on your planet. They wanted to know what it was all about, which we thought was pretty ironic since that was why we were there.

Nevertheless, they came to Earth for a visit. They didn't need any ships because they could move spiritually, and they could have bodies on Earth. Their belief at the time they made the journey was that the strain of ancestry would be from what you human beings would call the animal world. They felt that this form of their ancestry would have to be able to get around easily, so it would be nice to walk on two legs because that's what you normally do. Yet it would be good to have something about them that appears to be not human because there were quite a few human beings on Earth at that time.

They came in a group of about thirty people. You have a couple of pictures of them that are accurate, and that is pretty much how they look: long-haired and walking upright, big, fairly tall but not gigantic, certainly not gigantic, probably not even as tall as some of the tall human beings on your planet. They said when they came to your planet that they attempted to explore the source of the strain of their ancestry and they found it quickly. They were astounded. How could this possibly be?

They had among their group people who were very clear and knew exactly what they were looking for. In that form of thought/feeling, you might say, the people who were attuned to that would simply land, but it wasn't from the sky. If you saw it, you would have seen someone slowly appear. The spirit was there first, and then the physical body formed around it. You can imagine what that would look like.

Everybody arrived at once, and immediately the people who were attuned to it turned and faced exactly the source of their ancestry. I can only say they were incredulous. Their ancestry was a tree, the type you call biloba. Have you heard of it? I think you would spell it B-I-L-O-B-A, and that was the tree. Of course, all who were tuned in to it agreed because they were looking at the same tree, which was vast and very old — quite ancient, you would say.

They weren't able to decide in terms of years at that immediate moment how old the tree was, but they realized that the tree represented 10,000 generations. A generation for us on our planet is roughly equal to about 2,300 years on your planet. This tree was beyond ancient in that sense. It was vast; the trunk of the tree was about — oh, I am tripping over your measurements — something like 800 feet across. It was vast. There were other smaller versions of the tree around it, so it was obvious that the tree was perpetuating its existence. There were a great many of these magnificent, wonderful trees.

The Knowledge of Trees

After our people got over their initial surprise, they wanted to know about life and how it was and how we got to where we were and everything. The tree was what you would call — there is a term for it. I'm sorry. I do not have it. The tree was a being that could answer all questions to all groups about who they are not only en masse but also about who they are individually. So when the people who were attuned, as I said before, which I think was three in that group, asked, they each received different information.

The information agreed on how we got to where we were and the connections and all that business, but the information differed because the tree assumed that people individually also wanted to know about where they were from and their background. So all the people got their personal information just for themselves, which differed, and all three people got all of our group, or cultural, information exactly the same.

At first, they weren't aware that the tree spoke to each of them privately. They were amazed and started talking about what the tree said about where we were from and so on. But then one of them said, "I couldn't believe how the tree (they didn't call it a tree) knew all about my life." One looked around the group and said, "Now you know all about my life."

The other beings were like a cartoon with question marks above their heads because they did not know what the person was talking about. That's when they discovered that the personal information was included with the overall picture. Then everybody got as close to excitement as possible for people who are known for their calm outward demeanor. Everybody got almost excited, and that's when all things were explained.

They were intrigued, and it turns out that our species (who we are in our time in the future) are sort of an experiment. We are originally of this tree, which is hard to accept when you are mobile and walking around. It's hard to imagine that there is any connection to this massive, beautiful tree but also to something that doesn't walk around and stays in the same place.

As a human being who doesn't stay in the same place all the time, you can identify, yes? If you had to stand in the same place all the time, it would bother you. So you have an idea how we felt: On the one hand, they were totally mystified, and on the other hand, they couldn't remain mystified even when a moment like that came up. Immediately the tree was like grandmother and grandfather rolled into one. They instantaneously knew whatever they had been dumbfounded by, and the answers were there — personal as well as overall for the group, our civilization, and culture.

Tree Experiment

To get back to the explanation, our group found out that the trees wanted to experiment. There was more than one tree, so I will say "they" when speaking about the trees. They felt that life would at some point be much more numerous on the planet, and they knew that human beings walking around on two legs would become more of a factor. Therefore, they needed to understand what that would be like, meaning, "What are the feelings?"

The trees knew about human beings from other planets, so they patterned us after the human beings that they had met before coming to Earth. They also felt it was important that our people should be far enough away so that human beings from other planets would not discover who the trees were and their connection to our people for a long time. So we, in our time and place, would be able to develop our own culture. Then they would know what it was like to be human beings by connecting with us through our dreams. That way, they felt it would be the least amount of distraction to us and our culture. So that's what happened.

Then at some point, we went back and discovered another strain of beings that they had also created. It's getting complicated; that's why I'm trying to condense some things that would take probably twenty-five years to explain. So all these beings — we in our time, the tree in that ancient time, and the Bigfoot beings — are connected. The biloba tree said that they had, over time, experimented in creating a few other forms of life on Earth — sometimes prompted by requests from other life forms and also by what you would call a deity and other times simply just wanting to see whether something could adapt.

One of these being types that they wanted to see adapt is what you now know as frogs. They did not create frogs but rather a strain of frogs. This particular type of frog had a slight purplish cast, and there are not many of them left on your planet. But they were in abundance at one time, and that's all I'm going to say about that, because I think we are getting pretty far afield, and you probably have questions.

Yes. I looked the tree up, and the biloba tree is in Africa, Australia, and China. Can you tell me where the tree was that your people talked to?

It would've been Africa because we felt that was the area where the most advanced civilizations of human beings were, meaning they would be less likely to interfere and less likely to be so enamored with their tools that they would forget how to create. So they were still aware of how to create and be polite toward other life forms as best they could.

That is an amazing story. Which group is seventeen generations ahead of you in your natural time?

The Bigfoot beings.

How did these biloba beings from Earth create both of you in the future? Do they travel in time?

All beings who remember who they are travel in space-time, meaning the "travel in time thing" is a side effect of traveling in space. It is kind of a difficult formula, but it's sort of a portion of the $E=MC^2$ formula. Meaning that in order to travel great distances, or if energy moves great distances, it has to move in a flexible fabric known as time, which is basically what that formula means. Therefore, to cover the ground, so to speak, the ability to move from one star system to another is based primarily on motivation and desire.

A web of creation covers the universe; it is love. Love is not just tolerant of things that are incompatible with love; love superimposes over all that is incompatible with it. So even on your planet in your time now, when you have violence and anger and all of that, what superimposes over that and is actually underneath the beings who are doing the violence — their souls are purely love — and the connection to all life forms, no matter how violent they are, is love.

Bilocation

All exists in the matrix of love, and this is how love can happen. This is how you move without bringing along violence. The moment you leave the energy effect of the planet where you are now, not unlike life after death for your physical body, all that falls away, and you are strictly in love and you move. But what if you want to go some place as a physical being? Say you want to go to another planet or star system? You want to do it safely, benevolently, and easily, but in your past you had violence done either to you or by you, sometimes both.

Focus on your spirit self, which has an attuned energy. Everybody can feel it even though they don't feel it all the time. If you wake up gently from sleep, you feel it for a moment or so; attune to that. Then imagine what a place looks like in your galaxy or your constellation or some other galaxy. If you look up at the sky at night, see something, and maybe get a sensation of color or whatever, you say, "Oh, I'd like to see what that is." Just close your eyes, and you are there. You leave behind all violence, which stays on Earth.

You go in your spirit body, but you leave your Earth body here so when you get to the other place, your spirit body doesn't have any trace of violence. Just like after death. So I think you call this bilocation. [Bilocation, or sometimes multilocation, is an alleged psychic or miraculous ability wherein an individual or object is located in two distinct places at the same time (https://en.wikipedia.org/wiki/Bilocation).] In bilocation, you have a body in both places, but the physical Earth body remains where it is so that no violence is brought to the place that you are going. You can use all your abilities as a spirit being that you have when you are in your spirit self without any trace of violence or even discomfort of any form. This is how you are able to travel safely, benevolently, and easily, experiencing no harm and causing no harm to others.

What is your culture like in your natural time? Are you embodied or in spirit?

We are embodied, yes, like you. We look pretty much like you. I think there are a few minor differences, but other than that, we are basically human beings who are slightly different. Our heads have a little bit different shape. Our jawlines are a bit more prominent; our chins are a bit more prominent. But we think that there are people on your planet who have that shape of jaw and chin.

There are a few other minor differences I won't mention, but I wanted to mention that one so that those of you with that jaw and chin don't feel that you are not like other human beings. You are directly or at least genetically, some portion of you, connected to us and thus connected to the tree we mentioned.

Oh, there are people here who have your DNA too?

Well, that's not surprising when you think about it.

Are the yeti still here on this planet?

Yes, but not often on the surface. They are well below the surface in places that are unreachable by drilling equipment or fracking equipment or anything like that. There are places that are not reachable by such methods, and it is not possible to interfere with their lifestyle. You don't get there by a passage; there is no tunnel. You get there pretty much the same way I mentioned — by traveling in space-time. It's their natural place to be underground, but if for some reason one of them needs to come to the surface, he or she can bilocate to the surface so that they have a body they feel comfortable with on the surface. Below the surface, they are not as hairy.

Are they in another dimension beyond ours?

Well, obviously the bilocation process utilizes other dimensions. So you could say that in a way, they are, but if you met one physically on the planet, he or she is definitely in the same dimension as you.

Okay. Do you think that tree is still alive?

No, human beings got there and said, "We can make a lot of houses out of this." They didn't all say that, but that was the thought at that time. Of course, if they had known the nature of the tree, they never would've done that, but they didn't know, so a certain amount of forgiveness is possible, given the situation.

Are you still in contact with the spirit of that tree?

Oh, yes. The reason I am here — and you might reasonably ask how this relates to your time, a phone call from the future, and all of that — is that we feel that in order for you to understand each other better, it would be useful to be able to gently exist in someone else's culture without causing any harm, discomfort, or distraction in any way. We feel — and this is important — that it would be good to bilocate and just sort of stand there but not create a body, be there just to observe.

The sensitive people there might see you as a dot of light. But they will see lots of dots of light, so they won't differentiate and say, "Oh, that's someone from the planet," most likely. But if they do perceive at that level that there is love, it's not a problem. There are a few people on the planet who can do that.

In order for you to understand better, especially regarding the people with whom you are disagreeing or fighting or warring, and to understand why they are who they are, it might be good to spend some time with them, maybe in a family situation. Do not spy on them, because you won't be able to use bilocation for that, as it can only be done in love. This means that you can sort of extend there, and be there, and you will remember only that which is of love, and you will leave only that which is of love. So there will be no harm, and you will not be able to use anything that is harmful; otherwise, you can't do the process.

We think it would be good for some of you who are sensitives especially. You don't have to learn how to do this; just do it more and write about what you've seen. Talk about how much the people you saw are like people all over the world.

As those of you who like to travel know, people are people pretty much wherever you go. You might be vastly different culturally, but mostly you are all similar. We feel you need to remind yourself how similar you all are in order to be able to make the leap to the more benevolent version of Earth. We know about this and that you will be able to go. This way, you will be able to do it in love, as love, with all beings welcomed.

Some of you may say this is too advanced for a lot of people, that some people aren't ready for this, or that some people will misunderstand, and that's true, but it cannot be abused. In order to do the process itself, you have to be in love, meaning you must be the energy exclusively of love. Otherwise, you cannot do it. So it is safe. It is like a safety mechanism for all beings.

That's wonderful!

The Broman

The beings we call yeti or Bigfoot, what is their name for themselves? What do they like to be called?

Well, I will have to ask if they want to give that — just a minute. They won't say their actual name, but they give you this name: B-R-O-M-A-N.

Broman, all right. How do they live underground? Can they grow food, or is there sunlight? How do they live in the middle of Earth?

Keep in mind their advanced nature. Sometimes they eat for pleasure, but they don't have to. Sometimes they breathe for pleasure, but they don't have to. Sometimes they swim in water for pleasure, but they don't have to. You get the general direction.

What they particularly prefer to do is live in areas inside Earth without changing those areas at all. Some of the areas are very beautiful, and some of them have a glow so that you can see. It's not bright, but there is a glow, and they live there if they want light. But they find generally that in areas where there is not much light — you would say dark — there is some light, so they prefer that darker form of light.

How do they live in that time ahead of yours in your future? Are they embodied in that state? Do they have a culture?

You know, it would probably be best to ask them.

Ah, okay. Let's get back to you. Have you shared with your culture and your planet what you found out about your ancestry?

I wasn't part of the group that went back to 1400 BC.

All right, did those beings share with everybody? Did all of you accept and understand it?

They didn't tell everybody. The scientists and educators shared it with each other. But you know how it is in your time: Word got around.

How many beings are there of you in your time?

Approximately 370,000.

Oh, that's all!

Well, that's quite a bit if you imagine yourself in a group of 370,000, but we don't live like that. We are spread out all over the planet.

Are you the only beings on the planet?

No, there are several. There are lots of what you call plants and trees as well as other life forms. Some of those fly but not too many others. There are a lot of roots for the trees above ground, so you have to know how to carefully step on them so that you don't create any discomfort. Or you have to know the pathways to travel so that you don't have to step on them. Even if we did that, there would be something between our stepping on them and the tree roots them-selves; we would know to do that.

But our proximity, you understand, it is like personal space. Do you understand personal space? That's the personal space of the tree roots, so they may not always be comfortable with that. This is a roundabout way of saying that I don't know how many other types of beings there are. We've seen the flyers. We have two legs, but I've only seen one type of being who has four legs. I'm not really sure what they are, but I've taken a quick scan of your four-legged beings, and they are not like any on your planet. Since I don't know anything about them, I can't really describe them. Four legs and no tail, a body, a neck, a head — but they are not like anything on your planet. So I don't really know who they are, but they are love, so, you know.

Okay, so you don't have technology; you live a natural life. Do you live on the land?

Yes, exactly, we do not need technology, and neither do you, but it's temporary for you. It is a way to explore. We think that the reason you are exploring technology to such a great degree is that you are probably going to be, at some point, helping out beings who have explored it to even a greater degree. You will have to be tolerant, patient, and understanding with their enrapture, as you might say, with their technology, some of which is quite amazing and wonderful, and they are still creating using technology, which isn't necessary.

Well, that's all very wonderful, then. I am delighted that you came.

A Gift from the Biloba Tree

I will make a closing comment since we cannot linger indefinitely. The questioner has asked various insightful questions, but I would like you, the reader, to ask the most important question in your life. You can ask it as many times as you want in your life because that question will change over time.

Think about it for a while although some of you will ask it immediately because it's pressing, a pressing need, you understand — not the question somebody else thinks is important. You ask the question that you think is the most important to you in that moment. Of course, five minutes later something else might be important to you and certainly all throughout your life. Just ask the question out loud. Whisper it if you want to.

I am not saying you will get an immediate answer, but the spirit of that tree is still on your planet. You might just get the way that tree likes to work, which is in your dreams. Good night.

PROTECTION FROM EARTH'S VIOLENCE

A Visitor from the Future

JANUARY 28, 2019

Welcome.

Thank you. What do you want?

Is this someone about the book Phone Calls from the Future*?*

Yes, the book *Phone Calls from the Future*. Our people were on your planet not so far in the past, but we were not on the surface. Still, one of our people managed to find a way to an area that is now a cave, due to shifting lands, underground earthquakes, and so on. We came with the intention of leaving a message that might be interpreted by some people. Really, how do you leave a message for people in the future? It's difficult. But as they were standing at the opening of the tunnel, which over time became a cave, they looked around and decided the best they could do was draw a star map.

They knew the contemporary people of those times would have no idea what it was. They might be interested if it were detailed or colorful, so they used a tool not much different from a laser on the stone inside the cave and tried to make a mark that would last. It was not sandstone or anything like that. They drew a general picture of your solar system with something like a dotted line. For us, this represents the wavy line of our planet, which is in your galaxy. That's what they did. I do not know if it remains in your current times, but if so, it may have been misunderstood, or perhaps not much of it is left.

What I can see from here using the instrument we have is that the wavy line is still there, but I'm unable to see the drawing of your solar system (basically just a sun and various planets). I am unable to see anything but the wavy line. So if people are wondering what that wavy line means, now you know where it's from. Apparently, it has survived for 40,000 years, and you cannot expect things to last forever. I am like a history professor in your time, but I am not sure how to offer my assistance to the cultures living in your now version of Earth.

Distressing Conflicts

When our people (obviously not me) were there, what they found most distressing were the wars, conflicts, and even simple arguments that resulted in violence. There didn't seem to be even then (although there were exceptions) ways of bringing about resolutions for creating peace. Not necessarily calm, happiness, or love, but peace. That's what our people found distressing.

Also, we do not have the capacity to look back great distances in time even in our now time. At that time, we couldn't look back much further, but it wasn't difficult to see the surface (even though, as I said, we didn't go to the surface), since we had access to something you might call a window or porthole. The porthole (how can we say?), we could look out, but others couldn't look in. It was obviously not stone, but it might have looked like a pretty rock or something like that from the outside.

We could see evidence of previous conflicts — not everywhere, but our people traced evidence of these. Apparently, changes on the surface of Earth were to eliminate what we think (correct me if I'm wrong, because I may not have all the answers, as historians generally don't) was some kind of unhappiness with the planet itself. It showed a tendency to bring about some change that would alter, at least temporarily, the surface populations — which is, I suppose, a nice way to say eliminate the surface populations. Of course, when that takes place, it usually happens with some form of water. It tends to be the last word, unless you are fully prepared on a well-stocked ship. Such evidence was apparent in at least one or two places. I don't know what I can offer. I have the records of the people in those times, but I'm not sure what you want to know, so you can ask the questions.

A Similar Planet

Why were your people here?

As an observational outpost. That's a good question, because there is a similarity in our planets. Our atmosphere is almost the same as yours, but it's more oxygen-rich. Yours, even at the best of times, when (I think) there were a lot more forms of life that would exhale oxygen, had less. But our planet is more oxygen-rich. Other than the fact that our planet is a little bit larger than yours, it is surprisingly similar. We have oceans, lakes, and rivers just like you do. We have about the same amount of surface land; on a percentage basis, that means we have less surface land than you do but our planet is bigger. It is enough surface land for us (our people) and the other forms of life we live among.

We are not human beings, but we are humanoids. I'm not going to describe too much the way we look because it's not very important. I will say that our bodies are comfortable with the prevailing conditions on our planet, so we don't need to wear many garments. Usually, we wear something light and comfortable, but we do not have cold or unbearable heat. I think the word is "temperate."

Feel free to ask questions about us. Basically, we landed on your planet because of its similar appearance to our planet, as we approached from space. The similarity is apparent even from a distance, if you have instruments that can see long-distances; but we didn't have those at the time. We were told by beings from other planets who had such instruments that there was a planet on the other side of the galaxy that looked almost exactly like ours, only a little smaller. Naturally, that aroused our curiosity. While we did not have ships at that time that could travel great distances, others did; so we went with them.

Faster than the Speed of Light

It took some training and adaptation to be able to tolerate the energy of those ships, because in order to cover such distances, you must travel in a form other than your own physical self as you know it. The people who went had to train for such conditions not only to be ready to go but also to be ready to come back. We would have to hitch a ride on the way there and on the way back. That's what we did. Now we have one ship for our planet that can go there, but it operates much more gently so that we can travel great distances across the galaxy in our physical forms. It does not require us to be transformed, at least for a temporary trip.

I mention this because your people will undoubtedly befriend a group like we did in order to get such traveling done. You will need to be mutually compatible. Perhaps they have already made contact. I do not know. I think one group has, and one group tried and did not have a good experience. They essentially said, "Don't go there."

I think for a while there wasn't much activity. Another group felt you were somehow directly and, to some extent, genetically their pasts lives (which I find a little hard to believe because they look so different than you do). They said, "We are going to go, and that's that." Of course, they didn't say it exactly like that, but I'm trying to talk the way you talk. Correct me if I use your language in a way that might be offensive.

Sure. How did they travel, then? They needed a physical body on Earth, so did they pick one up when they got here, or how did that work?

They started out with their own bodies. In order to migrate in the vehicle, the vehicle traveled a little faster than light speed. If you have to put a number on it, I'm not a mathematician, and I don't have those figures. But the vehicle travels fast enough so that it travels in light, and that is essential. If you are going to travel in a straight line, which is the fastest way, you cannot be crashing through the galaxy, because you would hit planets and all kinds of stuff. But if you are traveling in light, you can do that. You can zip right through a planet without harming anyone or anything, including yourself.

In order to do that our — oh, I'm getting a tap on the, what you might call, shoulder. I'm not supposed to tell you, exactly. Essentially, they floated, encapsulated in a liquid. I do not know how, but there was something around them. I can't say more. In any event, they were able to make the journey. Even though the bulk of the journey took hardly a moment, one of them had her hand on her arm and was a little nervous about it, squeezing her arm gently the entire time. She was not comfortable with the idea of becoming something else. That person's journal said that for the entire journey, including the longest (distance) part, she was doing that, and there was never a moment when she wasn't physical. That's all I can tell you.

Okay, so they came here to observe and had the ability to see around the planet and know what was going on. They didn't have to travel around the planet once they got here?

No, they didn't have that ability. They just had — oh, I see. You thought it was a small place they were in underground. You may not realize this, although I think your scientists in your now time (at least some of them) know it, but in those days, there was a vast underground system for travel. They were not alone, as there were many people living down there, including people who look very much like you. I don't know if they are still there, but this system deep underground was very (I suppose you would say) modern. You could travel great distances quite quickly in tunnels that were tubular; that is all I can describe. It is probably what you might think of as futuristic or what other planets might look like.

Getting from one part of Earth to another from deep underground is very pleasant. You would get in this tube thing that always had various types of peoples in it, and it went one direction or another. Really, you could travel anywhere, but you were deep underground. Then people who had demonstrated they were doing something scientific or observational (like a historian) were allowed access to certain points where they could get to the surface without actually emerging on the surface. Usually, it was on some high ground on the surface, and they could look through these windows or portholes and see great distances — you know, 40 or 50 miles at most, using some kind of magnifying system. Probably you have that now. That's how it was done.

Has your culture changed much in the past 40,000 years?

Well, I don't think it has. I'm looking at our history, and it is not about how one family evolved and became this. It's more the general pattern of culture. A historian in our times would probably in your times encompass the jobs of anthropologist, sociologist, and historian all in one. I don't think our civilization has changed at all. Others might not agree with me, but that is my opinion.

The Cape of Good Hope

Even though they could travel all over underground within the planet, do you know where they were from? On what part of Earth did they have their base?

Is that important? If that is important, then it was down there some place you call the Cape of Good Hope.

All right, good. How long did they stay here?

There was a change several times, and not the same group was at the Cape of Good Hope. But I think they were there. I'd have to get the calculations, and that's not my strong suit, so just a moment. It would've been close to four years of your time.

Oh, is that all?

Figure 11.1. The Cape of Good Hope

Well, really when you think about it, why would you want to go away from your planet, your culture, and your loved ones for that long? I think the longest any individual stayed was about three months of your time.

What did they do with the knowledge they gained? Did they take it to those who were interested?

It was quite obvious that violence is a factor on your planet. People could see that, so when they came back, they went to a planet near ours that specializes in, what you would call in your time, healing. All the violent things that they had seen (which of course affected them deeply) were cleansed from them, so they would not remember the violence. Also, the physiology of their bodies had no aspect of what you might call stress mutations in the cellular structure. We feel that your bodies — correct me if I am wrong — are constantly exposed to stress mutations, because you are in the midst of it all. Your bodies must be constantly undergoing stress mutations in your cellular structure. I'm not a medical person or person of healing, but I'm tapping into the language that is relatively compatible with your contemporaries.

Have we ever heard of the place that you are from, or have we talked to anyone else from there?

I have no idea if you have. Perhaps. Did you ask two questions? I only answered one. Oh, you asked: Have you ever heard of us. I don't know. You would be more likely to know what you have heard of than I would.

Do you have a name for your culture or your people?

Yes, but I am not allowed to say it.

Who is not allowing you?

Oh, it's not who it is. It's a matter of politeness.

I see.

It is most important, because you are on your planet and living your life, to make the best of it and not get distracted by what is going on, on other people's planets. If you do that and get distracted, you will have a tendency (and this is my sociologist self talking) to pay less attention to your primary objective, which is to live as well as possible and to help others do the same.

Live in the Now

Are you from the future in the sense of the time that we were in before we came here? You're in the natural time, aren't you?

I am afraid I don't know what you are talking about. I can only say what I have said, and I think you think I know all about you, but I don't.

But did you have to come by time travel for your people to get here 40,000 years ago, or are you in a time similar to the time we are in now?

Here is the situation: The speed of the vehicle we hitched a ride on (you would say) does time travel. But time travel is not fast enough, so there is something faster than time travel. I do not have a word for it; there is no direct translation in your time. Since there is no direct translation on your Earth, this can only mean that there is no way to describe it. You would say this is time travel, but it is much faster than that.

Oh, time travel has a time to it.

Time travel is not the fastest, but it is the closest that our civilization and other civilizations (I think I can speak for them as well) would use at times. Not to be redundant, but at least some of you can understand, if you can do the math, what it might mean. There is no point trying to describe something that is infinitely faster than time travel if it has no current relevance to any of your cultures. What is the point of describing it? Then it would be something you would want to do, need to do, have to have — which we think is problematic for you. I can understand, because we also have imaginations, how this can become addictive.

This is much truer of your bodies than ours. Our bodies do not produce chemicals that would cause us to become addicted to anything, including behaviors. We want to protect you from becoming addicted to needing, wanting, having to have, your body to stimulate these chemicals that draw you away from the immediate time and experience that you are living in. That might be perpetuated because you like the feeling. Thus, you can ignore what is happening in your immediate time experience and not make changes that would be helpful for you and others. Understand, I am not talking to you as an individual but as a representative of human beings' Earth cultures.

Yes, okay. I don't know if you can see this, but is Earth more violent now than it was 40,000 years ago?

I cannot tell, nor would I want to, because I would have to go to that other planet to be cleansed. I know you meant no harm with the question.

Ah, no I didn't. Then I'm assuming that we are.

A moment, a moment, one of our friends that took us there will answer your question when I'm done. They apparently can protect themselves from such questions and observations.

Can you say who they are?

I think that they would be much better at saying that themselves.

Practice Yoga

All right, do you want to say anything to the people who will read this, then?

Yes. In your time, we feel that you have many distractions, because even human beings on the surface of Earth 40,000 years ago had a great many of them. It apparently could cause problems. If you are living in conditions where there are disagreements and arguments that lead to violence, I recommend that you find, as an individual, a way to clear your mind, relax your body, and improve your general way of coping. I have been informed by our experts that such a practice is available in your time. It apparently includes some beliefs that may not be comfortable for all of you, but it could probably help a great many of you. I recommend the study and practice of yoga. Good night.

Oh, thank you very much for coming. Goodlife.

PROTECTION FROM VIOLENCE

A Zeta Reticulan

Greetings.

Welcome.

I'm one of the beings who has been visiting your planet you identify with our star system Zeta Reticuli.

Oh, you are the ones who brought them here.

Not we as individuals but our culture, yes.

Are you speaking from your home planet, or are you part of the group that is contacting humans?

I will not answer that for our safety and the safety of those in that project. You must not ask questions like that, because you must consider our safety. This is just a teaching for you, and you can take it out of the transcript if you like, but it is also instructional for astronauts and cosmonauts.

Okay, I will leave it in. He said you have the ability to protect yourself from our violence.

I think you asked the question: Is Earth (meaning human cultures, I take it, on Earth) more violent than it was 40,000 years ago in your now time compared to the time they were talking about.

Yes.

I can answer that question. I would say that individual human beings on the surface of your planet are not any more violent in your now time than you were 40,000 years ago. However, your weapons and the weapons you continue to develop are much more dangerous and tend to end life. This is not only for human beings but for all life, which apparently (and our peoples believe this absolutely) has to do with your tendency to (as you call it) commit suicide.

Because of various apparent reasons of the moment, which might happen in any given life for all kinds of reasons, there is a general feeling of missing one's component parts. This does not refer to physiological parts but to the awareness of one's overall being. To put it in the most obvious way, you are missing your spirit self, and this is perhaps why there has been a strong effort, including by our people, to help you remember. Your spirit self knows all about other types of cultures and appearances of people from other planets; it is not offended by their looks but loves all of them. The idea of variety is a delight. This is why we created that rolling image that I think you published.

Yes.

We created that to help those of you who were trying to bring more of your spirit into your day-to-day life. You would look at it at first and say, "Oh, what is that?" Then when you slowed it down, some of those different pictures (even if you didn't know where they were from) were very familiar. Those feelings would jar your memory, and that memory is in your spirit. For very few people on Earth, it would have been an actual physical experience. Some older people in the past had contact with the Zeta Reticuli civilization. But for the most part, the majority of people on Earth now, who have a sense that this is a similar life form that they know (or they have heard of), this is a memory from your spirit.

When you look at the pictures, it makes you say, "Oh yes, I know who that is." You have a sense of familiarity or even friendliness, and that has to be a memory from your spirit. You would've either been such a being, perhaps, in what you call reincarnation, or more likely, you would have had friends who looked like that. Your overall spirit, of course, encompasses all the various lives that you have lived and, to some extent, those lives that you will live in the future. However, memories from the future sometimes interfere with a current life, so you don't always have them. I don't know if that answers your question; perhaps it's more than what you asked.

No, that's good. But are you saying that the distraction of our daily lives is what we are using to cut off our spirits?

No, I didn't say that.

Okay, in which ways are we not connecting to our spirits? What's keeping us from connecting more?

I understand why you would ask that question. But how many times are you criticized as an individual for not doing something the right way? You are not doing "this" and "this" and "this." I'm not going to answer the question, but I will rephrase it.

Okay.

I'm going to say, "What ways do the things we are doing allow us to remember and attract more of our spirit to our day-to-day selves?"

Excellent.

Some of that is remembering dreams that are enjoyable or happy or that you wake up from with a smile or a laugh. For some of you who have difficult lives, this does not mean that something you have done or been involved in that was violent for one reason or another makes you laugh or smile. It means that if you've had a pleasant or even a funny dream, when you wake up and it makes you laugh, this is a way.

There is also your imagination. If you can stop what you are doing, even on what you call a coffee break, and take a moment to imagine what it would be like to live some place that is completely peaceful, calm, friendly, and enjoyable, where there are wonderful things to do, wonderful people and friends to be with, and you never feel like a stranger (and any other details you can add), this will also help you remember and be more of your spirit self along with your day-to-day self. Good night.

Thank you for coming.

NEW PLACES TO CHANNEL

Zoosh

All right, it's Zoosh. Can't stay long.

I thought we were going to do a book where the people who created what I call the old space ports and old ruins that are left on the planet from 50,000 or 100,000 years ago were going to come in and talk about them. But they haven't done this so far.

I think what Robbie just said to you is true. This is what I want you to do if you can, and it will not be that difficult; it will probably be pretty easy to find out which ruins have been channeled on before. Obviously, there would have been Stonehenge, where all kinds of people have channeled and written about it and then the ones where they have not. You can include scientific writing about it. The ones that, as far as you can tell no one's channeled anything from or put out material about if they have (or it hasn't been published in any media format that you can trace) are the ones to focus on. But even if you get something that people have channeled about extensively, even through this channel, don't eliminate that; it's possible different ruins were used in different ways in different times by different cultures.

Oh, yes.

It depends on what you want. It is your job, because you are in an altered state (that's why it's so important to record it), and I know you like to take notes. But we'd like to excuse you from taking notes. I know part of the reason you take notes is so that you don't have to listen to the recording. The long and short of it is yes, it's up to you to say, "Oh, did you do this?" Do that not from thought. Bring it up when you're in that altered state, because in the altered state, you will know for certain what they're talking about. When you come out of the altered state a little bit more, you can ask a question. Just say, for the purpose of the recording — you don't even have to ask if it doesn't flow — "I got that it was _____," and then say whatever it was, just to put it on the recording, okay?

Okay.

This is good, because it involves you more and it gets you away from taking notes. We think that taking notes is not a good thing, and we have said that from the beginning. We understand why you do it: so that you don't have to listen to the recording and you like doing such things. That's how your mind works, and you like mind-body connections. You love that. That's why you take notes, and you know this. But it also does not allow you to engage fully. Now, I realize that over the phone, it's difficult, and in person, it is much easier, but this is what you have for now. Okay?

Okay. I do keep writing notes. Originally, I thought I was just going to write down the questions I wanted to ask, but I tend to write a lot.

This is not a criticism. It's your favorite way to allow your body to communicate fully with your mind and your mind with your body. The mental and physical bodies are not complaining about that. They like doing that and stimulate certain chemicals in your body that support it and make it feel good to you. Yes, it feels good to you, and that is why it's so attractive. That's why in the beginning, you wrote down a little bit, but then you wrote more and more because of the stimulation of those chemicals in your body. You can read all about that if you haven't already. This is typically human, and you can't really avoid it, because that's the physiology of your body. But we don't necessarily think it's best. All right, good night.

Good night.

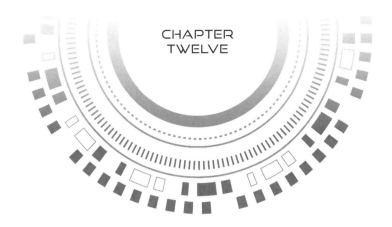

EARTH'S HISTORY OF
ET VISITATIONS

Copper Miner

FEBRUARY 13, 2019

The Temple Mount was built by Earth people. There is nothing particularly interesting about it, but I will talk about why it was built where it was. Why was everyone attracted to building in that one spot? It's not as if there weren't other places they could build it.

So we visited your planet some time ago, and we left in that location something similar to what you actually have now in your electronic communications systems. Say, for instance, that you are approaching your home, and you have a button in the car that you push so that as you get to your home the garage door opens. What we left was something like that: a receiving unit that would respond to a call. It doesn't make the call itself; it is a receiving unit. It is a thin film, more like a compressed energy, but if you were to see it on the surface, it would look shiny, almost like a form of paint. If you were to touch it, your finger would go through it, and you would sense a kind of tingly feeling. The reason we built it there is that

Image 12.1. Temple Mount, photographed by Francis Bedford, 1862

the location was suitable for an underground facility. The vestigial remains are deep underground there, deep enough that it is not really possible for humanity to reach them. That's probably a good thing because there are some objects there that you could probably hurt yourselves with unintentionally.

In terms of the original Temple Mount, as I said, that was built by Earth people. The Temple Mount and all of that business came later because the elders of various groups and sometimes younger people felt the energy of that place. The energy could be felt by sensitive people and very young people, from three to five years old and sometimes a little older, sometimes well up through their whole life. The sensitive ones will feel that energy and understand that this is the place to do something special.

We had been seen in our ships, and we visited the place quite a few times, really; we were still coming to visit up until about maybe

40,000 years ago. We created that "call" to the receiving unit, and the response made it possible for the ship to fly straight through the surface of the land. The ship flew at a high speed — not thousands of miles per hour but about 80 or 100 miles per hour — straight into the ground.

We were observed many times. When we came up to the surface, we emerged more slowly. We went into the surface at an angle, but we came up with the ship flattened out and directed straight up. The ship looked like a flying saucer. It emerged slowly out of the ground. Needless to say, because this was thousands of years ago, the Earth people were quite impressed.

We did not communicate with the Earth people. Because we looked very much like them, we felt that if they communicated with us it would alter the future. But we needed to be on Earth at that time, so we came and went as we needed to. The energy of the receiving unit remained for some time after we were no longer using it, and I feel that's why people were attracted to put something there.

Even though we were there thousands of years before the stories, stories essentially live forever. Many times, you will make up a story in your mind or even fantasize something that you might do for a time. I'm sure that many people on Earth do that. These stories will come up in bits and pieces, not because of what we did but because they are basic stories that exist and live on. So I will not put too fine a point on it, but I will say that the energy we left there created and influenced the writings of the times. When I say "writings," I don't mean that people were writing things down, but they sometimes chipped something in stone to leave some kind of a picture message. Eventually, writing came along. Various temples were built in that place, and the old stories still existed because they were handed down from one generation to another. In those days, people didn't wander too far from where they were born. All right, that's my opening statement. Now you can ask questions.

Miners from Another Planet

Well, first let me say welcome. Why did you need to visit that area?

The area has an element several miles down that we do not have on our planet. I think it is quite common on your planet, but we didn't have any. So we came to take some, which is not unusual. Such things go on all over the universe. It is sometimes frowned on if too much is taken, and we are not allowed to damage the surface of the planet. But as long as you go deep enough and what you take will not be missed by the planet or by any peoples who might exist there at some point in time, then it is allowed.

The element we were mining is called copper. We have none of it on our planet, and we needed it in small amounts. The closest I can come to describing the amount we needed would be if you were to pinch a little sand or maybe salt — a pinch of salt, as you say — between your thumb and your finger. That is the equivalent to the amount that we needed in creating this mechanism. I'm not going to talk about the mechanism too much because it's part of the drive system for the ship, and at that time in our civilization, we were just starting to make our own ships.

Before that, ships had been loaned to us, but eventually we were taught how to make them ourselves. We were given instructions for a rudimentary version, something we could start with, and we needed the copper. So we were looking for it, and we were able to find it at that location. Since that location had an abundant amount, we knew a little bit would not be missed.

Okay. Can you say who gave you the ship?

Initially, we were given the ship by a civilization that you will meet. You may have met them in the distant past. They are from a nearby ... no, I can't say. It's an odd situation here, but I can't say. Apparently, your past people interacted with these people a lot, and they hope to have that interaction again. I can say that they look just like you.

Okay, so first they loaned you a ship, and then they gave you one.

No, they never gave us one. It is not about ownership. They gave us the knowledge to build a rudimentary ship ourselves. But they didn't give us a ship; they loaned it to us.

I see. You built your own ship. So are you technological on your planet? Do you normally manufacture things?

No, but they thought it would be something we would enjoy doing. The ship would fit us. It's nice to sit in a chair that's comfortable and our size. We are about your height considering that the average adult is maybe around 5 feet, 8 inches to 5 feet, 10 inches tall.

Were the seats on the first ships too big or too small before you built your own ships?

There was more than one ship, but I'm using the seats to give you an idea. Everything was at a height that was not practical.

Okay, I was just looking to see if the beings that loaned you the ship were giant size or Zeta size.

Oh, I see. Well, something that needed to be interacted with was a little bit too high on one of the ships and some things were a bit too low. But this is on the same ship. You have to keep in mind that it's very possible that the ships were loaned out to various groups. The ship was not new when they loaned it to us. These ships last basically forever. So maybe the ships have universal controls. If you're very tall, then you can reach them, and if you're very short, then you can reach them.

Finding Inspiration in Nature

Can we ask where you are from?

We are from the galaxy that you reside in.

Have we heard of you before, would we know your name, or have we talked to any of you before?

No.

Can you say anything about your culture?

Well, our people are wanderers. We look exactly like you. We like to walk around. We don't walk in any machine-type things. We just like to walk around on our planet. Our planet is about two-and-a-half times as large as yours, but there are only about 120,000 of us on the planet at any given time, but there are other types of beings on the planet as well. There's plenty of space to walk around. We like to visit the other forms of life. We have some plant life, which has amazingly beautiful flowers, but I don't think they're any more beautiful than what we remember seeing on your planet when we were there. Some of them have very large leaves, and you could actually hover a ship under a single leaf, the ship being from side to side approximately 40 feet.

It's a big leaf, and it grows on a stem that is about as thick as an old tree trunk. We consider these plants to be elders because according to what we know about our time on our planet, those plants have always been there. Apparently, they were there before we were there. We have been on our planet for over 500 million Earth years. So imagine a single plant being older than that. Another thing about that plant, and the reason we like to visit it is that it's a good place to contemplate problems. Our culture doesn't have problems, but sometimes when we go to other cultures, we are somewhat confounded by why they do things the way they do. But if we go to this plant and stand under one of the lower leaves, it heightens our inspiration. It doesn't give us answers, but it helps us to put bits together so that potential answers are available to us.

You might wonder whether we visit these cultures simply out of curiosity, and the answer is no. One of the things we do is to function as intermediaries between individuals or groups of people who are having a misunderstanding. We do not interfere in misunderstandings that would lead to battle or fighting or anything like that; we simply help with issues that have caused the groups of people to no longer communicate as well as they once did.

Usually, those groups don't remember why they are not talking to each other, so you can see why it would be confounding to us. We have to try to remember for them. To do that, we need to have heightened inspiration, and that's why we stand under one of these leaves. When you stand under the lower leaves, it is about 50 or 60 feet above you. It is very cool when you stand under the leaf because the surface of the planet sometimes gets a little excessively warm, and shade is welcome. It is nice to have that cooling-off place while simultaneously getting your inspiration heightened.

We sometimes have our inspiration heightened when there isn't any reason to put something together, meaning that it resolves something. But as a result of just going there, sometimes our intellect is heightened. This can be valuable when attempting to do this diplomacy between groups. It allows faster inspiration and allows us to quickly head off something that would create further arguments between these groups. I don't have all your words, so I may be using multiple words to describe something that you could say in one word.

You're doing great. How do you know what needs to be the result? Do people come to visit you, or do you commune long distance?

What happened — and this is why we had ships loaned to us — is that it was known that it was something we could do. It was understood that we had this capability. Travelers would come to us and ask for our help to resolve problems that they were having on their own planets or planets they had visited, where people and groups were estranged from each other. The visitors, whoever they were and wherever they were from, knew about it but didn't know how to make it better. So they loaned us ships, and that's how we came to have the ships and go around to these other places where there were problems. Eventually someone said, "Well, maybe you'd like to build your own ships," and naturally we said yes. That way, we could make the ships a little more comfortable for ourselves. We built them to fit us.

This plant — was there only one plant or many of them on the planet?

There are many of them. The planet is very large and there are some places that are difficult to get to because there are deep valleys. You have things like this where you are on the surface and then you get to where the surface drops off. There are places like that across our planet, which restrict where we can go. Granted, we could take a ship and fly over these valleys, but what we feel — and this probably has to do with our inspirations — is that if we get to such an impassable place it might mean that we are not meant to go past that point. Yes, we could fly over past that point but maybe that area is meant for other beings. The reason I feel this is that we have winged ones that fly over us. One of the winged ones that frequently flies over an area where the land falls off told me that it is true what we feel. We have quite a bit of space where we can wander, and these areas are very well-suited to our people. But the places beyond those points would not be suitable. I didn't ask why; I felt quite pleased to know that our feelings were right.

A History of Visitations

Okay, so the last time you were here was 40,000 years ago. When was the first time in our terms?

It was about 120,000 years ago. But at that time, we were not gathering the mineral. It was just a visit. Your planet looked quite a bit different then. It had a lot more plants. In fact, plant life was dominant on the surface. Mobile life — meaning that which walks on two legs or four legs or more — was not found as often. I think that our people were intrigued by the plants. There weren't any with those big leaves, but there were magnificent trees, and it was typical to find trees that were 90 feet across at the base of the trunk that reached a quarter of a mile up to the sky.

The people — the many-legged and sometimes the two-legged — took their own track up the tree for whatever reason. Those with many legs would go up the tree because there was food on the trees that they liked and was good for them to eat, and the tree was fine with that. It has something to do with the trees' seeding process. The humans sometimes climbed up about 100 feet or so to sit on a branch. I don't know why. Perhaps they simply enjoyed the experience.

So 120,000 years ago — were there civilizations on the planet? Were there ET colonies, or was it developed in any area?

They were usually either underground or in some rocky area, like what you call a cliff. It was not unusual to find cliff houses. But as far as advanced civilizations compared to your current civilizations, I think there were a few underground places. Of course, there was the one that we went to in order to request permission — just to be polite — and visit with the dwellers then. But if you are talking about civilizations as you know now, the answer is no. However, we didn't go all over the planet. We just went to that one place. So I am not able to say much about your planet.

Keep in mind that we weren't studying your planet. Initially we were just visiting because there was a base there. When I say base, I am just using your term; there was nothing military going on there. There was just an outpost, so we went to visit. We loved the surface, the plants, and the people; everyone on the surface was very pleasant. They all seemed to have enough to eat, shelter, and whatever else they needed when they needed it. I think in that area at that time it was heavily forested, and when it rained and you were a human being, you could stand under something to avoid getting wet. But then again why do that, because the rain was usually warm and refreshing. It was like getting a shower bath; why wouldn't you like it? So being rained on was a blessing.

So the human beings you saw on Earth lived, you said, underground or in caves and the cliffs.

No, I'm sorry. It is good that you brought that up. The ones who lived underground were advanced civilizations, meaning probably not from Earth at that time. Those are the ones who lived underground, but the others lived in a hollowed-out area — not exactly a cave but in a cliff or something. The land looked a lot different then.

So they were like hunter-gatherers, then? They didn't farm?

No, no one was a hunter-gatherer as far as I could tell. The human beings did not kill. They ate fruits and vegetables that grew wild. There was plenty for everyone, so they were gatherers.

Were the people at the outpost your people or others that you knew?

They were not our people, but they were one of the peoples who originally asked us to help resolve problems, as I mentioned before. So we were flying by and thought, "Let's go visit our friends." Of course, the planet was beautiful from the sky, so who wouldn't want to visit? I'm sure that in the past, you had an abundance of visitors. It was so beautiful. It was like ... well, I don't know how to describe it. Other planets are beautiful but Earth is especially so.

Maintaining Diplomatic Relations

I will ask a personal question, and if you don't want to answer it, it's okay. How long do you live in our terms?

About 800 years or something like that.

So then, what was the most interesting resolution you've personally been involved in or heard about?

We weren't interested; we were performing a service. We didn't find it interesting in terms of your thoughts that you have now. You might pursue a subject because it piques your curiosity and you want to know more about it. But it's not like that for us. So you have to rephrase your question.

What was one of the most helpful interventions that you either participated in or heard about?

I can't really answer that, so I will answer where your curiosity is. One thing that was done was there was a planet where everyone was related. I don't mean simply because they were the same type of beings; they all came from essentially one family. But for some reason, they couldn't remember that they were related. I'm not going to describe what they look like, but they all looked exactly the same. Some of the people had hair, and some of the people didn't have hair. Then they became estranged from each other. So here you have this massive family. There were maybe 80,000 of this type of being on a planet, and about 60 percent of them had hair and about 40 percent of them didn't. These aren't exact numbers, but I'm using your terminology. They didn't communicate with each other very much, but when they did, they weren't unfriendly. When they were around each other, they were polite. But they weren't close as they once had been. So we went there, and we were able to discover that the different groups originally were related.

They don't want me to share too much. This comes up in diplomacy. Keep in mind that if I'm telling you something about other people; it is like you telling a secret. If you had a secret someone trusted you with and then you told someone else that secret, you would be going against that promise.

Oh, I didn't know it was a secret. Okay.

Yes, it is always the case with diplomatic relations. It is always a secret. I did not know this myself until just now. But I was advised that I could not go any further because it is not meant to be shared.

Pay Attention to Your Feelings

You said you had a history of 500 million years on your planet. Do you have a cultural history of where you came from?

No, apparently some things do not exist in time. The thoughts come up, and we think that it must be some completely different situation because we can go back that amount of time measured in your years, and we cannot go any further. To us that is an exact parallel to coming to the drop-off on the land. We feel we are not meant to go any further back. I think in your time from what little I know about you, you are used to pushing past things that seem to limit you. Sometimes you are successful with this, but other times you are either not successful or may cause harm to others though you may not mean to do that.

Maybe you didn't know it was causing harm. Sometimes you have to pay attention. If you see something in front of you that would cause harm and you don't want to do that, maybe you have to look up or down. Maybe you have to look closely when looking down or up, or you need to look to the sides. In short, if you are prevented from doing something in some way, like coming to the end of the land and there's a drop-off or something like that, maybe you are meant to go no farther. In ancient times in some civilizations — and perhaps in yours — when people traveled from the land to the ocean or to the freshwater lake, of course the water would be drinkable and they would be happy to have a source of water to drink. But it would not occur to them to go beyond that point because they didn't think of the water as anything other than a gift for them to drink and not to use as a means of transportation.

So my advice to you in your time is to pay more attention to your feelings. You're like us: you have instincts; you have feelings, and granted we are living in a more comfortable situation. For you, it is harder, but try to pay attention to your feelings. What do they tell you? Go here, not there; pay attention. I feel you will live happier if you do so. Good night.

ANCIENT CULTURES MOVED STONES THROUGH LOVE

Visitor from the Past

FEBRUARY 18, 2019

We did not have a stone quarry. We did not cut the stone ourselves. We spoke to the stones and said, "This is what we would like and need, these portions of you; would you like to participate?" This was all done in love and friendship. Because the stones existed near where we were, some of them wanted to participate as an act of friendliness and love. We said, "This is what we want," and drew a picture on the ground, in the air, or more often, with our fingers on the stones. Sometimes we had to walk for miles to draw on a stone, guided by that stone's love and desire to participate. The stone guided us by the feeling of moving back, and we also moved back until we didn't get the feeling anymore. Then the stone broke off and moved slowly to the ground in the form we wanted and needed.

Then came the time of moving the stones. Sometimes pieces of stone came right away, moving the way I mentioned. Other times,

Image 13.1. The Stone of the South at Baalbek, Lebanon, is the largest worked monolith on Earth, weighing in at a staggering 1,242 tons. It is even heavier than the Stone of the Pregnant Woman, which weighs an estimated 1,000 tons, that sits on the other side of the road in the quarry.

a stone came part way and then decided it wanted to move more slowly. We had to be patient and enjoy friendship with the stone.

Stones Have Feelings Too

Often stones have a sense of humor, so there was joking, laughter, and merriment. Even though stones do not seem to talk, they have all the feelings humans have. More stones joined in when they were ready. We could not move them much; sometimes they moved themselves.

We woke up one day to find a stone that didn't want to come along had moved quite a distance toward the structure overnight. Then we laughed and felt the merriment in the stone itself.

Stone is alive; when you know this, your world gets a lot less complicated. Once you know that stone is alive, then of course you realize everything is alive. Then cooperation surrounds you — love, compassion, kindness, patience, and all good feelings.

Could all your people do this or just some?

Everybody. That's why I was surprised that you cannot; it has apparently been lost in your time. That's why I made an effort to describe how it was done to the best of my capability (I'm not a teacher).

Can you say what you are?

Can you say what you are?

I am a woman who runs a publishing company and talks to people through a channel.

I'm not a feminine energy, but I will say I'm someone who loves my family, my friends, and my life and their lives, and I am someone who lives as well as possible.

Jealousy Destroyed Civilizations

In times ancient to your own, there were many issues that we feel might be relevant in your times. Very often, people were distracted by their personalities and could not do the work at hand, whatever that work was. Because of such struggles from within, people often wanted to do what was right but the personality (you say ego) would take over in a struggle to be recognized and valued. In those ancient times, we had that, I feel, just as much as you do. The reason that some things lasted, meaning structures of civilizations, as long as they did was that people found a way to make something like a family.

Even though there was, at times, "this" boss of the family or "that" boss of the family, it wasn't always the same person. We feel that custom might've been lost in your times, because in your times, there are too many bosses. This happened in ancient times as well, and when there are too many bosses, everybody wants control. One person's idea of the perfect system does not always match everybody else's idea. This is why civilizations came and went.

When a group was too caught up in the control issue on an individual basis, the group became vulnerable to other groups who envied or were jealous of whatever they had. Maybe group B became jealous of group A and wanted whatever it had. Because group A had become vulnerable, group B was able to challenge it. Then no matter how beautiful the structures group A built were (for example), group B would go out of its way to destroy those structures even when they found them appealing. I am just saying this because it is relevant to your times. They would put their structure in its place even if the majority of people disapproved. This is why civilizations seemingly rose and fell. But just because a civilization could build something monumental, that might have lasted for a long time and still has vestiges in your time (at least when people dig around and find them), that doesn't mean that the civilization was superior. It means that things worked for a while, until others decided that it was their time.

We feel this is a human trait on Earth. I cannot see your time very well, but I can tap into whatever emotional progress you might have made. I don't see any. You might think that sounds judgmental, but you asked for someone who could speak to your contemporary issues while still rooted in our common origin (in the past).

I recall that the group A and group B scenario of the past is exactly what happened to us. We became too infatuated with our individual needs as a result of having a smooth system (not as smooth as yours, perhaps, but a smooth system). A smooth system means that basic needs were all taken care of, and people would sometimes have what you call leisure time to think about what they as individuals had and what other individuals had in the broader group, resulting in jealousy.

Everyone Needs Support

What was always missing in those times was a full and complete unifying factor. That happened in our times. We needed something we didn't always have: emotional support for all people, not just for babies who need it or older ones who are getting ready to die. Even when people are functioning in groups (sometimes families, sometimes structures you call organizations), they still need this.

It's easy to lose track of who needs what and when they need it. In your time, you seem to have structures in place that attempt to provide for basic needs, but what is still missing is emotional support. "Emotional" is not the word I would use in my time. We would say you need to be able to provide love and compassion, even when people's needs of the moment seem to be trivial to you as an individual. They are not trivial to them. Maybe they are simply unable to explain them very well. Perhaps it's something that has built up over time and they have strong feelings about even though they can't put it into words. We failed as a society to provide them as much love and compassion as we did for our young ones and our very old ones. Our society became overly distracted and vulnerable and thus easily conquered. We think this is also happening in your times.

I can see into your times a little bit, and it seems you have many more people. This makes things more complicated. But I feel that with love and compassion, a great deal can be accomplished. Even if every individual's needs and wants cannot be provided for exactly the way the individual needs or wants, friendship can make a difference. I recall in my time that I had friendship, connections with family members, and love. Because of friendship, we could laugh about all the things we wanted or needed to — even desperately needed sometimes. After a while, we thought maybe it wasn't that important, because life went on, we learned things, and other things became more important. It seems in your time that love, compassion, and friendship are missing sometimes even among family members.

I am not saying this is the case for all people in your time. But since there are so many people in your time, it seems that groups of people from other places (or even groups of people in your own place where you live but you don't usually associate with) have these issues. It might be difficult to communicate with others even if you want to help them, because different groups have different ways of communicating. It was the same in our time, and sometimes one group's ways were not compatible with another's. You have to find ways that can help you all be friends in your families as well as in different countries all over the planet. I don't know whether this is the kind of thing you wanted me to talk about, but it is a similarity between our time and your contemporary time.

It's wonderful.

Love Moves Mountains

In addition to that, can you tell me about your time on the planet?

As an individual?

No, your people and your society. You built the foundation of Baalbek, is that right?

What is that word you are using?

Baalbek is a huge complex in Lebanon that uses monstrously long, huge pieces of megalithic stone.

Oh, I know. You cannot move these stones in your time?

No, not when they weigh hundreds of tons.

Oh, so maybe I am not able to speak to your times after all, because this was something simple to do. One person could move such a stone, but in your times, this ability has been lost. That's a terrible thing to have lost, this natural human skill. It's all based on love, you know. After you ask the stones to move, essentially what happens is that they float along the ground, sometimes skimming the surface, other times well above the surface. To move them, you say, "You're needed to build a structure to protect the place you live

Image 13.2. Baalbek Temple complex, size perspective

so that you will be able to thrive." Then you went to where the stone was. It could be a mountain or perhaps stones nearby. The stones were formidable, and you asked whether there was any stone that would like to be a member of your family for a while. You haven't put the stones back yet? You found the stones and left them there, is that it?

They're still there, the structures.

Know that we promised to put them back at some point. That will have to happen, because we made the promise. Maybe our souls will have to return and put the stones back. Stones, of course, live much longer than human beings. I'm going to check, a moment. [Pauses.] The stone says we still have time. I will get the measurement in human time. [Pauses.] We have 100,000 years to put it back. This does not mean in 100,000 years we have to start moving stones; rather, we have to see to it they are put back. This means that people will be able to move these stones. It's hard to explain how this can be done in your time, because you've lost it.

Moving stones involves love and compassion. There are people in your time who can move little things. These people were born with the skill and were discouraged from using it. For some reason, they are disbelieved even though they can demonstrate. Perhaps they have a small metal object, something you might use to clip papers together. They might put such a thing in front of them and move it without touching it. Ah, I see. You think in your time this involves will. It is not the mind; the mind is not involved (other than its basic function). The mind is involved neurologically but not as thought.

Love and compassion for the object are involved, because in order for an object to move — even a small object moved by people in your time — the object must love the person who is about to move it even if it has never been exposed to that person before. This can be done because the person loves the object — not as the object is now but what it was. This reminds the object what it was so that it loves what it has been and also its temporary appearance (whatever form it takes in the human world). I don't know whether I am making myself clear.

Yes, absolutely.

Stone Structures Saved Lives during Floods

Objects and human beings have relationships of love. A human being might make motions with his or her hand without touching the object. As long as the person loves the object as a friend, as you love a good friend or even a close friend, the object will move at least sometimes. When the object is no longer prepared to move, that means it wants you to do something for it — maybe just sit there loving it.

The object might be all right with being picked up, or maybe it does not want to be picked up. You have to be able to reach for the object, and if you get the feeling not to pick it up, then don't. The object might want you to love it at a distance without touching it. In short, what I am teaching you here is something that I think you have records of people doing, so what I have explained to you is exactly the same but for big stone. It doesn't matter what it weighs; it doesn't matter the size. The relationship is the issue. One must love the object and what it is.

Very often, a stone is willing to love a human being such as a child, because a child is innocent. But human beings might also be loved as adults by stones if they do something funny or playful. It is all about how you relate to the stone. This is the same way that people can move the paper-connecting object in your time. We think such people exist in your time, and we think there are also people in your time who can move large objects, because the way to move a small object is exactly the same as for large objects. That is how the stones were moved in our time.

How long ago in our time did you build this humongous platform?

Something like 40,000 years ago.

Why did you build it?

It was the base of something, what is left in your time — and what does it look like? Just describe it. You used a term to describe it: "platform"?

Yes, a huge platform. Can you give me a minute to pull it up and describe it?

Yes.

Okay, hold on.

Image 13.3. Baalbek Temple complex, aerial view

I will tell you why I am asking. The reason I am asking is that I find it hard to believe that the entirety of what we created with loving assistance from stones is still in existence in your time. This is why I want you to describe to me what it looks like in your time.

Yes, okay, it's a huge slab that has deep walls, and in one place, six columns are standing. Then there's another place that has two sides of a building standing and very high columns but no roof.

You can stop now.

Okay.

This was originally a structure with walls. People lived in it or sought shelter in it when (as you'd say) the exterior conditions were not safe. This does not have to do with other human beings. It just has to do with the environment — rain, wind, and so on. People came and went, but sometimes there was loss of life because of floods. So we thought it would be good to have a structure where, even in the deepest floods, there were levels that people could go to above the water, and they could use foods stored there that had been grown, dried, and preserved, along with fresh water. Basic necessities were available on higher portions of the structure, even though none of this was used except in emergencies. I think maybe in your time you have similar things; if not, it would be good to make some.

Just building a structure higher off the ground isn't always the best way. If you are going to build a structure where there might be large objects blowing about in the wind, you cannot expect a weak structure to remain standing. But if the walls are very thick and the stones want to cling together and are loved by the people they are supporting, all happens in love, including with the food that is stored. It is possible to create a society that is supportive, and such societies, we thought in our time, would live together because they were so perfect. But I described earlier what happened. So perhaps in your time you have not been able to find any of the old preserved foods, and this doesn't surprise me because they were preserved in vessels that would not ordinarily survive.

We sometimes shared some of our preserved foods with other people. Visitors came and went, and occasionally we found out that they had done the same thing. In one civilization I can remember, the people came and visited us while they were going from one place to another, and they did not represent a threat. They stayed for a few days, and we supported them. They were good people. They mentioned how they also made vessels and stored dried fruits in them. That both our civilizations had developed this on their own made us feel a close bond with them. I remember toward the end of our civilization (although we didn't know it was toward the end), we promised we would meet again. But because our civilization didn't last much longer, it didn't happen, and I suppose they wondered what happened to us.

How long were you on the planet?

As a civilization?

Yes.

I cannot be certain, maybe 3,000 or 4,000 years, something like that.

Really? What were your people known as? Are they in our history books?

Oh, you do this thing. What are your people called?

Well, here we are named by our country. Here, we are Americans, and there are English, Chinese, and Japanese, like that.

Oh, I see. We did not do that. We were just people.

What the Stones Chose to Build

I'm looking at one picture here that has a flat surface and three human beings standing on it, and the steps go up about three times as high as the human beings. Then there is one intact wall on the end and a column on each side. It goes up around 100 feet, and the whole end of the building is totally intact. I can see one side, the end, and the left-hand side. So that is still there, if that is something you built.

[Laughs.] I'm surprised that lasted. That is what the stone wanted to do. The stone wanted to form some structures that would remind it of its tiny portion. I will have to come up with your words here, a moment. "Tiny portions" it is, and it resembled the crystal structure of the tiny portions of the stone. We could not do this in the structure we were creating, and we did not understand why the

13.4. Baalbek Temple complex, inside temple

stone wanted to do this, but I understand it in my now time. The stone was attempting to re-create something that reminded itself of home. So that is why the steps (as you call them) seem to be made for giants, but we were not that.

The columns have heavily incised vertical indentations top to bottom.

We think this might have come afterward, because they weren't there in our time. You're saying "carved"?

Carved, yes.

We did not do that. We left the stone and kept it simple. We did not do that.

Okay, maybe this is something that was built on the top of your structure. I don't know. Can you say where you are from — what planet or galaxy?

I do not understand.

When you came here, you came from some other planet?

No. Did you?

Well, I did. Okay, so you were on Earth as part of the people on Earth, and you built this?

That's my understanding, yes.

Okay, I thought it was built for a spaceport or something — you know, to land flying ships on. Can you say where you are now or what your life is like now?

I am no longer a human being, but my life is different and probably does not relate to your life. It is a pleasant life, and there is no suffering. Oh, what relates is that there is love, there is compassion, there is friendship, there is patience, and there is kindness. I think those things exist in your time as well, and it might be good to celebrate the good feelings more often in your time. Good night.

CHAPTER
FOURTEEN

GOBEKLI TEPE, TURKEY — ANCIENT PLEIADIAN HEALING AND MANIFESTATION CIRCLES

A Pleiadian

FEBRUARY 21, 2019

[**Publisher's note:** I asked for someone who lived now in the future who had been involved in the building of the stone circles filled with T-shaped columns and columns carved with strange animals that we call Gobekli Tepe in Turkey to speak through Robert Shapiro. I asked, if it was possible, whether they would also speak to us about their perception of our time now on this planet. This didn't get recorded.]

All right, thank you for the opening remark describing the site; it helped. Now, I may or may not be able to advise you in your time. But the purpose of the platforms that you refer to was to create a location to provide services to our people that would last and create a generational connection to our people in the future. As it happened, our people did not stay there. The reason, for the most part, was that it was not fully understood by our scientists how outwardly expressive your planet is. We didn't expect so much wind and other

Earth motions, so even though the areas — the platforms — are still somewhat active (not much anymore, since our people are not there), there is still some slight support for the creation of what was literally asked for.

Initially, the elders — or the one picked in any given group or family — would stand in the center of the circle, or as close to the center as possible, and speak of what was needed, desired, or what would simply be enjoyed by us in that part of the planet. After that request was made, a pictorial in stone was created — you call it a carving — requesting certain types of beings we considered friends. These were not considered a food source, as our people did not eat other beings but rather certain types of "others" we found pleasing to be around.

Of the circles uncovered, from what you have stated, we think this might not be all of them. According to what I'm looking at, there were fifty circles. The others either have not been uncovered or perhaps something happened over time and they are no longer present. I don't think they will create a disturbance to your people, but I do think certain aspects of our behavior have caught on. If you look at some of the carvings in the stone columns, there was a stance — a way the person would stand?

Yes, there are circles with stone columns that are shaped like a T with carvings on them, and some people with their hands against their hips with their fingers coming to the fronts of the bodies. A few have been excavated, but there are many more that scientists in airplanes have seen by means of ground-penetrating radar that are not uncovered yet.

Aside from that, I would simply say that some gestures were not typical for human beings to make at that time on Earth. It wasn't typical for human beings to take a certain stance with hands on their hips. So that, I think, is what I was referring too.

Oh, yes, there are carvings just like the ones in South America that have hands carved coming around toward their bellies (image 14.1).

This is important for those of you doing spiritual work and other things. Those positions are intended to show that the speakers (who would have been at the center of the circle or as close as possible) would stand with their hands in that position on their bodies. The position of the hands request that the pictures shown (the beings in those pictures carved on the columns) be present on Earth physically. That's what the hands on that part of the body meant, physically. It wasn't for a food source; however, some people might have speculated that. This was to instruct succeeding generations of our people — in case it was forgotten, since that was possible — that was how you stood. In this way, the request became not something that occurred in a dream or in a vision but actually manifested physically.

Image 14.1. Carved stone column showing dantian, the "stance" position

Can you say how long ago you were here?

Our people were in that location thirteen eons ago. Now, to us an eon is not the same as it is to you, and I am unable to translate what it means in time. But I can say that after our people left because of Earth's expressions of herself — wind and storms and so on — it is possible that others came and used those circles, at least when they were on the surface. But over time, things on the surface usually are no longer there.

Was your creation of these circles after a flood or before a flood?

Oh, I see. I do not think a flood was a factor in our people leaving. There were rivers and lakes, yes, but if there had been a flood before that, we were not aware of it. It might've happened after we left.

How long were you here? Can you say that?

I'll try to say, even though our time measurements are different from yours, and they don't seem to equate. This is what I can get for you: If you take your average human life span in your time measurement and multiply that by twenty-three, that would be approximately how long we were on the planet.

Okay. That's about 70 years times twenty-three, which is 1,610 years.

I know you're saying something for yourself or for some other, but it doesn't relate to me, meaning I am not a mathematician.

Compatible Communication

These circles were ceremonial centers, so where did you live when you were here?

We lived in the open. This is why we did not leave at those times when the weather was calm and pleasant. Occasionally, there would be others who lived locally on Earth who were born and raised there. They were compatible with the weather and Earth, and I think they had no struggles or difficulties. They usually avoided us, probably because what we created with the circles was not anything they did. So apparently with human beings on Earth at that time (I don't know if it's still the same), when things happened that were completely different from anything they knew, there was a tendency to avoid the area. So most of them avoided the area, but occasionally braver beings came to communicate and inquire as to what we were doing. We explained as simply as possible. They nodded and sometimes stayed for a meal, and other times they moved on.

Image 14.2. Carving of beings being asked to come to Earth

I am looking at one of the carved columns in a circle right now that has a crab on it, some geese, and some other beings I can't identify (image 14.2). So you asked those beings to be physically in your vicinity?

Yes.

How did you know they existed on Earth?

They didn't, as far as we knew.

Oh, you were calling them in to incarnate here?

Yes, they could very well have existed, but they didn't exist in that area. So we requested that they exist in that area, because we are compatible with them and we like the way they think and communicate. We felt that if we needed to understand Earth and the citizens of Earth better, perhaps they would be able to explain it to us.

How did you know they existed?

They existed on other places. The beings that we requested all exist on our planet.

What planet is that?

I don't think it would make any sense to you, but I'll do my best [makes a sound with tones].

Okay, is it in a galaxy that we've heard from and understand, or can you say where it's located?

It is in your galaxy, but not where you can find it. Propulsion won't get you there.

A Suggested Venture

How did you happen to come to Earth?

Well, one reason was that we had heard from our friends — the beings I referred to — who were near there on another planet but not in your solar system. They said there was a nearby solar system we might want to look at. Oh, I see now the connection. Our planet, if you approach it, is blue, white, and green, so that's why our friends must have said we might like your planet, because they have similar colors. The patterns are a little different, but the colors are about the same. Our planet is a little smaller than yours, but approaching your planet from space was an odd experience. It felt like we were coming to see friends or cousins. So we were a little startled that the human beings on Earth were not like us. They were very similar to us, but they were not like us, and that was a surprise.

Apparently our friends who advised us to go there thought we might enjoy it because of the similarity of appearance from a distance. We even have some similarities in weather: warmth, sunlight, rains, and occasional lightning.

One of the circles I'm looking at is filled with rocks (image 14.3). Did you leave it all open when you left?

They were not filled with rocks when we were there.

It's like someone deliberately buried them to protect them.

I think it's the other way: Someone after us may have covered them so as to not see them. There were some people who did not like the circles or did not trust them or felt they were unpleasant to their eyes.

Image 14.3. A circle filled with rocks after the Pleiadians left — partially excavated

THE PURPOSE OF
THE GOBEKLI TEPE CARVINGS

A Pleiadian Child

FEBRUARY 25, 2019

So you have been interested in the carvings, especially the ones that have depicted forms of life that do not exist on Earth [image 14.4]?

Correct.

Those forms of life did once exist on Earth but only for a short time. Some of them were brought by visitors, and some were the visitors themselves. But what was understood shortly after those forms of life came on their own, with others, or were brought by others was that this planet was not about that. This planet you are on is for experiencing (as you know for human beings and even for all other beings) individuality. Each individual (not every single one, just a few rare exceptions) for the most part experiences itself as one recognizable form of life. I grant that seahorses are an exception, but they are among the few.

When this was understood by those who were visiting, those forms of life felt it was important to leave a record of their existence.

Image 14.4. Forms of life that do not exist on Earth

They do exist in other places, and they are people. But on Earth, once that was realized, those forms of life either got back on the ships or were picked up by ships that came back to get them. It was not that they were uncomfortable on Earth, but the realization set in — usually due to "this" or "that" teacher — that was not what Earth was about, at least for the foreseeable future from that perspective in time.

I thought I'd start by explaining that to you. That's why those mysterious pictures are there, carved on the columns in those circles. But the pictures were left, as well as other impressions of what they saw at the time, or sometimes the pictures were just beauty and art for their own sake. Other times, they were ideas of many different forms of life that all have something in common.

There's a pattern on one of the pictures you sent to Robbie that looks like art, meaning it appears to be a decoration where all the forms in that decoration are pretty much the same [image 14.5]. That was a reminder that all life forms, at their core, are exactly the same on Earth: Animals are not soulless; they all have souls. But scientists — including those who know and believe in

Image 14.5. A reminder that all life forms, at their core, are exactly the same on Earth: They all have souls.

religion or philosophies that acknowledge the soul or self as a significant portion of life — have not realized or accepted the fact that all forms of life, including particles, have their own unique souls, which says, of course, that they have their own immortal personalities. So that is the meaning of that apparent decoration. If you have any doubts, ask the channel, and he will make it clear to you what picture that is about.

Healing Circles

Now, I am aware of the person you were talking to, but I will not pick up that thread. Instead, I'm going to tell you that I was alive in that time our people were on your planet. I was not one of influence, but I was there. We were not from Earth (I think I've made that plain already), but at that time, it was an accepted thing that you could come from other planets to Earth and stay for a while. Usually, it was encouraged that you stay underground in a place that wouldn't disturb the surface dwellers. But if you had something to say or do that might bring some happiness or improvement in life for the surface dwellers, you were allowed to do that.

Image 14.6. A partially excavated circle — one of fifty

The circles [image 14.6] performed healing, and in those times — even though the surface dwellers/humans had their own ways of being — they still had illnesses and injuries. If they could get to a circle or be carried to one, they could lie down in it and be cured. This did not happen instantaneously. They fell asleep, and the others sometimes sat at the edge of the circle (that's why there was a place for them to sit). But most of the time, they sat outside the circle and the person lying in the circle experienced a healing.

I know you are going to ask where we are from, and I can tell you we came from the Pleiades. In some of the previous material I think you may have published, the way the Pleiadian people (on one of the planets) would come to the end of their lives was to lie down on a walkway that was often beautifully formed and looked like what you call tile (although the designs could change according to the energy that they were exposed to), and they died there. It was not unpleasant, unhappy, or dramatic. As the soul slowly left the body (I'm going to call them tiles even though they weren't that, but that's how you would relate to them if you saw them), the tiles transformed. The circles radiated, and it was like they were expressing joy and happiness and sending love to loved ones or friends or family. Then there was a bright spot in the middle. The soul or spirit was gone, and people removed the body.

So that's just a reminder, but in terms of Earth with those built circles, it was decided that what was needed (given that most surface dwellers were nomadic and that you couldn't tile the whole planet) was a place with beautiful structures that attracted people. At some point, someone went there with a wound or a disease and lay down, and others noticed that they got better. So that's why we were allowed (granted, I wasn't doing it since I was a child at the time) to build these structures, because it could improve the quality of life for the established surface dwellers.

Bird-Headed Beings

The previous speaker said that the people in the area did not like to look at the circles, so did that mean they didn't understand their function, they weren't willing to ask about it, or they didn't want to learn about it?

Is this something I said or the other one said? I'm not going to comment on what the other one said. I will explain, however, how it came to be that there were stones piled in there and all that. Is that what you are asking about?

That's part of it, yes.

That came along much later, when people on the surface forgot what those circles were for. They would just walk by, look at them, and walk on even if they were sick or hurt. This is not unusual in your time, that people forget things. If the awareness of what something can do, even though it's ready and available to do it, is not present, people might come to misunderstand it, or they might judge it in some way. In the case of the circles, sometimes there appeared one of the beings who designed it (at a distance, because they were no longer there). They came to see how the circles were faring and to see whether everything was still all right. It was one of the beings in the carving, the ones that don't exist on Earth, with a sort-of bird head.

The ones with the sort-of bird heads designed the circles [14.7], and they sometimes traveled through light, and then the light was in the circle. Then you could see them. This was an example of a being that was more than one thing. Of course, since they were unknown on Earth, some people became suspicious, and they put rocks in there. The so-called tiles were the same as the ones in the Pleiades, so the designs could move. They covered up the tiles, and then the beings could not really be there because the circles were covered.

Image 14.7. The bird-headed being who designed the circles

The Pleiadian version of the tiles is alive and was the route that allowed the beings to visit because they could connect there. But once they were covered up with stones, and in some cases dirt or just time, then they couldn't come anymore, because the tiles did not function the way they did on the Pleiades. At that point, the designers changed the Pleiadian version of the tiles to an Earth version with a fixed pattern. They felt that would be the safest because the circles would probably be uncovered by people or by something Earth was doing with wind and so on, and if people did not know how to use them, it could accidentally alarm them. So that's why the change was made.

So right now the circles that are being excavated and opened no longer have any power in them?

No, they don't have that power. But at some point, when there is contact between Earth and extraterrestrials, then it might be possible to return them to their original functions.

Spiritual Education

Can you ask somebody how long ago it was in our time when you were here and when they were built?

Let's see if I can get the figure. It is a little confusing, but I will give you two numbers: It's either 40,000 years ago or 400,000 years ago. I'm not sure which, but the figure 40 is stronger.

Do you know who Zoosh is?

No.

Okay. Do you have a spiritual teacher you ask things of when you need to know something?

No. There is a reason I don't have one. Remember to ask questions. Why don't I have a spiritual teacher?

[Laughs.] Why don't you have a spiritual teacher?

This is because I know what I need to know in my time. I was educated by my parents, and my parents are spiritual teachers. There are wisdom teachers. You probably have wisdom teachers you call elders or parents. That is not the case for me; my parents are still present and young. Oh, I see what it is. That is why I'm here. [Laughs.] I was young in that life on Earth, and I'm young in my life now, so that's how I can relate.

So what is the length of incarnation in your body? Are you still alive? Are you 40,000 years old?

I am not 40,000 years old. What makes you think that? Oh, I made a mistake; I didn't say it right. When I was on Earth, I was a child, okay?

Yes.

Where I am in my life now, I am a child.

But in a different life?

Not the same child. Is that clear?

Yes, that's clear. You came here on a spaceship, right?

Yes.

And you left because the weather was so nasty. Why didn't you just build structures to protect you from the weather?

All I can remember is that one day we were told that things were changing on the surface of the planet, but it wasn't going to happen immediately. It was felt that it would be better for us to leave, and being a child, I didn't have a vote, so to speak [laughs]. But things were changing, and my understanding at that time in that life was that things were changing for the surface dwellers, meaning the human beings, and to some extent for other surface dwellers. Perhaps it meant the surface dwellers were changing in some way; I don't know. But that's why we left.

Well, it could have been that an ice age was coming or a flood or something like that.

No one told me at the time. They just told me what I told you. That's all.

Is there anyone you can ask now about the reason they left?

I can go away and maybe someone else can come and answer. I am not offended. Sometimes I cannot answer your questions. If you want someone else to come, I don't know whether another will be available. I am a child, so I don't know, but I'm not offended.

No, you are a delight, but if we could find someone who has more answers to the questions, that would be great.

ZOOSH CLARIFIES SOME DETAILS

Zoosh

All right, this is Zoosh.

Welcome, welcome. Can you fill in some of the details?

I don't know. What did you have in mind?

The first thing is: What was about to happen on Earth that caused them to leave?

I think that the surface weather patterns were changing, and they had been advised by those who could look at the future that there were going to be sandstorms and possibly — well into the future — floods and so on. It was felt that it wasn't imminent that these things would happen, but there would be a buildup, a change of energy. During that change of energy, the surface populations would change. Some of them would get upset, some would get angry, and some would start fighting. This is not unusual. Even in your time, this happens. Sometimes people get anxious and upset, and there are fights and various dramas, and then comes a big storm with thunder, lightning, rain, wind, and all of that. Afterward everything is calm again, and the fighting goes away. That kind of thing would have been upsetting to the peoples there. They would not have been able to tolerate that, so it was the buildup of that energy they needed to leave at that point.

Right. The being that was just here said 40,000 or 400,000. Is either one of those numbers correct as to how many years ago they were here?

Just a moment. You know how they got those two numbers? Well, the reason is that they were here on third-dimensional Earth. You are not on third-dimensional Earth. What the being told you was really very accurate: It was either 40,000 years ago or 400,000 years ago, because you cannot measure time. Even equating the youngster's time and your time, it didn't work. He equated at first to third-dimensional time, and then he equated it to the "in-between stage" you are in now, and that's where the 400,000 came in.

Well, scientists are carbon dating it as 12,500 years ago.

Then that would suggest —

The 40,000, yes.

I would leave this in the manuscript because it is important for people to know that a wide variety of time, recollection, and remembrance — which is sometimes a little different from recollection — is quite flexible now. This is part of the reason people can experience the same event in the same moment while standing right next to each other, and each has a different remembrance or recollection of it even twenty minutes after it happened. Time is in flux.

Ah, that's right. You said everything can change, and it can change for the better. Yes, I like that. Okay, there are depictions in South America with the same position of the hands. Did another group of the same people go to South America, or did some of these people go to South America?

No, not the same people.

Some other people from the Pleiades who understood what that meant, then?

No, that has a meaning in your now time.

What is that?

Dantian.

Dantian? I don't know that.

Look it up. It has a meaning in your time.

Dantian is loosely translated as "elixir field," or simply "energy center." Dantian are the "qi focus flow centers," important focal points for meditative and exercise techniques.

The lower dantian is particularly important as the focal point of a breathing technique as well as the centre of balance and gravity.

Taoist and Buddhist teachers often instruct their students to centre the mind in the navel or lower dantian. This is believed to aid control of thoughts and emotions.

Source: https://en.wikipedia.org/wiki/Dantian

More Details

All right, I asked why, if they had a spaceship, they lived on the land without any protection from the elements. They told me why they left but not why they lived that way. Do they live that way at home in the Pleiades?

The reason they lived that way on Earth was that there was nothing to be concerned about with the elements. At the time they were there, it was that way on their planet. That's why they were attracted to this planet in the first place. It was calm.

Ah, okay. Is there anything else you can say about those fifty circles that I don't know to ask?

The fifty circles all functioned in exactly the same way. What if there were forty, fifty, or sixty people who were all ill at the same time? It was not like they could take aspirins. They would all have the opportunity to lie down in a circle and be cured.

Did that happen very often?

Yes, it happened several times during the time of understanding of what the circles were for. Keep in mind that people were nomadic, so the same people weren't always present in the area. They tried to leave some kind of message in the dirt (but those messages didn't last) or something like that for others, telling them what it was to be used for.

Did I understand the child to say that once they manifested all those beings that had not been here on Earth, they realized that they shouldn't have and the ET ships took them away?

Yes, that's a simple way of explaining it, and the simple way is often the best way. The ships didn't take them away. It's just that they got on the ships and said, "Oh, we are not supposed to be here, because we are more than one thing." I think the example was given about a seahorse as the exception, and there might be a few other exceptions of beings that appear to be more than one thing at once (such as a duck-billed platypus or something like that). There are a few life forms on the planet that are still vestigial remains of more than one thing.

Oh, I see. I didn't understand that. Did someone create them that way, or was that their natural form from some other planet?

It was their natural form. They are people, and human beings have a tendency to separate themselves and even cherish the documents that said they are in charge, something like that, or documents that have been misinterpreted over the years, through various translations, suggesting that human beings are in charge of nonhuman beings. That is not true, but in time this will be acknowledged, and then maybe, if all goes well, people will actually learn what other forms of life have to say to them. They may not speak your language, but it can all be done telepathically.

Oh, we look forward to that. Okay, that's all the questions I can think of, and I really appreciate you coming in and clearing this up. There's so much speculation now from archaeologists and ancient-astronaut theorists as to what these circles were, when they were built, and how they were used, but this should clear it up a little bit.

Well, that's one of your jobs with Robbie — to offer alternate explanations that people can choose to believe or not. But alternate explanations can sometimes lead people in the right direction. Then they can explore that direction and maybe find out other things. As with many things, sometimes they won't actually have to do any exploration physically. They can just look at the data and reinterpret it according to another point of you. This happens all the time. There is hope that someday it will be reinterpreted correctly, which it has many times, but not acknowledged as being valuable. In the end, it will. On that note, I say good night.

Thank you.

BIRD-HEADED BEINGS IN GÖBEKLI TEPE

Culanaro

MARCH 27, 2019

I am Culanaro. You have a question about the so-called bird-headed beings. I will speak for a few moments now.

Wonderful. Welcome.

The nature of our existence is to visit species who are attempting to help other species. Sometimes it is just an individual. Other times it is a small group, and sometimes it is a whole society of beings. We appear in the form of their bodies, meaning that in the case of visiting human beings, we look sufficiently human in order to be accepted. But we have heads and necks that resemble a bird's. It is important to draw that distinction. We have, on occasion, been depicted in various forms as having a bird head. You have seen many birds, and they all have distinct features.

We do not have feathers or long beaks, but there is no doubt that the form of our heads and necks (which are part of our actual form) are birdlike. The rest of our actual form does not look human. Occasionally, if the people we are assisting are very accepting, we will show up in our actual form, which does not look human and is not really birdlike, just different. It might have been pictured fairly well in the carving you are asking about [image 14.8]. But the bird head is not that prominent, not such a big beak.

Anyway, that's enough about that. We are beings who naturally emanate an energy that can help to transform disease, discomfort, and even mental illness in all forms nonviolent and violent. In some civilizations, violence is considered a disease, and some people on Earth think of it that way. Of course, it's not necessarily something you can approach therapeutically if immediately confronted with it. You might have to return "like with like," and we understand. Of course, survival and protecting others is very important. However, we see violence as a disease, and most people have experienced it at least once during their lifetimes (that is, Earth people in your now times) and often more than that.

14.8. Carvings of bird-like beings

Your main personality will exert a modifying influence that will cause the temporary outburst to be expressed, and then it is over. As long as it can be expressed in a way that does not harm others, it can be done as a form of therapy. For example, you get angry some place that is not around people or beings as far as you can tell — not around animals and possibly not around trees unless they are very old big ones. In which case, the trees will have the wisdom to know that it will pass.

It is best not to have any weapons if you are going to do this. Jump up and down and do whatever you need to do to let it pass through your body. Some people just run, and that can work because you move your arms as well as your legs, which is a whole-body form of transformation.

A Friendly Planet

If you were to approach our planet from a considerable distance, you would feel its energy, and it would calm you. Even if you were a benevolent being, you would feel a sense of camaraderie; you would want to visit, and you would be welcome. Our planet is not in your galaxy, though, so the chances of you visiting it as a space explorer are not high. However, you can make a request, if you wish to be able to visit our planet and be with our people, at the deepest levels of your sleep. This is almost always allowed, because at that level, the portion of you that travels is totally benevolent and radiates a similar energy. You may not know that, but it is so.

We live in small family groups on our planet. We don't do things like you do. We just live as well as possible and consume foods that grow on various plants that we can reach from the bows, you call them, of trees. We do not have tall trees as you do on your planet. We love the tall trees on your planet — so magnificent. On our planet, the trees are not much more than 12 or 15 feet tall, and that's fine, because the lower bows have the cherries or berries. If you were to consume them, they would remind you of cherries with no pits.

The upper bows are for a group of beings who fly; they are not birds as you know them. They are more like the being you call the dragonfly. I don't know if you know this about dragonflies: They are very friendly on your planet as well. Some people want to make them into pets, but that is not a good idea. If a dragonfly visits you, then just let it know that you like it and that it is welcome to return, but let it remain free.

If you are a flying being, you must be able to fly where your wings take you. I don't know if you know this about winged beings. It is this way for some birds on your planet, but it is mostly for the many-legged. Often they don't think about where they are going. Their wings can operate independently and will take them to where it is best for them to be, for themselves and for their people (meaning others like them). Perhaps they are being led to where they can help the human race, which is part of the reason they are there.

Dragonflies eat mosquitoes, so if they are around, it means you also have mosquitoes. They can eat hundreds and hundreds of mosquitoes in a single day, so if you have many mosquitoes, you will want dragonflies to be your friends.

Circle Energy

We have visited Earth a few times in the past, usually to visit groups of people. Sometimes you call them societies or peoples who have been initiated to help others in their race of beings. I do not mean the human race; I mean nationality, not different shapes or skin colors. "Nationality" does not mean a city, state, or what you call a country. It means a society or culture. Perhaps they even move around, but they are complete unto themselves and have their own pursuits.

We visited such societies if they were focused on improving the quality of life for others and themselves. That's a very important lesson, not just directed within a society but, when possible, directed outside of their society to help others. The people we visited in the past of your time were instructed by us; we made the first circles, and they continued.

The circles have a specific measurement (you know all this, so I am not going to go into it); they sometimes have designs or patterns. The patterns are for those who need to be stimulated visually. Some people are like that; they do not necessarily feel the energy unless they are visually stimulated. Others can simply approach the circle and the energy is sufficient, so they don't have to be inside it.

What you may not understand is that the circle has energy similar to our planet. You don't have to land on it to feel the energy. The energy is felt from a long distance. It would be approximately the distance from Earth to Saturn. That's a long way. Of course, we wanted to create the circles to do what our planet does. The reason more than one circle was created was that the people we taught to do this felt it would be useful. You understand this because on Earth the idea of having something that's really good, well, sometimes you want more than one of those things. We taught them how, and then they went on to create the others.

You also asked the question at some point about why the people who created the circles piled the stones in there. The people who created the circles (including we who created the first one, of course) did not do that. That was done later by people who did not know what it was and thought it was about the pattern in the middle. They covered up the pattern because they just didn't understand it. It was something not to their liking.

They didn't destroy the circles, interestingly enough, and it didn't stop the circles from radiating. How about that, eh? That's because the circles have been so deep in the ground for such a long time and have only recently been dug up. Is that right: People just recently found and dug them up?

They are in the process. They have only dug up a few, but they know how many there are.

So they built more. The circles then functioned just like our planet in that you don't have to be nearby for them to work. It would be good to remove the stones from the center for those who don't feel the energy. They are capable of feeling it, but for one reason or another, their lives have caused them to shut down this capacity. In short, they do not feel safe being sensitive, so they would have to climb into the circle and look at the pattern or even sit at the edge, stare at the pattern, and relax. The only way they will be able to relax is if several of their people are nearby so that they would feel safe. In time, it would work, and it would heal all their old physical wounds. It also could (if they accept it) heal their psyches or the bruising that caused them to set down their sensitivity.

They may not want that but might appreciate having all their physical wounds healed. If they have lost a finger or two, the fingers would grow back. If they were harmed by a spear or something, then the inner organs would re-grow and the surface of the skin would look unharmed. This might also cause some skin illustrations (tattoos) to disappear, and people would not like that. They might have to put these back if they want them there. Those are just examples.

Now you probably have questions. All right, you can ask.

Circle Activation

In regard to the patterns, the beings from the Pleiades who told us about the circles also said that the original Pleiadian tiles had been removed. Did you know that?

No. However, the circle will still work. The pattern in the center is visual, as I explained, so the circle will still work. It will have to be re-energized once the stones are uncovered. There is one exception: It's possible in some cases that what they found are not the circles I am talking about. There are others who built circular structures, but those go very deep and are actually a different kind of thing. When they completely expose it and see no pattern at the bottom with (what you are calling) no tiles present, then it could be something else. Where on your planet has this discovery taken place?

It's in a country we call Turkey. I don't know if you can locate that or not. We call it Göbekli Tepe.

Yes, this is the place we went to, but we also went to a few other places. I will only mention one in the extreme southern part of South America, but I won't say where exactly. The area is not active, and if it could be made active, then the motion of sailing vessels would be easier, because the area is known for being stormy. When the circles are operating, the water is calm. This makes sense if you think about it: A human being who is violent must go through steps to first become sensitive and then to become calm. So it makes sense that the waters exposed to that energy would become calm.

If the circle is found, it can be reactivated. Over time, it has been covered, but it used to be on the surface. This is what you can do, for those of you who meditate or do spiritual work that involves good energies that you can feel that are calming and nurturing but not exciting and not simulating, You can say the following words to activate the circle, but only for this and only once. It can be done without words. But if you like words, you can say:

> "I'm offering a small portion of my energy
> to help activate the circle in southern South America."

You don't have to say it out loud. If you even just have the motivation to do it, you don't have to think those words. However, I recommend you do it only once, because it will work only once for you as an individual. If you do it as a small group (that is, you and at least three others), then you can do it twice. If you do it with a large group, you can do it three times, but do not do it any more than that. Saying this might help in time, not right away.

You will know that it is helping when you notice more days that the water is calm, not stormy. People keep records of these things, so it will be noted, and eventually, if enough people do this, then there will only be a few stormy days. It will be known when these storms will occur, so the ships can plan ahead. The storm will just be one, two, or three days because Earth needs to express herself. The rest of the time, it will be calm.

Will that work in Turkey also?

We recommend you do it only for the one in southern South America.

Pleiadian Interactions

Okay, now the Pleiadians, the two who spoke said that you were an example of being more than one thing, as if you were two beings or something. Can you tell me about that?

That's the way they saw us. You must keep in mind that we appeared from the shoulders down to be human beings, or a variation of human beings, that they would recognize. But from the neck up, we had a birdlike appearance, as I described.

I see. How many beings on your planet are like you?

Ninety-four.

On the whole planet?

Well, there are other species on the planet.

They also said that you could fly in light and that you could appear without vehicles.

Yes, but this is something you can do too. You just don't remember. You call it astral projection, but that's not quite it, since astral projection's purpose is to go see something. The purpose is not necessarily to be seen. Some of you call it bilocation. The simplest way to say it is that we travel in light. As we get closer to the surface where the beings are that we are going to assist (in the case of the Pleiadians), we gradually "formed up" in a way that looked similar to them so that they would be comfortable with us. This way, they could accept the fact that from the neck up, we looked quite different; there was enough similarity so that they were not alarmed.

Did your people carve the columns in the first circle that you built with those animal beings who are not on this planet, or was that the Pleiadians?

We did not do that. We did not put anything on the inside of the circle or on the base, what you call the ground. We did not do anything like that.

Okay, if I looked at you, would I see you?

Are you asking if I showed up, meaning right now, and sat down next to you, would you see me?

Yes, with my eyes where I am now.

No, and I will tell the channel something to tell you afterward.

Okay, could the Pleiadians see you at that time?

Oh yes, of course.

Oh, so they were from a higher dimension, then. Could the humans at that time see them?

See who?

The Pleiadians.

I think they had the ability to be seen if they chose.

I see. How did you know the Pleiadians? Had you helped them before?

We had helped them before, yes.

Did you help them build circles on other planets or in another way?

In another way.

Alareo

In Egypt, we have paintings that go on and on about beings like you are describing. They are human up to the shoulders and then have bird heads, such as the being Thoth and so many others. Are they a part of your people, and is there a relation?

In the area you are referring to, in the past there were groups of people who looked as I have described. Yes, you understand. At times, we went there to help those groups because they were helping their people and societies and they were also helping others whenever they could. Sometimes there was more that they wanted to do or that was needed for their people or others. Usually, it was for others. There was no common language. We went there and helped them make contact or whatever was needed.

Ah, at last, is there any way to ascertain how many years ago in our time that was?

No, because you are between time.

Can you say how far back from the third dimension?

Ah yes, about 90,000 years ago.

Is Thoth one of your people?

Where did you get that name?

That's the name on this planet, but he is also known by other names.

You're referring to the residual (or whatever you call it) carving, yes?

Yes.

That is one of our people.

Oh, well, he still channels through people and is a spiritual guide to humans even now.

It would help if you used the actual name.

What is it?

Just a minute. I will ask for permission. Alareo.

Wonderful, Alareo.

One thing you might want to know about Alareo is that Alareo is not a he.

[Laughs.] Oh really! A she, oh my goodness, we might ask her to talk at one point. Okay, so what are some of the other ways you help different beings? Are there some that cause you particular joy, more than others?

No, they all are joyous because we do not go to help unless we know for sure that it will help. Meaning you must be able to communicate, be trusted, and be compatible with whomever you go to see. We are pretty happy on the way, as well as when we arrive and leave. The feeling is the same.

Do all ninety-four of you go out at different times or only some of you?

Never more than two or three, ever.

Ever — oh, and you are one of those!

Yes.

Do you live a long time?

We live a long time, yes. In my time, I don't know of anyone who has died. This is not very unusual on other planets. The ninety-four of us have been here on this planet for as long as I know. I am not aware of us ever having been anywhere else.

Well, are you one of the beings who came to Egypt in that early time?

No.

No Stimulation

I had such a good question, and then it evaporated. I will probably think of it after you leave. Is there anything else that you can share with us that we would find relevant about your life and what you've learned?

In your time there is much distraction. There are even some people who are stimulating distraction for you. I feel that it would be useful for all of you to pick at least one day per week, or even half a day, and make that your time to rest and relax and to try not to think. Have a day of no stimulation, because you have a life now (well, most of you) that is overstimulated. This is from either work that must be done or family responsibilities and so on.

Try to pick at least one day or a half day for each individual to rest and relax. Think if you like, walk if you like, or sing if you like, but do nothing to stimulate yourselves like you are stimulated at other times. In this way, you will find that you will be able to become calmer and maybe even sensitive enough to become your true magical self. Good night.

Thank you so much.

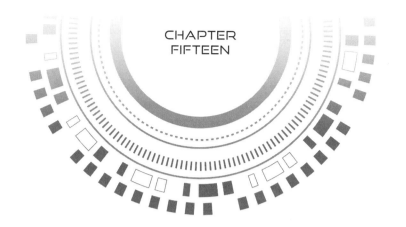

ANCIENT PEOPLE RESCUED FROM THEIR HOME PLANET SHARE STONE-WORKING TECHNIQUES NEAR CUSCO, PERU

An Ancient Visitor

MARCH 14, 2019

On our home planet where we resided in the past, we did not have much surface to live on. The planet mostly consisted of fluids. There were some stone outcroppings, covering no more than twenty-four or thirty square miles of surface over the entire planet. That land was considered special, and it could not hold many people. But we were visited regularly by friends from other planets; almost always they were friends. There was lots of compassion from those who visited, and they often offered to take us some place else in order to have more ground to live on. As you may know, being a citizen of your planet, the idea of leaving the home you have been born and raised with for something completely unknown may appeal to a few but not to the majority.

The decision was made for us by our home planet because over time the fluids began to move up and portions of the surface were beginning to disappear. Friends came regularly to rescue the people.

After a while, there was practically no surface available and all the people were assembled on various vehicles. It was suggested to us that since we had a great love for stone (because that's what was above the fluids) we might enjoy, until we could find another place, experiencing a planet that was what our planet had been in the distant past. We found that intriguing and wanted to know all about it.

This was the first we had heard of our planet having been anything else in the past. We wanted some information on that. The information was granted: at one time our planet had water, clouds, and blue sky; all of this you would recognize. It also had much land surface, but the population was in competition with other populations and even with itself. Ultimately, the planet dried out and became desert-like.

Eventually, a civilization could last even though it was difficult. Then the fluids came. The fluids were not water. It is hard to describe them — something like oil only denser; you might call it tar. It was roughly the consistency of tar, but it did not need to be heated to move. It was obviously not hospitable for life. We do not know why our planet did that, and we do not live there now. We cannot go back because it is completely covered with that substance. It just happened, and perhaps someday we will know why.

A New Home

Friends took us to Earth; this would've been many thousands of years ago in your time (I am not sure exactly how far back) when there weren't many people. We are not that interested in numbers but certainly no more than a few million people were living on the surface. I think there were quite a few living below the surface, but they did not take us there. They took us to high mountain ranges, because they felt that this was what we knew and would understand.

Now, the reason they would think that is that the portions of our old planet that were above the surface where the higher parts of mountains. They wanted to give us, at least temporarily, a place like that. We had on our old planet, besides underground streams and some water on the surface, stone. That's what we used to make dwellings and raise crops. It was not what you would call a bountiful life, but it was sufficient to survive.

You are going to ask how many of us survived and I will round off the number: approximately 5,000. That is the number of us taken to Earth's high mountain ranges, not only what you know now as the Cusco area but also to other areas that some of us wanted to try. When we got there, we could see that it would be easy to grow our crops because the soil was good and the people there were welcoming. This was very nice because we looked like them. Even though we did not have a common language, we could communicate well because we would think in our language and they would understand in their language. They would think in their language and we would understand in our language. This is something universal, so communication was effective.

At that time, the people already on Earth did not have much variety in their crops. Not all crops can grow at such an altitude. Since we had been at an altitude and didn't realize it because of the fluids, we weren't aware that we were on at a high altitude on our old planet. All our crops grew at that altitude, so we were able to raise crops for ourselves and freely share them with the people already on Earth, and they shared with us too. It was like moving in for a time.

Image 15.1. Group connections illustrated on stone structures
at Sacsayhuaman, near Cusco

A Gathering Place for All

Earth people had not done much with stone because they did not have to. There were other means of shelter, but we, on the other hand, had done everything with stone. We asked for their elders' and leaders' permission to continue to build with stone as we had always done on our planet. They wanted to know what we would do. We described the homes and other structures we would build and that we might even create something like a gathering place where we could all meet and experience more of each other's culture. This might involve singing each other's songs or chants and more.

It took a while to explain this, and the elders of Earth said it would be all right, but it must be made clear that all people are united and that even when people come from other places (meaning us), they are like us (Earth people). There were initially only a few of us because we did not want to suddenly arrive with 5,000 people. The arrival, even though they accepted how many of us were there, would be shown in stone — celebrated, honored, and indicated throughout all patterns as well as possible, especially in places that had to do with gatherings or residences. They preferred we show the mixing of the different cultures, and we promised that we would do that.

So began our time of stone carving. The carving was done as quietly as possible. You might ask why. Keep in mind that the peoples on Earth were not used to loud sounds other than what came from the sky in a natural way such as thunder and perhaps sounds made by high winds. The sounds that came from moving stone or cutting it is best subdued. We felt it was important to do this because politeness is essential, especially when you are arriving in a large group.

It was like a challenge, because in the past on our planet, stone structures were created to be practical, useful, and long-lived (you might say). There was nothing about them that you would call artistic — no patterns, no curious connections. Well, I'll get to that. At first, it was a little challenging how to show such a thing without words. It had to be pictographic, meaning you had to be able to look at it and say, "This suggests that something is joining something else." In some pictures, it's very clearly shown that something (it looks like a notch in a shape [see image 15.1]) is connecting to something larger.

It wasn't necessary to create that in order to put the stones together. It was done to show that first came a small group and behind that group was a larger group that would come later.

Other things were done. There are places where it looks like a peg sticking out from the stone, and again, this was not meant to hold things together. It was to show the continuity and connection between people. Even though there would've been a vast population on Earth compared to our group arriving, we were able to fit into the larger population in a way that was compatible. However, even after fitting in, it was apparent that we were different.

In another picture [see image 15.2] that you sent to the channel, the large thing that looks like a stadium has, instead of the squared-off things, a swirling pattern that's reminiscent of waters. We loved the water on Earth and understood that our planet had once been like this. We felt that a gathering place would best be shown by a coming together. Imagine for a moment a wave coming to shore, only instead of the wave being vertical, you are seeing it from the side. The waves would come in and swirl together and form this large gathering place for people to come together to speak, tell stories, and tell about their origins. Our people, over time, discovered that there was a connection.

Image 15.2. Ancient gathering place

Forgotten Connections

We did not know (of course, the people who brought us here must have known) that there was in the distant past a connection between our people and Earth people. The people already on Earth and our people mixed their bloodlines (you would call them ancestors). The result is actually in your genetic makeup now. It still exists in the now times on your planet, but we did not stay. Remember, I said we were there temporarily.

We were on the planet in Cusco and a few other places around Earth. Keep in mind that in those places, many times the same or similar patterns were shown. Even though the bulk of our people stayed in and around Cusco, you will see those patterns in other places. Now, in your time, we feel that people have forgotten how connected they are to people from other planets. What we believe in our now time on our now planet (which is different from our old planet and from Earth) is that you have forgotten those connections. You are all very much alike, and minor differences in general features and skin color are trivial (from our point of view). They have become accentuated as if it should be a competition or grounds for separation.

It was always intended that there would be a merging of the bloodlines. Eventually, all people looked similar and had the merged bloodline appearance, bringing about a variety of people on Earth. Also, there were combinations of people so that there would be the gift of all the cultures and the good health of all the cultures. I realize that people on Earth do not have good health all the time. We feel the reason is that there have not been enough loving connections.

This is not something to be done by scientific projects but rather in the natural way of coming together and having children from love and happiness. This is meant to bring about a combined bloodline on Earth to produce people who would live, say 225 years or maybe 250 years, because of having the healthiest attributes of the genetic makeup of all the different types of human beings on Earth. I have been informed that this could still happen. There has been some progress, and we feel you can make more progress.

The problem in your time, of course, is that there are many diseases. At least three-quarters of this has to do with your now time and things in your food, air, or water that weren't intended to be there. We do not know whether you can all survive on the surface while your planet sorts this out, which might take a while. We think that someday you will either be rescued, as we were, and live temporarily some place else, as we did, or that (and we don't know this for sure because it didn't happen on our planet) you might move underground.

We cannot honestly say that we would feel good about that, but if safety and a long-term situation could develop with some form of sunlight underground, then perhaps. We think that it is more likely that the surface populations would be moved to some other similar planet. In short, like our situation, the reason I'm giving you so much background is that I want you to consider that if this happens (and it could, you see) you will have to be very polite and grateful to those who rescued you, as I'm sure you would be. But you would have to maintain that politeness not only with those who rescued you but also with each other.

Obviously, no one's going to want to rescue a group of people who are fighting, competing, and hitting each other. Why would they want that? They would want to rescue people they enjoy, who would be completely comfortable with their children, families, and crew. This gives you a little idea of what you probably ought to be working on in your time now.

An Attractive Profile

How long were you here?

Like I said, I'm not so good at math. Well, as much as I can understand, it was about 7,000 years.

Okay, can you say who brought you here?

They didn't look exactly like us or like you, but there was a similarity, only the tops of their heads were a little different. On their skulls, there was sort of a pronounced ridgeline that stuck out a little bit. But it was attractive on them, and it somewhat accentuated their facial features.

Oh I see, you want us to give you a name for them. I don't know. Nobody knew, but when people are rescuing you, you don't stop to ask, "Who are you?" You are going to say, "Thank you, thank you!" So we didn't ask them who they were, and they didn't tell us, but they seemed to know a great deal about us.

The teaching about who we were and what our planet was like in the past all happened on the way to Earth. I think the ships could travel quickly, but they took their time and in that way we were able to look out the clear screens or windows and enjoy seeing what we were passing by. Of course, it was very beautiful, and during that passage, they told us about our planet and how it looked similar to your planet, and they dropped little hints that we were connected somehow. Those hints made it easier to blend in with Earth people while we were there on your planet.

Can you say how you move the rocks or the stone?

Well, that's really easy but again problematic because you cannot see —

Okay, there is a group of stones that is absolutely humongous, and they are called by our people the Temple of the Sun, which was never finished. They are vertical stones that are just incredibly huge. What were they for?

I think this was for learning purposes. Of course the people on Earth wanted to know more about how we were creating stone structures. Some of them thought it would be useful to learn, so it wasn't for anything that was their home. That's why you'll see things (those stones), and wonder, "Well what was the purpose of this?" It was a teaching tool. That's the best that they could do. Their job was to cut the stone out making no more noise than we did and move it and then put it in place creating perhaps a connection between them. They were able to do this. It is important for you to know this, because it means that you can learn how to do this yourself. I will not teach this, but I will speak of it at the end with the other part.

But you are specifically speaking about these six huge red ones (image 15.3). I don't know how tall they are. They look like they are 50 feet tall or something. They are just huge.

Yes, I am speaking about those.

All right, now, there is a lot of construction here.

The reason I mention this is that if you look at the other pictures you will notice that there is nothing like that. That's the explanation.

Image 15.3. Megalith at Sacsayhuaman, near Cusco

You did the other stuff, didn't you?

Yes, we did the other things.

So you were attempting to teach them with these megalithic stones. Why so big?

Because there were many of them, many students — and understand it wasn't as if we were playing "the know it all," as you say in your time. Do you still say that?

Yes.

We were not doing that. It was just like sharing food, no different. When you live in a world of stone, you are used to big things. There were many students (over the years, there were different ones); altogether there were maybe eighty-seven students, but that's over the thousands of years we were here. The stones were brought together over time. First came one, and it had to be cut out quietly and moved quietly and put in place quietly so as not to disturb the civilization. It had to be sturdy, and we didn't want it falling over on anyone.

Okay, and the structures you built that look like windows in the stone (image 15.4) — were they windows? Were they living spaces?

Yes, they were places to live with nice ventilation where you could not only look out but also step out and perhaps have others step in, if you chose.

Image 15.4. Windows in stone structure

The Will of Stones

There are pictures here of these humongous structures you built. Did you use mortar? How did you get them to fit so tightly that you can't put a card between them?

The stones wanted to be that way. No stone was picked that didn't want to participate in a very specific place, not only because they fit perfectly but they also wanted to be that way, and stone that was carved also wanted to be that way. You have to know and be able to have a heart-to-heart connection with stone. Even though you don't think of stone as having a heart, if you were able to climb inside, so to speak, you would be living in a crystal world.

There is heart there, and the heart can be seen on the surface by the way the light reflects off the stone. The heart is colored with light. You just need to be able to do that, and then you can have heart to heart with the stone. It is not that the stone will then do your bidding; it means you ask whether they want to participate. If they do, then a perfect place will be found that they will like, and it becomes like the stones are hugging. They want to be there and they want to hug the other stone, and when you want that, that is love. The simple answer is the reason they fit together so well is because the binder was love, love from one stone to another.

Terraces and Stairways

Okay, here is another picture of terraces going up a high hill, and in there are stairways that people can walk up made from small stones (15.5). Did you do that, or was this done by people after you left?

No, we did that. We do that with our students. Sometimes it was only one, sometimes it was three, and sometimes it was seven or eight, but it was done to show what could be done. You might reasonably ask why. The reason is because when we arrived on Earth, the Earth people, while they were very supportive of each other, would sometimes have arguments. Sometimes the arguments would last a long time. We wanted to show them that the reason the arguments lasted so long is that this was an expression of individuality, and maybe it wasn't that they were really angry at each other. It was just that you could get along better with others.

Image 15.5. Stairway built to demonstrate connection

This is how we could show them: If the stones that were all just sort of tumbled down and askew, crumbling and rolling were exposed to some other surface and other stones, they might desire to be connected to that group and would be received lovingly. This is the way we taught that lesson so that people, instead of having arguments and then not speaking to each other for a while, maybe were meant to have other friends and be part of other groups. This was not meant to break families but to discover that the family did not have to be all things to an individual and that you could have friends. At that time in that civilization on Earth, that was not typical. So that's how we taught that.

Can you tell me where else your people went, because there are other places on the planet that seem to have the same architecture. Can you say where else your people went when you were here?

I think I already did say that. I just didn't use your names, but that's where they went when you see those kinds of things. It was our people, but I cannot be certain; it might have been the people who followed. For all I know, it might've been people who preceded us. After all, the people who brought us here seem to know a lot about things, and for all I know, they have done this before.

The Milky Way

Do you know any of the names we use for the places your people went to?

No. The only reason I have the name of Cusco is because of the pictures you sent to Robert.

Oh [chuckles], okay. Where are you now?

I am on my home planet.

Right but where is it?

Oh, you mean, what galaxy is it in?

Yeah, in some words that I would understand.

Well, I will have to ask, a moment. The scientific advisor says that we are in the same galaxy.

What we call the Milky Way galaxy?

That's what the scientific advisor says.

How is your life now? How many people do you have now?

On our planet, oh, maybe 80,000.

Is it a planet like ours, or is it very different?

Well, it is not like our old one, as it was in the past, and your question is relevant. It's similar in that it has water, clouds, land, and streams but no oceans. There are large lakes and bodies of water, but the sky is a light green color. There are many plants, and of course, they are green, yet some of them have different colors like you see on your planet, flowers and so on. The water is green. Other than that, there are similarities. There is stone that we have carved in various ways, including how the elders on Earth showed us, which we passed on because we liked very much what they said about these showing the connection between peoples.

Are you the only species on the planet or the only humans, or are there others?

We're the only humans, but there are many others. Of course, we have not moved any stones or done anything with the stones. That would be incompatible with the others' wishes. We have only moved stone around a little bit in order to create some structures (gathering places and so on), but we do not have to reside in stone structures. In fact, the surface is hospitable, so the stone structures we have created are small.

So you live on the land in the open?

Yes, it is comfortable that way; there is no need to build anything to protect us. Occasionally, there is light rain that feels pleasant landing on your body.

You breathed oxygen when you were here. What do you now breathe in the air?

I will have to ask the scientist. Oxygen, nitrogen, and something else.

Oh, it's the same with us. So if we came there, could we breathe it?

Just a minute. It would be difficult for you because it is oxygen-rich.

So how was it for you when you first got there?

It was a little difficult, so we moved slowly [chuckles].

So what happened after 7,000 years? Did the same beings come and take you away?

You don't have to ask multiple questions. You don't have to explain.

The explanation of the questioning happens in the beginning to create a relationship between us. But once you start asking questions, you don't have to continue to explain. I just thought I would mention that, because it could save you some extra words.

[Laughs.] Okay, thanks.

A Temporary Home

What was the catalyst or motivation for someone picking you up and moving you to that new planet?

Oh, I don't know anything about their motivations. They just came to say that a new planet had been found and that the people who live there would welcome us; that was it. We knew we were on Earth temporarily, and remember, we are generations from and obviously not the same people who landed initially. We also knew that the people who rescued us and moved us knew things. When they came and said, "We have found a place for you," we said goodbye to our friends, cousins, and relatives. Initially we said innocently to those of Earth, "Do you want to come with us?" But they weren't sure, and Earth was their home. Then the people who came for us said, "No, no, no, they cannot come with you."

It was clear at the time that the people of Earth were relieved that they were not going to have to go some place else. So even though it was a loving relationship, apparently everyone was comfortable with that. There had been connections on Earth with families and bloodlines united, but our people always remained a little bit separated. That was intentional because we knew someday they were going to come back and take us some place else. Families would not have to be broken up. Do you see?

No, I don't see. If you interbred with the people who were here, then the people who married with the natives got separated. I don't understand.

They kept separate. The idea of marriage that you have now was not in existence then.

So they might have had relationships but didn't move together and you became part of Earth families?

There is no similarity to how it is now. If people felt love for each other, they were romantic and were places and did things. But our people explained it to them gently from the beginning so that no one was fooled about how we would someday be leaving. It would not be good to have anything like a long-term relationship. But, you know, it was all done very politely, lovingly, and gently. Of course over time, there were a certain number of offspring, and they were loved by both parties. You have to remember, when we first came to the planet, we had no idea how long we would be there. They just said they'd be back someday when the perfect place was found. They didn't say it would take 7,000 years.

How many of your people left with the ones who moved you to the planet?

We kept our population about the same because we did not know that we should do any differently. They rescued an original number of us, so what were we going to do — become hundreds of thousands or millions and expect them to rescue us all? No, we kept our population about the same, and we had to be respectful, you know. Respect is essential, especially between different species of beings. They resembled us, but they didn't look exactly like us. They were very kind and generous with us. But we could not make assumptions about their generosity.

Yes. How long did your people live at that time, in our years?

No longer than 275 years and often shorter than that.

But what about the native people? Did they wonder why they didn't live nearly as long?

How do you know?

Excellent question: Did they?

It wasn't unusual for them to live 175 years and after a time, our people started to live only to that age too. On our now planet, we live no longer than 275 years, sometimes not that long.

You said you didn't look exactly like the natives here. What was the difference?

Very minor.

Have you ever had a desire to come back, or are you very happy where you are?

Oh, we are very happy where we are. After all, if you think about it, our friends were always looking for the perfect place for us. Just imagine 7,000 years of them traveling and living life yet all the time they were "keeping an eye out" for a perfect place, and we were "keeping your eye out" for their return. "Keeping an eye out" — do you still say that?

Yep.

They were keeping their eye out for us, and they found the perfect place.

Do you have anyone you can ask questions besides the science advisor, and do you think they would like to talk to us?

I do not know.

All right, we will ask to add an explanation.

I'm going to make a closing comment. Now, I do not normally, say, as an individual "do this" and "do that." But the theme of this book is future peoples who have connections to you, sharing our ideas, our ideals, and so on with you, so that's why I spoke the way I did. I want to leave you with one thought: In your true nature, genetically as well as emotionally, you are so much alike. Don't make such a fuss about how you are different, except as individuals. Some people are artistic, and some people aren't. Some people are athletic; some people aren't. That kind of thing is fine. Those are individual differences. But from group to group you are almost exactly the same. Be happy that you are living on a planet where you are surrounded with sisters, brothers, and cousins of the heart.

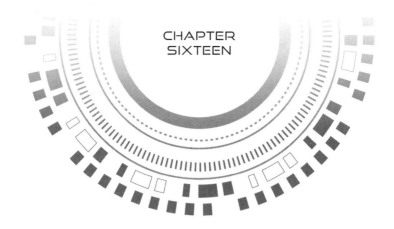

THE RESCUE

A Being from the Ship That Rescued People
from the Tar Planet

MARCH 18, 2019

Hello. Welcome.

Thank you. Was there something you wanted?

Are you the beings who carried the group of people who were on the planet where the oil came up and made the planet unusable and brought them here to Earth? Was that your group, your people?

Yes. It wasn't me personally, but that was our vehicle.

How did you know about these people? Had you visited them in the past?

We had not visited, but we went near the planet, because it was unusual for people to live on high mountain places surrounded by truly inhospitable matter that was dangerous for them. Even though we hadn't made contact, we routinely made a detour in our travels, you might say, to go closer to that planet in case there was an emergency.

Around that time (as you were told, perhaps, in previous talks), we noticed that the liquid was rising and that people appeared to be nervous. That's when we made contact, and of course they did not want to leave, because it was their home. But we informed them that as far as we could calculate, the liquid was going to cover all the ground where they were. Of course, they were interested in what we were saying.

We took them aboard the ship. (It's a big ship.) They were concerned, because it was not in their personal experience to have ever been on such a vehicle (or on any vehicle, so you can imagine their initial reluctance). Simply seeing something that was completely beyond their comprehension was why they were reluctant in the first place. As things got more uncomfortable on their planet, they had a change of heart. Keep in mind that we weren't required to pick them up or anything.

Some species, when they know they are going to die, just accept that. Other species, if offered a chance to continue their lives, will reach for it. So they reached for it — all of them. Apparently in their group, they did not make singular decisions (as you might say). They were individuals and they all had identities, but big decisions were made as a group. That is why no one stayed behind. A moment, I'm going to have to speak a little quieter. Can you hear me all right?

Yes, you are fine.

All right, so when the people came aboard, they were nervous. They had been told there was another world just perfect for them. In our communications, we didn't make something clear and they misunderstood. They thought the other world was going to be the vehicle. We didn't reveal that there was another planet. But even if we had, we don't think they would've understood. Sometimes interspecies communication is challenging. You probably know this.

The people did not understand at first that they would not have to live in such a strange machine. (They were not a machine society.) The ship was a strange object, and they didn't realize we were people; they thought the object or ship was talking to them. You see, the problem was that they were not an object society, but they thought the object had come to rescue them and that they were going to have to live the rest of their lives on the object. That was pretty frightening. But when they came aboard, they were happily surprised that there were beings on board that sufficiently resembled them. We explained to them that we were there to help them go to a place that they would like, not on the ship. They eventually understood. We got them to the planet. Did I answer your question? You can ask it a different way if you need to.

Unexpected Shifts

Okay, when you brought them here, they told me that they knew it was temporary, because you were going to find them the perfect planet.

Yes, that is true, and we had an idea when we brought them here of where the perfect planet was. When we initially told them we knew of this perfect planet, we didn't realize that in the planetary systems you have, the planets that go around your Sun and everything are moving. What you may not know is that galaxies do the same thing. The galaxy made some kind of move that surprised us. Galaxies — well, it's a matter of scale, do you understand? You understand motion, because you move as a being. Planets are larger beings, and they move; and galaxies are even larger beings, and they move. A move happened that we didn't expect, and we could not take them to that planet, because we literally could not see it anymore. There was no connection, so it was like, "Oh?" Your planet was sort of just in case.

We said we would take them to this planet just in case, for a time, until we were able to take them to the perfect planet. When they saw this planet, of course they felt that they had come to a wonderful and fabulous place. The whole planet was very similar to that tiny top of the mountain where they had been living. They were thrilled and felt this was great. We told them it would be temporary, but of course with different languages, even when there are translations and so on, you do not get the innuendos. When we told them it would be temporary, they thought it would be temporary in their lifetimes. You understand?

Yes.

It wasn't in their lifetimes. Fortunately, since they were not a people that wrote things down, they carried knowledge and wisdom along in stories. The stories were passed down for as long as it took for us to reconnect, because of galactic motion with that perfect planet. Then we came back, of course, and by that time, they had adapted to living on the planet and were used to objects and beings using objects. Then with that whole thing of objects in the sky with voices they could hear, they realized it was not the object talking but the people in the object talking. Even though they loved their life on Earth and had become quite adept at interacting with objects, they felt, "Well, somehow this other place is going to be better." They couldn't even imagine something better than what it had been, but it was better.

Yeah, they explained to me that they thought temporary was a very short time, and it was really 7,000 years. They kept the same number of people by interacting with the natives and breeding but not taking those people into their society.

Yes, but I think they did it very gently, and there was never any dishonesty. There were marriages, but it was (you may not have this on your world now) people marrying but not marrying out of their extended families, meaning their culture. You as an individual remain a portion of your culture and the other person remains a portion of his or her culture, but you have a life together, have children, and so on. Generally speaking, the children would belong to the mother. They may not have made this clear to you, but the people who bred (as you call it) with the original Earth citizens that were found there were always men from the culture we interacted with. Okay?

The children were those of the mother of a person from Earth, and that was always the case so that people would not be wrenched away from literally a portion of themselves.

Right, that explains it, then, because they said they expected you to come back at any moment, and they didn't want to have more people than you brought there.

The child is a portion of the mother, and the mother is a portion of the child. You see, even though the man (the father) provides a small portion that becomes the child, the child and the mother are one being. This exists in your now time as well. This is not well understood in your world, perhaps, but the child from the mother is the mother. Your physical mother is you as well as you are a portion of your mother, because you grow inside your mother.

Father is the person who provides a small impulse to trigger that reproduction, that re-creation (that's the word, not reproduction) of mother. It's like mother is re-creating herself when she has a child. Every time she has a child, she is re-creating herself, and that re-creation is always a part of her. Those re-creations, those children, are always a part of mother. We feel that's not understood very well in your world, but it would make a big difference, we think, if it were.

No, I have not heard that before.

It would be good for you to speak of that to the other beings you talk with and feel good about, because you might learn something about yourselves as a human race.

Keeping a Promise

Okay, the other thing they told me was that they were so grateful after such a long time that you persevered to give them what they needed. It was 7,000 years, and they were amazed that you would focus on their problem for that long.

Well, it was a commitment, you know. When our people make a commitment, we stand by it. We made the commitment and that was that. It wasn't as if we were constantly searching for 7,000 years. We knew exactly where the planet was, but we couldn't connect with it. We waited 7,000 years for that reconnection to happen. We were doing other things, but we certainly were not going to leave them on the temporary planet. We were not going to say, "Oh, well, that's good enough."

I would like to ask about several areas in South America and around the planet where the rock-moving and rock-placing skills are similar to those in the place they spoke from in the area of Cusco, Peru. When you picked them up from here, were they all in one place, or did you have to go to different places on the planet to get them?

I see. Again, this is a translation problem. When we dropped them off on Earth, we didn't leave them all in one place. They were with us long enough that some people wanted to go "here" and some people wanted to go "there," and so on. That's what we did. They didn't all go to one place.

Were they all close to one another, such as in one country, or were they all over the planet?

Well, I think they were all on one continent. They had strong telepathic connections with each other. Keep in mind that we told them it would be temporary, and we didn't know at that time how

Image 16.1. Machu Pichu, near Cusco

long it would take to reconnect with the planet. We thought at that time that it would be happening at any moment. So the idea of being scattered around the planet was not a problem. Only later did we realize, "Oh, this is going to take a long time."

We think this is an issue for your people too: You make a promise and it doesn't happen in your lifetime, so you might write it down. Would what you wrote down last for 7,000 years, and if so, would you be able to find it again? That would be difficult. But they had a strong connection to their people. As far as I know, at that time, they were all placed on one continent. Let me check. They were on one continent, but you don't have that many continents, from our point of view. You have North America and South America?

That is one continent, and then you have Europe and Africa, that is one continent — that kind of thing. Do you understand?

Right. So they might've come to North America?

Not come to it, but it might've been one of the places where they were dropped off. They were all dropped off on one continent. That, I'm sure of.

Okay, it's just that there are so many interesting ruins, and I'd like to find out if all the ones around the place we talked about last week were their work.

Yes, I completely understand what you are talking about. You are talking about similarities that exist in various civilized remains, yes?

Yes. "Ruins," we call them.

I understand completely what you're referring to, and it's very possible.

Okay, one more question really concerns me: Planets are conscious beings, so why would the liquid flow up to the top of mountains and then flood them?

It was a liquid planet that apparently brought the stone up (the mountain, you would say) for some reason. We think that happened during the time when water was on the surface. At some point, the water receded under the surface and that sticky substance — which is like a very dense version of oil, almost thicker than tar — came up to replace it. That's the best I can think of: It was just part of the planet's existence. The planet did not expect to have human beings on it.

So they came from some place else at some point, then?

Apparently.

Okay, now I'd like to ask you: Have you interacted with beings on Earth? I swear, there is a picture of you out there some place, but I can't find it.

I know what you mean. Someone did a sketch; it's not a photo. We think it might be in a book that was originally in a different language.

Then incorporated into another one?

Yes, perhaps.

Would it be a Wendell Stevens book?

I don't know about that.

Traveling Through Matter

So tell us about your civilization. You're a space-faring planet and you travel all over?

You didn't say that quite right. Can you say it again?

You have spaceships as well. Just tell me about where you travel.

Well, we tend to travel around the galaxy that you are in. Our vehicle is very large and can easily accommodate us. We go home sometimes, but home is quite far away. The vehicle travels — ah, you may not know this — by an energy between sound and light. There is a thin connection that allows something like what you might call a slingshot effect. When you travel at such speeds, it appears, from what I can understand, that matter is not harmed when you travel through it, even if it is sensitive matter. It is similar to an infinitely small vein or tube. If we need to travel great distances, that's what we do. It does not seem to disrupt anything or anyone, but it is controversial in our society, and some people feel it does disrupt. It's hard to explain exactly where we travel, but it is in and around this galaxy.

To help other people, to trade, or to explore?

Just to do it. We have always traveled. Trading does not come into the picture unless people need something that we have or we can acquire from some other place. We are not merchants, if that's what you are asking.

Can you tell us a little bit about your society — your culture and your people?

Maybe a little bit. What do you want to know?

How many people are there on your home planet?

No, we can't say that.

How many people in your ship? Is it a small percentage?

It is a small percentage of our population, yes.

Are they the same ones, or does it change?

Oh, we do not live for thousands of years. Our life cycle doesn't equate to yours very well. But I'll give you a comparison: roughly between 250 and 350 of your cycle of years. Your cycle of years also changes, so you'll have to take that into consideration.

Yes, we've moved dimensions a little bit. Can you say how long ago you brought these beings to the planet? Because they didn't know. They knew about the 7,000 years they were here but not when they came.

Oh, it was maybe — I know the number I have, but it doesn't equate to the time you are in now. So it really is meaningless.

Well, let it equate to the third dimension and that will give us an idea.

About 40,000 years ago.

All right, what I meant is, if you go out on a journey and there's, I don't know, 100 or 500 people on your ship, on the next journey are they the same people or do different people go?

It depends. Some people like to travel a longer time and some people don't. Some people like to travel once. It's maybe not very different from your people. Perhaps there are people on your planet who like to travel all the time.

Some don't like to at all, yes. So on your planet, are you a technical society? Do you have machines, buildings, and that kind of stuff?

The vehicle is not a machine. It is a living organism, not unlike our bodies or your body. It depends on the perception of the individual. If you came on board right now, you would say, "Oh, this is a machine," because you would see it that way. But for us who are on board, it is more like being in a living organism, and we are like the blood cells in a living organism. We see things much more softly and gently. From your perception, having been influenced by a society of structures and artificial angles, what you know to be absolutely true (as a result of being a portion of your mother) is that there are no 90 degree angles. Everything is rounded. To us, it is like that. But since you have been raised with artificial angles, I understand that one might find a 90 degree angle in crystal. Nevertheless, you know what I'm talking about, yes?

Yes.

You would see it in the form of a machine. It might be a 90 degree angle, it might be an 89 degree angle, or it might not be a completely precise angle. In other words, you would see it as a machine, but it would be a "softened" machine. That is the best I can describe it.

Yes, okay. It's a lightship.

But it is also a sound ship.

Ah, that is the first time I've heard that.

Well, that's why I described it before, but yes, it is sound. When we are in the ship, we hear the sound. If you remained on the ship long enough, you would hear the sound too. The sound is also the same sound that Earth makes. This is why we are able to find such planets: We knew that the people we picked up on that other planet were used to hearing that sound, because the planet they were on had it also. It was just a matter of listening to the galaxy to find those sounds. That way we could find the perfect planet, but we also found this other planet that you are living on now that made the same sound. So we felt a temporary place would be possible, you see, and we found it through sound.

Is that the first time you came to Earth, when you brought those beings here?

Yes.

Have you been back other than to take the people away?

No.

So how did someone do a drawing of you?

The only explanation I can come up with is that they must have had contact with some other group of beings who were in contact with us. They might have taken a ride on a ship, and it might have come to our lightship.

They saw you, then.

That's the only explanation that makes sense to me. It's not impossible that if they had a ride on a ship, one of our people might have been visiting that ship. But we have not visited your planet.

So you don't have a name that we would recognize?

I don't know if you would recognize it.

Can you say it? I know some people don't like to.

I can say it, but I won't spell it for you.

Okay.

On la fune.

Okay, obviously those are sounds that we would not recognize.

I think that sound exists in at least one of your languages.

Oh, all right. I will check the recording against the translator.

Knowledge Sharing

If I looked at you with my present eyes, would I see you? Or are you at a different frequency?

You would see me.

I would, okay. Do you have special interests, like philosophy, art, or science?

Yes, we are interested in all these things, and that is why we have a vast library of knowledge on the vehicle. Some people who have visited us find our library very pleasant and very interesting. From what our people who interact with the library are able to determine (we sort of tend to do this as a hobby), not only do they keep the knowledge that has been acquired through interactions with other forms of life about their people (to the extent that other people want to share it) but they also tend to make projections based on what they feel would happen to these people, as a group and as individuals. So in a way, it's accurate to the extent of what we know from the truth we were told — or at least the truth of the individual with whom we interacted.

It is slightly less accurate about the future of that individual and that society. That's why I say it's more like a hobby. They enjoy the idea of projecting how "this" or "that" would happen, but they keep it to themselves. They don't tell the others, "This is going to happen to you" — none of that. It would interfere with their lives, and we don't tell other societies the projections. But we sometimes follow up.

It is not unusual for us to come in contact with a society more than once if we are on a similar flight path or cross through their coordinates. The people who interact with the library sometimes find out how close their projection of the future of people or society became real. But they don't tell anybody; they just keep it here. I thought that might interest you.

That sounds absolutely fascinating. Do you do it for yourselves too?

No, they just do it — there's no other way to describe it — for fun.

It sounds like fun.

Encounters with Planets

How do you choose the planets you go to? Is it by sound or because you've heard of them? What are the criteria?

We don't go to a planet just offhand. But you are close to it. If it has any portion of that sound, then we are inclined to go near. If we feel welcomed, then we will perhaps go to the surface. But we have to feel a strong sense of welcoming, so there is not an abridgment of our society or the societies we encounter. I will try to put it in your terms. You might be walking somewhere and see someone or something that is momentarily startling — not necessarily frightening but startling. It causes a fear reaction in your body. We have to avoid that and approach very slowly with just a portion of the vehicle. If we get the feeling, all the way to the surface of the planet, that it will be comfortable and safe, then we have an encounter — but only then.

Only with the shuttlecraft or does the whole big ship land?

As I said, just a portion.

Ah, so your interactions are always only with beings on a small ship, not with everyone on the big ship?

Exactly. Everyone and everything has to be completely compatible. By this, I do not mean tolerant. There has to be love, kindness, gentleness, and welcoming, and it has to be, as you might say, 100 percent. If it is even slightly short of this, then we back off; we might come back to try again another time if we happen to be passing.

Well, that wouldn't work on our planet now, but maybe it could in the future.

We are going to have to stop soon. The channel is having a hard time. I will make a closing statement: We do not judge you.

We understand that you are living in extremely difficult circumstances. Some of you might feel your circumstances are quite safe and comfortable, which they might be temporarily. But until you fully understand the fundamental connection between yourselves and your mothers, you will never feel truly at home on Earth. We recommend that you explore that feeling and understand that all people on Earth right now are a portion of their mothers, and those mothers are a portion of their mothers, and so you are all truly related, not only to each other but to Earth itself. Good night.

DOLMENS: ET GIFTS TO ENSURE EARLY HUMANS' SURVIVAL

Visitors Who Taught Humans
How to Build Dolmens for Survival

APRIL 19, 2019

All right, greetings.

Welcome.

Thank you. You are interested in the structures your people call dolmens.

Correct.

Years ago in your time, our people came to Earth because there was danger to the human race that preceded your current techno-logical era, including use of basic hand tools. There was a possibility that your people would not survive. This had to do with other beings who were dangerous to humans, such as lions and hyenas. Human beings, of course, are quite vulnerable — no natural defenses other than instinct and awareness.

In areas where there were migratory groups of human beings and also some areas where there were settlements, we created basic

Image 17.1. Montana dolmen

structures for their protection. They knew about using wood, but they didn't have tools to cut down trees, for instance. They gathered branches and so on. We put the basic structures together while nurturing and encouraging the societies.

Among their people, a few knew how to move small stones without touching them. We helped them to discover that it didn't matter how big or small the stones were; they could move all stones without touching them. At the time, they didn't understand, so they needed nurturing and teaching.

We looked similar to them, so there was basic trust from the start, because we were clearly trying to help them and keep them safe from those creatures. An interesting thing about life then is that human beings were living on natural Earth, meaning there was no digging to create foundations and so on.

The surface of the planet everywhere was stable with the exceptions of earthquakes, volcanoes, and slow-moving glaciers. As a result, there was no disease. Disease was unknown. The people usually died from interactions with other species, so that was the big risk. I thought you might be interested because in your now time there is a lot of digging into the ground for various reasons. This brings up materials that were once on the surface. If the digging just goes down a few feet, it is not an issue. But digging down, say, 30, 40, or 50 feet and further increases the chances of bringing up materials that were never walked on by people in ancient times, and that would have created disease. Digging also creates disease in your now time, but it is not the only factor.

On your planet, the unearthed materials are sprinkled around the surface everywhere by the wind. Before we arrived, that knowledge had been considered by a previous visiting civilization. They were the ones who planted the forests and the trees. There were some plants before their visit, but there was nothing vast such as a forest of trees that would drop their leaves, which would eventually turn into soil. That had been already established by the time we arrived.

Our people (not me personally) knew that they could stay for maybe six or eight months, but then they would have to return home, not because they were in danger but because they had other things to do. During our stay, there were quite a lot of us here. About 4,000 of us came to make sure there would be good coverage all over the planet in order to show the people how to make these basic structures, which still survive today.

Imagine the huts with tree branches and soil stuffed in them they had been living in. They were not really meant to serve any purpose other than temporary shelter. People could hunt and gather what they needed and run back into the hut to be safe when dangerous Earth life forms were around. I'm not talking about dinosaurs. I'm talking about big cats, bears, hyenas, and so forth. However, there is a limit to how much damage a bear can do through stone compared to wooden branches.

There were enough people trained on Earth who could move stones without touching them to provide the hope that the skills for building would last indefinitely. Over time, with a much greater population and wars and so on, that capability died out. But it is still in your genes. It is in all races of human beings. That is why we want to talk about it, because you can still do this.

Encourage Children

Parents, notice when your children have an interest in something like that, especially if they do things without having been stimulated by movies, TV, or books. When children demonstrate interest, skill, or belief that it is possible for them to move stones without touching them, then I recommend you encourage them. Just say, "Maybe it is something you will learn to do." Don't tell them it is just a dream. Try to recognize it as real.

The younger the children are, the more likely they will believe it. When they are in their early years, especially before they begin formulating words in your languages, they will still remember a lot of who they were. The remembering might be from having been on other planets or from their greater spirit selves and so on. They will think that it is completely normal.

Are you referring to the ability to move large stones with thought or sound? You are not saying what "it" is.

Not with sound or thought, as thought is not involved. However, it would be good to have a picture in your mind (but not a thought) in order to find an area where such stones exist. There were many such areas, but they were not everywhere. In those times, if there weren't stones in that area, we moved them there and built one or two structures. Then we encouraged the people to try. You move them with gestures and with energy. It is a feeling.

Again, parents: your children may not be able to communicate it in your language. They might start making gestures, particularly a gesture using either hand (you cannot see what I'm doing, but you can imagine) in which they flatten it out a bit with the palm up and then make a scooping gesture, which looks like lifting something up. That's pretty much it. If you see your children doing that, they might be trying to do something in the world in which you now exist or they are demonstrating something that has been done in the past and feel they can do in this life — even though they may or may not remember what that is. As they get older you can remind them about it. Don't try to force them to do it. Just tell them: "When you were young, you used to do this. Do you remember?"

These megalithic sites are on major earth energy grid lines. Did you do that deliberately?

Well, energies like that offer support, you see. You cannot expect everyone to have the energy capability, because as I said, only some people in those groups could move stones without touching them. Usually it was the younger ones, but some others also had this ability. If they didn't have it, then they could assimilate it from the energy in that particular area. It was a supplemental energy. Also, the people who had the ability to move stones without touching them could use that supplemental energy to do so more frequently. You cannot do it constantly. You have to rest, and of course, you have to eat and sleep and so on.

But if you were in an area where there was supplemental earth energy, you could do more or even climb up to high places and do things up high. We put a few things up high to demonstrate that in case there was a need, particularly to get away from some threat, then they could also create something like that. That was the whole purpose. There wasn't any symbolic purpose involved. It was strictly for survival.

Okay, can you say how long ago that was?

Well, as you know, you are not in a stable calendar time now. But I will give you a range that would cover it. It was from 50,000 to 170,000 years ago Earth time.

So 50,000 years ago from the third dimension, right?

From where you are between dimensions.

Galactic Travelers

Where else did you go on Earth to do this? This particular picture is in a state called Montana in the United States.

Search for it on the internet yourself and look at it, because we were all over the place, all over Europe and everywhere, not just Montana. I know about what you sent to Robby, but he went to the website and found out it was all over the place.

Can you tell me something about you and your people?

Anything in particular, such as my favorite color? What do you want to know?

Okay, you said you look like humans, so where are you from? Is it from a place we have heard of or we don't know about?

We are in your galaxy, and you will probably encounter us in your travels at some point. But we are not anywhere nearby, so if you encounter us, you will probably be on some other civilization's vehicle that travels fast and far. But we are in your galaxy.

Okay, so you are not who we call Pleiadians?

No, no.

How much do you look like us?

We look pretty much exactly like some of you, and keep in mind that you have variations of appearance even though you are all human beings. If you want to know certain characteristics such as our skin color, we are — oh, I don't know how to call it — tan. I don't know about your color wheel, but if you had one here, I could point to it. I guess if you had a cup of coffee and added maybe three or four tablespoons of cream to the coffee, it would be about that color. We have eyes that look Asian.

Do our Asian people come from your people?

Oh, no. There are people who look like that all over the galaxy and in the universe as far as we know.

Obviously, you travel all over the galaxy. Did you create your ships, or did someone give them to you?

We got our initial ships from other beings. They gave us two or three ships because what we had was not quite adequate for what we wanted to do. We were able to build new ships for traveling, and then we gave their ships back to them. I think you'd say they loaned us their ships. We traveled in them for a short time and then said, "This is very nice, but of course it was built for other people, so let's create and build something like this for our use." You do this for yourselves, correct?

Yes. Are you on one planet or several planets in a solar system?

We are on two planets in a solar system that are not as big as your planet. There are seven planets in the solar system, and we are on the third and fourth planets. One has some water but not as much as on your planet. The other has hardly any water. There, we live underground, because there is some water underground; we are able to cleanse it and use it for everything we need.

When you were here, could you see the humans and could they see you?

Yes, we were of the same dimension.

All these years later, where are you now?

We are in the same, what you call, third dimension, yes?

Yes. Obviously you started to travel to help people. Is that the main reason you travel?

No. We initially wanted to travel to see what was out there. Your people are not the only ones who are curious. We wanted to see what was out there and whether we could find friends. We were given some guidance by the people who loaned us the ships about where to go and not to go, where to find others like us, and so on — sort of a road map. As a result, we were able to explore, and the more we explored, the more we learned.

How did you know about Earth and the fact that there was a need for safe structures?

The people with the ships told us. They said that there was a human population that held promise for the future of the planet and that they would need some help to survive. When we felt ready, they thought it might be good for us to go there and share some skills with them. But they didn't say we needed to hurry up and go. They said there was time and gave us a framework for how long we had before it would be imperative to go. If it became imperative to help and we were not able to, then they would. But they are not human beings, and they felt that it would be better for human beings to go.

Help from Zeta Reticulans

Are these people who loaned you the ships anyone we have ever heard of or know about?

Yes, they are the Zeta Reticulans.

Oh, great!

Yes, they are very helpful people and are known around the galaxy for being helpful. I can't say around the universe because I haven't been everywhere.

Okay, was this a talent or ability that your people had on your planet, to move large blocks of stone?

We had that ability, but the Zeta people informed us that, as far as they knew from their contacts with other human populations, all human populations had that capability. It is apparently in the genetics.

Oh, and when you got to Earth, where did you go or where did you first start on the planet?

Well, 4,000 of us went there, so there wasn't one place we started. We just fanned out all over the planet to where we could see there were groups of human beings or settlements. It was all over the planet — everywhere human beings could be.

Your 4,000 people split up into small groups and lived on the planet with these early humans, then?

Yes, and with the vehicles of course. We didn't come with 4,000 vehicles. There were around ten or twenty people per small vehicle, and then one larger vehicle for the smaller vehicles and so on.

Would we call them shuttlecrafts?

I suppose you would, but I think the term is too diminutive to be used. That is more a fictional term, which comes about as a result of people in the transportation industry. No, I wouldn't call it a shuttlecraft because it is a little too mundane for the quality of the vehicle.

Did your people live on the vehicle?

We sustained ourselves on the vehicle, yes. We didn't eat the foods that the people ate on Earth unless it was possible. At times it might be deemed necessary in order to establish a sense of community and trust. Then we might have to go back to the ship and release those items, if you understand.

Well, that's absolutely fascinating. How long do your people live?

Oh, about 700 years.

I don't remember whether you told me: How long were your people on the planet?

Well, we could only stay about six or eight months.

Oh yes, and you only made one trip right?

Only one trip, yes.

Natural Safety

You just built shelters? You didn't build what we call Karnak or Stonehenge?

No. Although, I must say that Stonehenge resembles the type of things that we built, but Stonehenge is different. It is not the skeletal remains of a building as far as I can tell. But it is possible that it was a building at one time, and it might've had a roof. I think that some of your people have decided that it had a roof at one time.

Do you know who built it?

No.

The humans you interacted with — what percentage of them could lift the stone?

I'm not a wizard at math, but I would say about ½ to ¼ percent. That's not a mathematical term, but you get the idea.

How did you find these people?

Well, we didn't look for them. We went there and communicated in such a way (you call it telepathically), saying, "We understand you are in danger, and we want to help you to build better shelters," and so on. Then we demonstrated building a shelter, and very often, someone said something or a youngster did something. It is not that there were secrets. There were no secrets. People just spoke up.

Wherever we find this type of structure, was it from your people's influence?

Well, I cannot say that for certain, because there were probably other visitors from other planets. I can only say that the structures pictured on the website, yes, those are ours. I cannot say that every single one was because of our influence.

Do you know who came before you to plant the forests, or does anyone know anything about that?

We don't know, and I just explained it because I wanted to suggest that at some point in your future we hope that you will build on the surface and let the earth, forests, leaves, and trees do what they do naturally to create a safe environment for you. You don't have to really do anything. You just need to let the leaves settle, and eventually that will turn into something livable for you. It is a natural thing that is meant to happen. But the more you cut down trees, the less leafing trees you will have. Then you're going to have a problem.

Are you saying we can live on the surface but should not dig deeply into it?

You can do whatever you want to do. I'm talking about not only living but thriving and perhaps saying goodbye to a lot of diseases. Diseases may seem to be in your bloodstream, but they are not. Good health is in your bloodstream, and it is dependent on other life forms that make life easy for you, such as the forest and the ways Earth has of building up her landmass on the surface, not necessarily through volcanism.

I don't have a lot of scientific terminology. I know about trees and I know about leaves. We have trees and leaves where we are.

A Simple Life

You said you live underground on one planet, but what about on the planet with water? Do you live in structures?

We live on the surface in simple structures, but they are not made of wood. We are thankful for the trees and leaves. Even if branches fall, we do not use them. We have a material that is similar to fabric.

Do you use it to create your structures?

They are not structures as you understand them. Keep in mind that we don't have to deal with storms and things like that. It rains only lightly and gently if at all.

How do you live? Do you educate your young in schools and universities or anything?

There is no need for universities, because we don't need a lot of words. We live as well as possible and encourage our people to do the same. We sing songs and tell stories. I don't know how to explain it to you. It is a simple life, and we like it. Just because we can fly around in vehicles doesn't mean we make a habit of it. At times, we go places and do things, but we do not have a technological society. The beings encouraged us to have such vehicles. I know you want to know all about us, but we live a simple life and that's all.

You don't travel all around the planet?

We can travel all around the planet.

Do you have small ships, the kind that you can come to Earth with?

Yes, but frequently we walk. Do people on your planet do that?

Not in most developed countries. They drive cars or use—

Nobody walks? What do they use their legs for?

Well, some people walk. I don't know. I live in a small town and I drive a car.

I am not trying to quiz you. I assumed that we were a lot alike, but maybe I am incorrect; maybe you do not walk. We walk, and we like to walk. We don't use vehicles unless we absolutely have to, because if you walk, you can see things, smell things, and enjoy beauty. We like that. The idea of rushing past something beautiful when it is showing you such beauty, we would not do that.

Perhaps the flowers would like to say hello. Rushing past them is impolite, and at the very least, we should stop and admire the flower and tell the flower how beautiful it is, even though it might know that already. It is always nice to be told that. The flower might move and acknowledge us, and as far as I know, you can do that on your planet as well. I think some of you walk, and perhaps personally you just don't know.

Many people walk, yes. Many people hike and go on vacations to places where they can hike, walk, and see the world.

I think people walk more than you know. I think maybe it would be good for you to know about this. You don't necessarily have to do it yourself. I can see that you are unable to do that at this stage of your life, but it might be good for you to know that it happens.

The reason I say this is that it might help you to feel better about life. When you are getting on in years, it is often pleasant to notice the young and what they do; it is life-affirming. That's my advice.

Yes, that's very good advice.

Simple Interactions

Okay, so this was all those thousands of years ago. What about in your time? Have you gone out to other planets?

No, I have not.

Do any of your people still go?

Occasionally we do, but we have not gone on another massive trip; that was a one-time thing.

It certainly was appreciated, because it allowed us to be here.

You don't have to appreciate it anymore; the appreciation came at the time.

What are your interests in life? Is there anything special that you care about or that you study or want to know about or want to do?

I like to walk, and when I see beauty, I like to interact with it. No one picks flowers here. If we see a flower, we like to interact with it and look at it up close if it feels comfortable to do so. Some flowers are shy, and you can only get so close.

Do you share your planet with other species, either like you or what we call animals?

This is a confusing topic, as the people on Earth were baffled by the other life forms that were violent, and from what we could tell, there was something not right there. But we had to accept that that's how Earth was and apparently still is in places in your time. What was your question?

Do you share your planet with other species?

Yes. There are what you call birds.

Oh, all different kinds?

Different colors. I don't know if there are different kinds.

Do you have any origin stories, and do you know whether you came from some place else? A lot of people who help other people were asked to come here by the Creator.

I don't know anything about that.

But as far as you know, have you always lived on those two planets?

I have and everybody I know has.

Do you have children?

Yes, I have a son.

How are they educated? Do you teach them, or do you respond to their questions?

They usually don't have any questions, but we are friendly with each other. I love my son, and he loves me. I don't know what to say. This might be something that I am not good at explaining.

I just wondered. For example, when people want to be artists or to dance, paint, or learn about nature, what would they do?

If you wanted to paint, what would you paint with? The paints have to be manufactured from other products. We don't live like that.

What about dancing? Do you dance?

Sure, we might dance, and sometimes it is fun. If we make music, we sing. We live a simple life.

I see. You must understand that because of the way we live here, that is a little difficult to fathom.

I think some people understand it. In your times, it is difficult to live a simple life, but it is possible. Your society is just, perhaps, overly competitive, but that will change in time. Right now, you are living in an unnatural situation. In time, it will become more natural. The natural situation implies a simple, uncomplicated lifestyle. That is natural for human beings, because in my experience, we are flexible, capable, and adaptable to different environments as long as we have the basics. It needs to be reasonably warm, and there must be water and food sources, for instance.

We don't necessarily have to do something; we can simply enjoy life. That's what I recommend that you strive for rather than attempting to assimilate too many words. Good night.

Oh, good night and thank you very much.

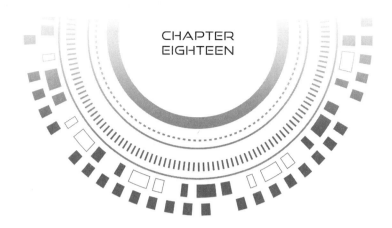

THE TOWER OF BABEL

Future Earth People

JULY 9, 2019

Welcome.

The Tower of Babel was real.

Okay!

It is a real thing that came to be known later on as the Tower of Babel. Initially, it was not a very high or tall creation. The tower had in it all the known languages in the universe and knowledge given by other peoples.

This was a gift to an Earth civilization many years ago, but these are not people you would know about. At the time, it seemed perfectly all right to have the tower out in the open. This was so that people could come to it, and regardless of whether they had a spoken language or simply had thoughts and feelings, they could communicate with anyone, anywhere in the universe if they chose to.

You might say that the knowledge in the tower was constructed

Image 18.1. Tower of Babel by Pieter Bruegel the Elder, 1563

by people who had expressed their thoughts, spoken about their cultures, or had given an overview of their cultures and who they were. All this was a portion of the tower. Well, I'm just going to call it the tower, and keep in mind that the tower was only about 30 feet tall. But you know it would've been considered something unusual. Also, it did not look like a structure that you would know.

But interestingly enough, over time, people built these structures out of stone initially as homage to the original appearance of the tower. It did have an appearance of being made of segmented objects, but the segments really are separated compartments of knowledge. It was round and thirty feet tall, but it had these segments. So you can understand this in your time because you have computers that have language and communications not unlike what I described.

A Universal Translator for a Promising Civilization
The gift aspect of the tower was something like a universal translator. The tower is very thorough, and such thorough gifts were not

usually granted, but that civilization on Earth was deemed by our people to be very promising. They had a lot to offer because they had interesting knowledge, capabilities, and capacities that had not yet fully formed. It was almost like having brilliant children in which you can see they could be so much more or go in many different directions. That was the kind of feeling our civilization felt, and they recognized this element in these people on Earth.

But looking back, you could say a mistake was made,. It probably would have been better to put the tower in some cave or place that was not out in the open so that succeeding civilizations that did not know about or understand it could not destroy it.

For a while, the tower existed out in the open and provided knowledge and wisdom to those who asked. It would never start a conversation, so to speak, but you could walk up to it. Let's say you were walking with a friend and said, "What is this?" If the friend said, "I don't know," then a voice was heard from the tower, answering them in their language, no matter what language existed in the universe, and it explained briefly what it was. So that gives you an idea of how it worked.

Initially, the tower was on the planet without being disturbed for about twenty years or a little less than that. The civilization that was given the tower was not a warlike species at all. They were not exactly an intellectual people, and they were gentle. Unfortunately, they were overrun by other people who just wanted their stuff. These gentle people had the capacity to carve beautiful things. You know, sometimes a people will see other people's beautiful things and want them, so it was essentially a crime, as you refer to it. The gentle people did not exist after that. The people who stole their stuff, well, it was just one more thing that they had done. However, to some minor degree, the genetics of the gentle people have lived on — not to a major degree but to a minor degree. This is not to suggest that every gentle person is from this lineage, but it is there.

A Diplomatic Gift

Can you say something about yourself and your people that created the tower and gave it to them?

No, we did not create the tower. It was something that others had shared with us on our travels. We were told that this was a way to introduce ourselves and bring something to people that we might find on other planets to give them a connection with life from other places. It was a gift. A simple gift is how it was introduced to us. They gave us about thirty of the towers, and we said, "Thank you very much," and then we went about our travels. We accepted them as one might accept a diplomatic gift. Do you understand?

Yes.

We didn't think that we would ever have a need for them. So the thirty towers were put away in a storage area on our ship. At times, our people occasionally visited the area where the towers were stored on the ship and interacted with one or more of them. People, especially children, are universally curious, and if they wanted to know about "this" place or "that" place and so on, they could visit the towers. The parents didn't think that was a problem, so that's how it went for quite a while.

But when we came to Earth, we discovered that this is perhaps exactly the place for a tower because these were exactly the kind of people that our friends who gave us the towers must have had in mind. It was what you would call an eye opener for us. Initially, our contact with Earth people was diplomatic, such as, "Hello, who are you? We are so-and-so." It was that kind of thing. But when we realized that they had somehow knew that we would come to Earth and had come across the towers that we had on our ship, well, that caught our attention. We realized that these new friends were insightful, but we did not realize until that moment how insightful they really were. This changed our attitude quite a bit, and after that, we made a point to stop at the planet to visit more often.

After leaving Earth, where we left one tower, we disseminated seventeen more of these towers at other places. We still retain the remaining twelve, which we have on the ship for our people to use. To this day, our children, especially the young ones, interact with them. So this was quite a learning experience for us as well.

I know you are going to ask, "When did this happen on Earth?" It happened about 85,000 years ago.

Have we ever heard anything else about these gentle people or any myths or stories about what they had built or anything being left?

You are asking whether I know anything about that. No, I don't. But keep in mind that your times are not complete for us in our knowledge, and that is because of the violence. You might think that you are not violent all the time, and certainly, that is true. But violence has a way of damaging and destroying other things.

You see, records are not just written in words. For example, since you are in the written words business, it's good to know that records are also feelings. You can think of it this way: If you were reading a book that was very pleasant with no violence and suddenly there was violence on one page, well, this would mean that we could not have that book in our culture because of the one page. So this is how even one act of violence can destroy the whole thing. It doesn't destroy it in the sense that the book doesn't exist anymore; it means it just doesn't exist for our people. So the reason I say we don't have full awareness of who you are, what you've done, and what you know is because of that. I cannot answer your question that way.

I understand.

An Advanced Civilization from the Future

So who are you and your people? Are you from an alien race that we have ever heard of?

Well, I don't know how you possibly could know us. Oh, because of what *you* do! Oh, all right. Well, I know you expect me to know these things, but I don't know that.

Well, what are you called? What is the name of your civilization or planet?

Oh, I see that you don't understand. We are from Earth in the future.

Oh, okay.

We are Earth people but just from the future. I am sorry for not making that clear. Perhaps I did not understand your request, but yes, that's who we are.

So you came from Earth's future.

The future Earth that I am from does not have the exact same appearance of your current Earth, but it is in the same orbit, so it has to be future Earth.

You are on that Earth now?

Yes.

Okay, did you come from the future back to this gentle civilization to give them that tower or were you then part of another civilization somewhere?

I am not sure what you are asking, but I will explain this to you: I know that your people are slowly moving toward a new version of Earth. But the version you are moving toward is not the same version we have. We are on a version of Earth but not the one you are headed to. It is a version of Earth and in the same orbit, so I have to assume that it is in a different dimension.

Can you say which one?

You number them, eh? We would be more inclined to color them, but I will see whether I can get an interpretation for you. You would understand it as the ninth dimension.

Wow, that's wonderful!

We are still in the exact same orbit, so I have to assume that theoretically you could say, "Well, that planet is there right now," and that would be true. But even if it is there right now, we are still about 250 ... You know, I was just tapped on the shoulder by a scientist who says that putting it in years won't make any sense to you because it just doesn't work. Do you want me to continue?

No, that's fine. I understand. Where were you at that time? Were you in the same ninth dimension 85,000 years ago when you gave the tower to the gentle people on our planet?

Yes.

Ah! So for how long? Can you say?

Understand that the gentle people were gentle like us, and that's the reason the gift was given. It was like finding cousins in a way. They didn't look exactly like us, but they were very similar. My people said, "Oh, this is so wonderful! It's good to see you, and maybe you could use this." It was that kind of thing.

And they were all wiped out. How terrible.

Well, they are immortal, of course, just like everyone else.

Yeah.

But their civilization ceased to exist. Those who came later (the ones who stole the gentle people's stuff with all that violence) did not know what the device was. They were not even curious, and no one approached it. So it actually stood there for quite some time afterward. Eventually, other people came along who didn't know what it was, and over time it didn't survive. However, the shape did. I'm just taking a quick look at your planet. Even to this day on your planet, one sees — well, I'm going to describe it. Since I see it, then apparently I am allowed to describe it. I think there is more than one. It is a round tower, and in some cases, there is an inner stairway that goes up to a landing at the top where people can look around. In some cases, there is an outer stairway, but it is constructed of segmented pieces. It looks like sometimes it is smoothed over with something, but I don't know. It is sort of like a lookout tower, and I think it is used mostly these days for pleasantries.

It could also be a lighthouse tower. It's tall and round with a staircase that goes up to the top where there is a strong light that can be seen at sea.

I really don't know. The thing that I see on your planet is roughly around the time in which I think you are living in now, but I really don't know. It is made out of some kind of stone, and it has an outside staircase so that people can walk up to get to the top. I think most people take photographs. So it's on a hill, or there is a valley just beyond that. It is just a place where people can stop and enjoy the scenery.

The Story of Babel

Well, you don't know, but it turned into a story about people trying to go to heaven to become greater than God, so God squashed it. We have ridiculous stories about the Tower of Babel.

Well, the important thing is this: Enough stories survived about the tower from other civilizations. That is what I understand. Enough information survived, and enough people apparently interacted with it before it was destroyed. So when it was working correctly and different people approached and asked a question, they heard the answer in their language or the language that they knew the best.

Later on, if many people approached the tower and one person asked a question, the people at the tower heard the answer in a language that may not have been theirs. In other words, it didn't always (especially at the time when it wasn't working well) answer the question in the language of the person. So you might, for example, ask a question in German and get an answer in French. But if you don't know French, it's not going to make much sense to you. You're going to say, "Well, it's just babbling."

[Laughs.] Well, the Tower of Babel.

"Babel" is an old term, and of course, it's been translated over the years. The story itself had to be transformed into whatever religious perspective managed to keep it alive. But I think that this is actually a good thing because it will, in time, create a means to interact with others who speak different languages. You probably have something on your computers now that allows you to interact with one person who says something in one language, and the other person gets it in their language, like a translator. This is probably already in your culture; if not, it will be soon. So perhaps the tower will be re-created by your people.

It seems to me that it can only do good because many times people have misunderstandings. Even though most people in my encounters (granted I haven't encountered many different kinds of people) have similar feelings and needs, they have more in common than one might expect. We think that you have other life forms on your planet, and most likely, you have a lot in common with these life forms even if they look completely different. You all need to eat and sleep and have shelter and so on, and that's a lot to have in common.

The Placement of the Tower

Do you know where on the planet the tower was placed?

It was a benevolent space, and I'll have to see whether I can get that for you. I think it was in the farthest northern area of North America. What is that called up there?

Canada or Alaska?

Well, it's in the center part of North America but very far to the north.

It must be Canada, then.

Well, it's in the center of northern North America, straight through North America to the northernmost part. I think it is still land. It was there, and that's all I have.

Well, the weather was different then; it's very cold up there now. When you were there, it was probably very different.

Well, these things change, don't they? Apparently, you are experiencing changes on a regular basis. Do you have seasons?

Yes, we have seasons, but also different parts of the planet have different weather. Some areas have a temperate climate and other areas have a colder climate.

Ah yes, I see.

Life in the Ninth Dimension

So you came from the future. Did you say that your people were traveling? Do you normally travel in time?

The ship can travel in time, and of course, the people have to be in complete and total compatibility with the ship as well as the ship being completely compatible with all people aboard. In that situation, you can build a vehicle that will travel in time. This can happen only if everyone, including every minute particle, agrees that this is something desirable. So as long as you understand that, then, yes, we can travel in time.

Are you talking about something your people in the past did, then? Do you live that long?

I am talking about something my people did in the past, yes. But I am now speaking as a spokesperson. I might be making it sound like I was involved, but I am actually speaking as a representative.

Even though you're in the ninth dimension, do you have a plasma body? You have a body that you live in, right?

I don't know why you think that, but our bodies are a solid substance to us. Understand that I try to explain where we are in the context of what you can understand. So I am interacting with you as much as I can, which is a very limited amount. Do you understand that?

Yes.

I said the ninth dimension because I think that this is something you can understand or appreciate. My body is solid, and all bodies here are solid.

But if I looked at it with my eyes now, I would not see your body, right?

Correct. You would not see my body because according to my understanding, all Earth's dimensions are all present in all places. You are in one of those dimensions right now, and you can see and totally interact within your dimension. But it would require a spiritual view to see into another dimension. With a spiritual view, you stay in your dimension but can look into another dimension. If you were to actually visit there, you would have to be insulated and protected somehow. You would not be able to come in direct contact with people. So if you are asking whether you would be able to walk and talk and be here, then no.

Can you describe a little about your life? Can you say anything about how you live and what you do?

Just imagine a gentle way of life that interacts with what you call plants. We consider plants to be people. We would never think about cutting flowers because it would hurt them. Plants and flowers are people to us.

We do not have rigid educational systems. If children are interested in something or show interest, then there are teachers for them. If teachers are not available, then the towers are available. We eat, sleep, and love each other.

You don't have technology, though, and your ships are lightships, right?

Well, it depends on how you define technology. If you define technology as "putting materials and things together whether they want to be together or not," perhaps that's technology where you are, yes?

Yes.

But in our technology, our ship would appear to you to be a light when it is in the sky. Yet when we are in it, it is solid.

But it wants to be put together? The pieces all want to be together?

Imagine you are in a nice place. Then let's say you would be interested in visiting some nice place on another planet, so how would that come about? Gradually, various particles would come together and form something to carry you and perhaps others who have the same interest along with all the things that support life as well as familiar things, such as plants and flowers and bees without stingers. I don't know whether that's the answer you expect.

Yes, it's fine.

Ninth-Dimensional Animals

So what about cats and dogs and bears and chickens and things like that? Do you have what we call animals?

Well, the reason I use plants as an example is so that you can understand that other species exist besides us. Oh, I see you want a specific species. Okay, let me try to understand what it means.

Are there any other species of any kind you share your planet with?

What does "animals" mean to you?

Well, I guess all other life forms on the planet besides humans.

I see. So plants, as you call them, are not animals?

Correct. Plants are not animals. Animals walk around on the ground, and fish live in the water. There is ocean life, such as dolphins and whales, and there are all kinds of creatures who live in the oceans. Then on land, there are still an awful lot of sentient beings that are not human.

Oh, I see. That is a good answer and what I needed. We have such beings as well, but we do not have any vast surface oceans; we have subsurface oceans. I have experienced one, and it is very beautiful and very calming. Of course, I am usually calm (speaking for myself), but by the subsurface ocean, I was even calmer. I literally cannot visit that subsurface ocean without immediately falling asleep. Then when I wake up, I feel refreshed. I think this might be a natural factor of oceans. I have heard from people on other planets that oceans often have that effect. Apparently, it is a means to be refreshed, and in some places, oceans have a healing capacity. Perhaps the ocean on your planet has a healing capability in which beings might go to be healed.

But I'm not answering your question. Yes, there are other life forms, and we interact with them much the same as we do with plants.

A Long-Lived People

How long do you live? Can you say that?

Yes, but it's hard to convert into your time. Keep in mind that our bodies are not temporary, but your bodies are. Perhaps this is because in your civilization and world, it is not easy, so you would not necessarily want to have — well, I don't want to express something about your civilization of which I know very little. But our bodies are pretty sturdy, and we are not diseased nor subjected to that. So I will interpret this as best I can in your years, and understand that any time I have mentioned years, you have to sort of figure that is a soft description.

Okay.

Our bodies would likely live about 25,000 years.

Aha. Yeah, we've been told that our lives are less than 100 years because it is so difficult here.

Yes, that sounds like my impression.

Okay, so —

A moment. All right, go ahead.

In the course of your lifetime, have you been able to come back to Earth, and are the people gentle enough that your people could interact with us on our level of reality?

No.

What do you do when you are traveling in space? Do you trade or help people or explore?

This is the only term I think you can understand: It is for fun. It is a pleasure to go places and see things and maybe see new things and share our culture if that is desired by the other people. It is a pleasure to have other cultures share with us if they desire it and we desire it. We think this is completely normal from what we've seen, and this is always happening.

Some cultures do not wish to have such interactions, and there are some means of knowing that as we approach the planet. So if that's the case, then we don't go there because we don't want to offend anyone. We go some place else.

Where are you in your cycle of having a body?

I'm about 17 percent of the way through.

Oh, you're just a young one. Do you have families the way we do? Do you have children?

We have children, but there is no pain or suffering involved in birth. Yes, we have one child.

Oh, that's great.

We are going to have to finish up pretty soon. When I asked you to wait a moment ago, it's because it's getting difficult to maintain the connection.

Artificial Intelligence Technology

Well, it would be nice to have one of those towers now if you could send it FedEx or something. [Laughs.]

I mentioned before that I think your people are possibly working on it. We think that you will need to have all your languages in it first. I would also recommend that you include all languages that are no longer spoken. So your people working on this will have to get that information. You may need to ask the elders of peoples in which very few still speak the language so that those are included. The more languages that you can include, spoken and unspoken (and probably this already has been done), the better the foundation of the tower will be.

Well, we have technology that can translate different languages to another with artificial intelligence systems. But I don't know anything about having them all in one place.

It's probably in existence somewhere in one of your educational facilities or institutions. Having such information available to the average citizen is not in place yet, but perhaps it will be soon or at some point.

We are going to have to finish up pretty soon because it's getting difficult to maintain the connection.

Yes, I am about out of questions anyway, and I really do appreciate your coming to talk with us. Would you like to say anything to the people who read this before you go?

I will do what I can. On your world, you have many things that are a struggle, and these are difficulties I believe you will probably find out how to solve.

I will recommend something. If you are having difficulties with a group of people who speak another language, it might be to your advantage to learn as best as you can or have at least a working knowledge of that other language. Then you would be able to find out what they are having problems with. Maybe it is something simple that can be corrected, but right now there is no common means of communication between you because the spoken word and the cultures are different. I recommend learning to speak or at least understand another language in a way that is compatible with you. This I feel would be helpful. Good night.

Thank you very much. Good night.

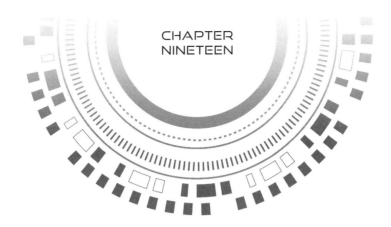

MEGALITHIC STANDING STONES AT CARNAC

Galactic Traveler

SEPTEMBER 17, 2019

Welcome.

Thank you. Did anybody ever follow the arrow?

I don't know about the arrow, but they found circles, squares, polygons, and all kinds of things.

Oh, the circles, squares, and other shapes were an attempt to leave general foundational elements in a universal written language. You tend to find those general shapes in all written languages. Circles, of course, might also be swoops and so on. But you didn't find the arrow?

Someone might have, but I don't know about it.

In that general area, an arrow was also left.

Pointing to what?

It was pointing to the code-breaker that you would be able to use to understand all languages. Of course, the simple way to do it is

with telepathy. People who have become too intellectual often forget that the simple way to communicate is to use telepathy. It does not require (as you know) an understanding of the other person's language. When you get to written language, which is important, then you need something other than telepathy. Unless the interpreter, or you might say "reader," of that language is able to put some portion of her body (perhaps her hand) on the written language and get the telepathic transformation from those who produced the writing. Of course, this works much better for physical writing than electronic writing, where the diffusion of the electronic process filters the input from the original person.

Something that is written, especially by the hand of a human, you can receive telepathically. The stone was left in more than one place. Sometimes they are referred to as telegraph stones. If you look that up (you might have to use a variety of searches), you will learn that the telegraph stones have been left in various places. On them will be versions of different languages.

Unfortunately, people have only tried intellectually to interpret what those symbols mean. What they really mean is that you can either stand near the stone or put a hand on the stone to telepathically get the messages that were put in the stone. That is how the stones work. The stone was left near the arrow. It wasn't a tall stone. I am being reminded by my friend that there was actually more than one arrow that pointed to it. Apparently the others did not last.

In the areas where those stones were found, search for one of the telegraph stones. It will have different symbols that look similar to letters from different languages. We are not sure, but we think at least one of those stones has been found and might have been transported to Scotland. That is what to look for. I believe one of those stones was found in the country not far from where you are speaking right now, somewhere near the corners of those four states that touch each other.

The Four Corners?

Yes, one of the stones was found there. There are others, so look for them, and use them telepathically. The reason all those things were written on them, or actually carved into the stone, was to let you know that it was the place of universal language. You can't leave that message for people when you don't know what kind of written language they will be reading in the future. You must hope that a child will put his hand there and say, "Oh, it means 'this.'" In your time, many people do not believe it when children say such things. I'm pretty sure children have come along and done that, or even sensitive adults, who telepathically knew what it meant.

The Line of Stones

How many telegraph stones did you leave in Carnac?

Just one but we left others all over the planet. Other beings also left that type of stone, and there are at least nine of them all over the planet. It depends on who you talk to. Some beings say eleven and others say nine. Different interpretations of history lead to different facts. That is what I know from here.

Okay, can you tell me why you set up those stones? They go on for miles, row after row.

Is that important?

Yeah.

Well, it was mostly to show people that in order to build structures, you need the stone's cooperation. In those times, stone was what you had to work with. There were structures there, but what you call the line of stones is residual. It was to show how you do it. Then we lifted the cooperative stones, and they stood partially underground. The surface of the ground has to be somewhat soft and liquid so that the stone can easily move up and stay standing in the ground. Then we showed the people how to add walls in front and a temporary roof. We advised that the roof be temporary or movable so that they could push it aside when there was no rain. They liked using something from trees for the roof, and there were a lot of them.

Figure 19.1. Standing stones of Carnac

The people had trouble keeping the stones standing in the ground because this required making the ground temporarily liquid — not like water, more like quicksand. Once the stone stood up in the soft quicksand, the ground returned to solid. You don't want soft ground to spread out where you are standing, because obviously you would sink into it. When the ground quickly turned back to solid earth, your friends would have to dig you out. It wasn't easy for them; mistakes were made several times, and some people had to be dug out. It was frightening, but no one died.

The teachings took place in the structure that we built, so now you can look at the standing stones as teaching tools. At that time, there were people living there who absorbed the teachings and went out and did it themselves. I think people also exist in your times who say, "Don't do it for me. Just show me, and I'll do it myself." You understand that attitude, of course. At that time, everyone had that attitude, but some of the structures they built didn't last very long.

Can you tell me — and I know years are not relevant — but something that gives us an idea how long ago in our now past you did that?

Let me ask. The information I'm getting is 14,000 years.

Who did you teach? Would we know about them now, or do we have a history of them?

Am I supposed to know everything you know?

[Laughs.] All right. Well, why were you there, then?

Didn't I already say that?

To teach them.

Sophisticated Interactions

Where did you come from before you came to Earth?

Well, we came from the world that we are on now, which in your time is along the outer edges of the galaxy you are in. From our time, our world is further inward because another outer loop formed. Have you been able to get a pretty good idea of what your galaxy looks like?

Yes.

You know where you are in the galaxy, okay. Then imagine where we are on the galaxy's outer edge, but from our time there was another entire outer loop created.

On the other side of the galaxy?

No, all the way around the galaxy. The galaxy goes around and around to build itself, do you understand?

Yeah, all right, so how did you happen to come to Earth?

We were informed by a friend who passed by from time to time and said that there were some highly receptive people we might find to be compatible because their method of learning was very similar to ours. Our method of learning is imitating what we have seen others do or what we have come to know others to do, which is broader than seeing. Since these people learned the same way, the friend felt that we would possibly find them compatible friends and that we might enjoy being able to interact with them. That was good enough for us. That's why we came to Earth.

Were you in a dimension that was able to interact physically with the beings on Earth?

Oh, I see. You are thinking that the beings we interacted with on Earth were humans.

I was, yes.

No, they were not human beings.

What were they?

I don't know if you have a word for that. They were a form of upright beings. Oh, I see. That is unfortunate. I see that in your time you think these beings who walked a little stooped over but basically upright were some kind of uneducated and uncultured Stone Age humans. That's what you call them. That's who they were, but they were very advanced, totally telepathic. They could do many things that you would probably like to be able to do yourselves.

As often happens, they were vulnerable to cultures more violent than theirs. Those beings were very kind, and they couldn't possibly behave violently. Sometimes people like that are seen as easy prey for others who are violent. My guess is that human beings might have eliminated them. I'm not saying your current human beings eliminated them — obviously not. Some beings you might consider to be more upright human beings would have found them to be easy prey.

Did they have a name? Do we have a history of them?

Well, you probably have some kind of Latin name for them. I described them to you, so you should be able to find information about them. Somebody came up with a theory of evolution, and people printed pictures, so I'm going on that basis. The evolution theory encourages people who can draw to show the idea of beings being less sophisticated by making them appear shorter and hairier or walking in a stooped way. This does not identify their quality of advancement spiritually, mentally, and physically. They have been identified by their appearance rather than by their quality of being.

I feel very sorry for you. You have lost this awareness. It is good you are functioning to put out the material as much as you are able in a single language. Some people in your time will consider that it has validity. Most likely, the young people will discover this at some point and start practicing it. Then they will remember who they are, and things will get rolling better for your kind.

Okay, what is your form? What do you look like?

We look like those beings I described who were vulnerable

looking to those who looked at them and said, "Oh we like those structures, and we would like to move in. So let's get those others out of there." Is that clear?

Okay.

Creation through Energy

Do you travel in light or in spaceships? How do you get here?

We travel in what you call spaceships.

Do you live differently on your planet now than you did then or pretty much the same?

Your question doesn't make any sense to me.

I guess I am looking for a level of technology. Did you make your spaceships, or did someone give them or lend them to you?

Oh, we asked for the spaceship "to be," and the energy that felt that it would like to be a spaceship came into being. Of course, energy comes and goes, so it can change into the ship. From your point of view, it is a lightship, but it can take a physical form when necessary.

Were these people you visited on Earth some of your people who came here previously?

Not that I know of.

Yet they were very much like you?

The traveler said those on Earth were similar to us in how they learned.

The way you lived on your planet when you came here, is it how you live now?

Yes, of course.

Do you live a long time? Do you have a long lifespan in our terms?

It is difficult to express, so I will give you a number that is going to create a feeling in you. It's not that the number is valid. Rather, it's the feeling in you that will be the valid thing. Are you clear on that?

Yes.

The number is 250,000 years.

Okay, to us that seems immortal. Where are you in that cycle now?

No. Don't get caught up in the years themselves. It's the feeling. It's the feeling of the years that I mentioned; did it generate a feeling in you?

Yes, it felt as if you live forever.

No, not in words. Did it generate a physical feeling in you?

No.

I think it did, but you are too focused in your mind. When you see the number later when reading this, you will notice the feeling.

However long you live, were you one of the beings who came here at that time?

No. That's why, from time to time, I stop to consult with our means of knowledge.

What means is that?

What is always present: you know what you know—

When you need to know it.

[Laughs.] Right.

Did your people, when they came here, travel around Earth? Were you aware of other cultures, or did you just stay pretty much in that area?

We took the Traveler's advice. The Traveler said we might find those people compatible. He didn't say we were similar. I used that term because I knew that you would understand it. In fact, the Traveler said that you might find that there is compatibility. Well, you know, the Traveler had never said that before, and we felt it was enough to decide to go. It was our decision to go. Then we discovered there was compatibility, and we stayed for a while. We didn't stay because the Traveler ordered us to. We stayed because we discovered there was compatibility. The Traveler didn't even suggest that we go. It was just a passing comment that peaked our interest.

Telepathic Building

Where did you get those big stones? Did you have to move them from far away?

No, they were on the land and under the land, lots of them. The stone under the land could be formed into a portion of a wall or structure. Some of the stone was in much bigger sheets. That's the size that they were, I think. Let me check for sure. All right, yes, apparently there was one stone, maybe two, of that size and shape. We asked the rest of the stone that was underground to come up. Yes, that's it, and we asked for the stone to come up in the size we already had above ground, which of course it did.

Is that how you build on your home planet?

We don't have to build on our home planet, but it works the same as how we acquire knowledge, which is, you know what you need to know when you need to know it. It's exactly the same thing as telepathy. You know what the other person is trying to communicate when you need to know it. This is because you hear it and feel it in your communicative form. You have, perhaps, a saying: "Everything is everything." If you think of it that way, it's the solution for everything. If you approach it as one thing at a time (with multiple classifications using different words and languages), it's a very slow process. I've learned that on your planet now, the communication is exceedingly slow. It's your natural state, of course.

Well said. How did you make the ground liquid or like quicksand? Did you ask it to do that?

Yes, exactly. We asked it to become liquid or like quicksand just momentarily so that the stone that volunteered to stand up in the soft ground would immediately be present and could stand in the ground. Then the ground would quickly become solid again, and the stone would be standing. The stones would then stand in the identical shape of the others.

You were teaching them how to build, but at the same time, you were putting forth images of Platonic solids on the telegraph stone. So you were leaving a teaching for others to follow, right?

That was the point, because those beings at that time felt that they weren't going to be there much longer. They knew that their doom was coming; they just didn't know when, and they wanted to be able to leave a message of some sort. We said we would help them with that. They carved one or two of the symbols on the stones. I think they did the spiral, and of course, knowing what we knew about the shape of the galaxy (and they knew that too), it was for them an obvious thing. One finds the spiral in other ways on your planet.

Oh yes. You may not know this, but did those beings come from some place else?

We're pretty sure that they came from some place else, but they did not come from our planet. Even though there was a significant resemblance between us.

The Traveler Ship

Did you ever discuss with their elders where those people came from?

That would've been rude.

Really?

Of course, it's like if you walked up to someone you didn't know but wanted to get to know and started asking them questions about their family. You don't know that that's rude?

I do that all the time. Well, I mean with beings like you.

Well, I'm talking about to walk up to another human being on the street that you don't know. You don't ask people about their families because that is rude.

Yes, in that case, it is rude. What is your life like now? How many beings like you are on your planet?

Well, it's hard to say because sometimes we are not individuals. We come together. At any given time, when we are individuals, there are maybe ninety of us.

Oh, that's all?

Yes.

You come together as spirit beings, then, right?

Well, yes, you could put it that way.

The purpose for that is what?

It is what we are. Everything is everything, and there is joy in that.

Do you travel much around the galaxy?

Usually only if we are drawn to some place. The suggestion from the Traveler has happened another time, and that's why we look forward to Traveler's arrival. Generally, we go to places where we feel attracted to, but if there's no place we are attracted to, we are perfectly happy where we are.

Tell me about this Traveler. Is it a being who comes to your planet every so often?

It is a ship that comes to the planet, and the ship has a personality. That's the Traveler.

So the ship just stops to visit and brings things?

Oh, you are thinking of trade and all of that business. No, we don't need anything. Ah, of course, you are thinking in your own terms. You eat food, and you build buildings. We don't do any of that. We don't eat food.

You live on light?

The same as you when you are your immortal self. We have bodies because it is our pleasure.

Ah, and you just manifest them, right?

Yes, but it is our form when we have bodies. That is always the form that we have. We never decide to be something other than our form when we want a body.

Forever Kind

I see, all right. Can you view our situation on this planet now?

No thank you.

Okay, I was going to ask whether you had any advice.

I cannot do that, because from what I've been told, it is not allowed and also not recommended.

I understand. Well, this is fascinating. I don't think I have any more questions, so I thank you tremendously for giving us this information. Do you have a closing comment?

Yes, I have a closing comment: Stay curious, be friendly, and practice kindness. You will need all three of these qualities now and forever.

Thank you very much. Goodlife.

NAZCA LINES: CREATIVE INSTINCT

Future Cartographer

SEPTEMBER 20, 2019

Mapping and geography.

You said mapping and geography? Well, welcome.

Mapping and geography at your service. We work on helping travelers to find where they want to go and sometimes help them out when they're lost. That was the purpose of those lines. Sometimes (well, I don't know whether some are still there) there was a picture that reminded beings (those who were passing by in a ship) of themselves or perhaps had something to do with one of their deities. When they saw the picture, they said, "Oh, this is important. We should stop." Then they looked at the other lines. Either they or the navigational system on their ship suddenly knew how to interpret them, and off they went to where they were meant to go.

We have made lines like this on other planets, mostly on moons. It is mainly because planets don't want their surfaces interrupted to do such a thing, but sometimes planets will say, "Okay, for a while." That usually means, "Well, someday there will be other people and beings here who won't really notice the pictures, or they will build a house there or something." It was like that on this planet. Essentially, the planet said, "Okay for now."

Growing Up on the Ship

I can explain my job to you pretty much in terms of a heading, but you are probably going to ask where we are from. I'm speaking in "we" because there is a group of us in the room right now; it's actually a vehicle. It is a big vehicle, and one would think of it as a residence, you know. I can't really say that we are from any particular planet. I was born and raised on this residence, and my parents and their parents all grew up on the ship.

My genetics set me up to be able to fit into this work very well. I find it fascinating, and that's fortunate, because otherwise I would've been bored. I like geography because I like seeing different terrains, including the forms of surface terrains and even seeing underground terrains. In short, I am interested in physical representations of matter. With this kind of interest, of course I would be curious about your planet, which has a variety of terrains.

Can you say what planet your ancestors came from?

I don't know if I can go back that far.

Oh?

I just said the previous two generations because I know you're curious. But I think all the family that I can trace was on this vehicle.

Wow.

I don't miss the home planet. Why would I? As far as I'm concerned, this ship is my home planet. It's what I know, and its vast. I have been here my whole life, and I haven't even explored the whole thing.

Time Questions Are Complicated

How many of your people are there?

Well, people come and go on a vehicle like this, but there is never any more than 250,000. In my time, it's been 70,000, but when we have 250,000, it doesn't seem very crowded at all. This ship has the capacity to grow as needed, so if there are more on the ship, the ship just grows to the needed space. I think the ship grew in my grandfather's time, and it was originally set up to easily accommodate 100,000 with all the things that you would need, such as support systems and all that.

But over time, there were more who needed to come to this ship, and the ship responded and grew. It had within it processes in which it could grow and adapt to different cultures and their needs and atmospheres and all of that. So all that is available on the ship. First off, you need to have a ship that loves variety and likes to do what it is doing; otherwise, it would be a chore, yes?

Yes. The people who come to the ship, are they born on it or do they come to join you from other places?

Oh, both. There are a lot of people on the ship now who were born on it, about maybe 48,000, but everyone else comes from other places. They don't always stay. They stay for a while, and then they go back home or some place else and keep going.

I see, and how long ago in our time did you put the lines that we call Nazca lines?

Oh, in your time — I am not good at that, and I've been asked that before. The ship refuses to tell me. I don't know why, but the only thing that makes sense to me (because I've put a lot of thought into it) is that it hasn't happened yet. It must be going to happen in the future, because if you ask something like, "How far back was it" or "How many years ago did it happen?" the question cannot be answered if it hasn't happened yet. Maybe it has happened in the future, and you are seeing something now that is only a portion of it because it hasn't fully manifested yet. That would make sense, you see, because if there are bits of it and it looks like someone stopped in the middle of a letter, it would make sense that it just hasn't been completed yet; this is what I believe.

Well, that's certainly interesting. When we look at it, we see long, straight lines and all kinds of squares and circles. Then we also see creatures such as monkeys or birds. What was the purpose of the animals?

There are no animals.

Well, the beings, then?

I'm going to answer that: There are no animals. There are only beings that come by, usually in ships and sometimes in lightships. Only very occasionally there are beings who come with only their lightbodies. They are beings from other planets. Just because you call them animals does not make them that.

Okay, so every representation, then?

Excuse me. I know I sound like I'm yelling at you, but it is just my personality.

Okay, that's all right. Every being we see outlined in Peru (most of these lines I'm talking about now are in Peru in South America), they are all beings who at some time—

A moment [being speaks to another on the ship]: Pauline, the session is going on. It will be over soon. Wait about half an hour or forty minutes. If you can still hear me, then that is unfortunate.

[Speaking to questioner]: The upstairs neighbor thinks that I'm shouting too loudly. Perhaps she is right. I will quiet down a bit. Go ahead.

Okay, so all these beings with their fascinating shapes have at some time or another flown over this area?

Yes, of course.

Wow.

Well, I can't say that because it's not complete. If my theory is right, then it is either they have flown over the area or they will.

Or they will, yeah. So there's one area that looks like a landing strip that goes on for miles perfectly straight over flattop areas and mountains. What was that for?

All I know for sure is it's not a landing strip, because airplanes are not going to get you from one planet to another.

[Laughs.] I know, but they call it the landing strip. What was the purpose of that, do you know?

It's just not complete yet. Otherwise, it's like an arrow saying "this way" and "not that way" or something like that. But, no, I think it is not complete yet.

Okay, we couldn't see the entire site until we had airplanes, and we thought this was all there was. Now we have found there are shapes all over the planet, because now people take pictures from satellites. Did you put them all over the planet?

We didn't, but somebody must have.

Image 20.1. Nazca lines, view 1

How the Lines Were Made

You focused on this area in Peru, your people?

That's what you asked for, yes?

Yes.

Then, yes, we are talking about the Nazca area.

Yes, so how did you make the lines? What did you use to make the outlines of the beings' shapes so large?

You are talking to me as if I am the one who did it. Remember, I am with maps and geography. Oh, you don't understand.

No.

You wanted to speak to someone who actually made the lines.

Well, not necessarily. I wanted to understand why they were made and how they were made and what they meant.

That's in geography. Maps in your time are used to find things or to show people where things are.

Yes.

Geography is about terrain and tells people, "Don't go straight ahead. There is a hill or there is a lake," or something. But our job wasn't to make the lines. You want to speak to whoever made the lines, so I will say goodbye.

No, no I want to talk to whoever decided to make the lines.

Well, that wasn't me, either, so I will say goodbye, and we will see who comes through.

COLLECTIVE INSTINCT

Future Geographer

This is the best that can be offered.

Welcome.

You are assuming that someone said, "Go there and do that," but it was not like that. When there is a need for something, then various beings in my time (and I think in other times and probably on your planet) just volunteer to do it. No one said, "Go there and do that." But in my time, we are actually in the process of doing the pictures now.

Now you are going to ask, "Where are you?" I'm going to say instead, "When are we?" We are about 30,000 years in your future.

We visited Earth and walked on it as you might visit a place to see what it is and talk to the people. Most of the time we are in our vehicle, which can imprint the surface of planets, which is not unlike, within this rudimentary example, you might see a printed circuit board that is intended to last for as long as it is needed. Although in your world, it is not for a long time. But in my world, I would not have been inspired to do what I am doing without a belief that it would last for as long as it was needed.

Are you on a future version of the same ship that the first being talked from?

No. Our vehicle is much smaller, and we have a small crew. Altogether, the number of the crew, which is never more than seventeen, is currently fourteen. Occasionally we get visitors, and that's why the number goes up.

You are 30,000 years in our future right now?

Well, I cannot say exactly, but I assumed you would want a general number based on your time.

Right.

That's the best I can do based on a linear measurement of time in which I do not personally live.

Right.

I don't have a means to consult on the ship. I just have to make the computations as best as I can in my mind.

Is there any connection between you and the first being who talked?

Who was that?

Well, the previous being said that he was from maps and geography, and he was on a ship that had 70,000 people with the capacity to hold 250,000 because the ship adapts to the size needed.

No, I don't know anyone like that.

Okay, but you're the actual group who puts the lines on the planet. You imprint them on the planet, correct?

Well, you are asking about a specific place?

In Peru.

The Nazca lines?

Yes.

Yes, we did that. Well, we are doing it [laughs]. It is difficult talking about this, because our time is different from yours. For us, very often if we have the picture in our mind's eye, as you say, of how we are going to do something, then I say, "We did that." Meaning we did that which we are planning to do, and then we do it. We live in a time that can only loosely be translated as "now," okay. We don't measure days of the week as you do. We don't measure night and day as you do. Everything we do is now.

I don't know how to answer your questions, but I will do the best I can. If I make any mistakes, you can print them as my words, if you wish, so people understand that there are other sequences of life available.

Okay, did you feel the need to create the imprint in the Nazca lines of what we call a monkey with a really, really long tail or a spider? How do you get the feeling what needs to be done?

The same way you would get a feeling: instinct. We have instinct too. Everyone on the ship has instinct. Do you think the crew was assembled and assigned to come on the ship? No, everyone on the ship had the feeling or the instinct that this is something we want to do, so we are doing it together. It's all instinct, and we know what to print based on instinct.

It's not as if we say, "Let's go 'there' and create 'this.'" It's not like that. We all have the same instinct to do the same thing. We start with instinct, and we follow the instinct every step of the way for what needs to be put on the surface of your planet as the Nazca lines.

In the Nazca lines, we have one vertical being against a huge high rock that has been called the astronaut. It has like a jumpsuit on and glasses or goggles. What was your feeling or need for that one?

You want me to analyze our creations, which are not based on linear progression. It is instinct: This is what is needed. This is what we do.

Was it intended for some being who looked like that?

No, you don't understand me.

Okay.

Again, you are speaking linearly. "Intent" is about linear. We know what is needed, so we do it. We do not say, "So-and-so might come along one day and be attracted to this." We don't even function that way; it is not who we are. We are now, not linear.

A Needed Task

Do you live on the ship, or is it like going out as we would go to work, and then you go home to a planet? How does that work for you?

You mean do we live linear lives? Because everything you see is linear. You see, we are having trouble with that, but I will answer as best I can.

Please.

I know that everyone on the ship came from some place, and there is no one on the ship who came from the same place. I have friends and family where I come from, and everyone else on the ship has friends and family where they come from. When we no longer feel that this is something to be done and it is completed, then as far as I know, we all go home. Everyone here is nodding their heads; they agree. When the task is completed, we all go home.

Where is your home?

My home is in another galaxy, so it will not make much difference to you. We travel in time, which is easy — the easiest way and easiest on your physical form.

Do you go to other places besides our Earth?

I am not making myself clear. You think we are travelers.

Yes.

No, I was home when I had a feeling that something was needed. All of us who are on the ship had the same feeling: that something was needed. Pretty soon there was a ship there, and I knew the ship was going to take me some place where I could do what was needed. At that time when I boarded the ship, there were three others. We looked at each other, and we knew why this was happening, so we picked up everyone else and continued on.

Do you ever get a feeling like that about going to any other planets, or so far has it only been this planet?

I have never had such a feeling before. It wasn't that I came to your planet. Do you understand? I came to that specific place on the planet where the Nazca lines now are. I was joining others who knew of a place that had this need, and that place is where the Nazca lines now are. We all felt the need, and the ship took us to where we would do what was needed. We didn't even know the name of your planet. We just went to the place to do what we needed to do.

Okay, but I'm trying to find out whether you have done this on other planets or in other places?

I understand, and as I told you: I have never had this experience before.

Only our planet.

Well, someone else on the ship has done that (followed instinct), something that needed to be done in another place.

Okay, so we won't see the fullness of your work until our future, then?

If you are still here.

[Laughs.] On this version of Earth, yes. Well, you see, we are told that it was people in the past who scuffed up the ground and created the pictures of the Nazca lines, but that just doesn't make any sense. They can't explain it, so that is what they tell us.

We are going to have to stop. The channel is getting tired.

Can you talk in the future?

Yes, let's do this another time, and maybe someone else on the crew will speak. But the channel is losing his voice.

All right, then we will talk at another time. Have a good day.

[Laughs.] Have a good now.

SUPPORT FOR EARTH
AND ALL WHO RESIDE THERE

Andromedan Who Assisted with Nazca Lines

OCTOBER 8, 2019

Now we will talk for as long as possible, and the channel is going to do the best he can. The Nazca lines are very much like a shiatsu massage that might be done to a patient by a practitioner, but they were done for Mother Earth. Sometimes the lines appeared on the surface as shapes and would be hard to explain. One was a little bit capricious in a way, but it has a good effect, and I will tell you about that one first.

I have been tapped on the shoulder, so to speak, and perhaps it wasn't so capricious. In most places on Earth, there are spirit beings in the sky, and sometimes when the clouds go by, they take the shape of these spirit beings, which can be clearly viewed from Earth. They look like a face, a profile, a ship, or even somewhat like an Earth person or perhaps another form of life on Earth.

Over the area where the Nazca lines are, there was a face defined by the clouds that was the spirit of that area. The spirits are specifically coordinated with the energy of that exact position on Earth, and they interact with Earth to help keep it stable regardless of what goes on there.

Of course you know that with human life, and sometimes other forms of life, things are not always pleasant. The land itself needs support from above as well as providing it to Earth below. I think it is good for you to know that. There is a shape of something that looks like someone, and the lines in that shape were done in honor to invite — yes, my companion is here nodding and smiling at me — a greater participation to support Mother Earth. But other than that, all the lines are there to heighten that particular place.

Mother Earth can also tap into that energy; it goes deep into the earth. What is visible on the surface is something like a positive shadow. In this case, we are using the terms "positive" and "negative" only as photographic references. Do you understand?

Yes.

A positive shadow is what you see on the surface. Even though the lines were made on the surface, the energy goes deep within the earth and resonates with Earth's core and those who live there (and you know who does). It is also available to all places on Earth since it has gone to the planet's core. That place was chosen by our teachers, who had some knowledge and interest in Earth as a planet. These teachers are not human beings, and you know them as "wills."

Well, the Nazca lines in Peru are the most prominent on the planet. Now that we have

satellites and aerial photography, we can see that there are lines, circles, and designs all over the planet. Are they for the same purpose?

We did not do those.

Okay, who is we?

I can only speak to you about the Nazca lines because I thought you had some interest in them.

Oh, definitely I do. Can you tell me who you are?

We are from a planet not unlike yours located in the Andromeda system. You're planet is perhaps one-fourth the size of our planet. We are not human beings, but we are humanoids, and we are on average a little bit taller than you. We have two arms, two legs, and a head, so we are humanoid. For instance, you would probably not be frightened of us because we are not "weird" looking. We are just not human beings, and that's as far as I will go to describe us.

Did you personally do the Nazca lines, or did your people do it long ago?

I was involved in the process, and so was my companion. We understand you are doing a book about people who came from the future to the present.

Yes.

We are in a way — oh, I'm being told by my elder not to interfere with that. Sorry. I can't interfere with something, so apparently it is my mistake.

Light in Motion

How many years ago in our time did you make these lines and shapes?

I'm sorry, but I do not know the answer to that. I cannot tell you in terms of your time. I can only tell you in terms of our time.

Do you live a long time?

Yes, but I don't know how to put it in your time. We are not immortal, but we live a long time.

Can you ask your elder to convert it for you?

The elder refuses.

How did you make the lines there?

Oh, that was very easy. It was done with the ship that we were on. The ship is equipped to do that. It is specifically what the ship does. It is not our ship; an elder said it was loaned to us, and we have had it for a very long time. If you were to see it, you would see what looks like a tube that extends from beneath it and does not cause harm to the earth. Imagine, for a moment, looking at a dusty place and then putting a tube in your mouth and blowing into that dusty place. The dust would move around. Do you understand?

Yes.

The tube functions that way but not with air. It is light in motion. I think I hear an elder saying that Einstein might have described that a bit. But with light as motion, things are rearranged on the earth according to the way Earth would like them. This happens for Earth to accomplish what it has requested. We were there because Earth put out the request for this. Perhaps the request went out for other places on the planet and others responded to that request. I do not know, but it seems like a possibility worth exploring.

Okay, then how did you know what shapes to create on the land?

Oh, I didn't know at all, and none of the people on the ship knew. Earth knew. We had the tubes, and Earth directed the tubes with the exception of the one that I mentioned that looked like the spirit in the sky; other than that, Earth directed the pictures and designs. We had instruments on the ship, and Mother Earth coordinated it all.

This goes for all the animals and the geometric shapes as well as the very long lines that go for miles and miles?

Yes.

Last time, when someone else talked from the future, and I don't think the being was from Andromeda, the being said they created the shapes by the feeling of it, but I didn't ask how they did it. Were there some shapes there that you did not create, or did you do all of them?

All of them.

Maybe others did it in different areas, then. Did you look around Earth at that time, and if so, were there many people then?

We didn't come for the people, so I do not know.

Okay, I was just trying to get a time frame.

I understand.

Knowledge of the Lightbody

There are also a series of holes that seem to go for miles and create a pattern when seen from the sky. Did you do those too?

No.

Do you know anything about them?

I do not. Perhaps it was the others you spoke of.

Yes, it could be. Are you in the same body now that you were in when you came here in our past?

Yes.

Are you still in Andromeda?

Oh yes, of course, it is home.

Is that the constellation or the galaxy?

Galaxy.

What do you do there? Can you tell us a little bit about your life?

What do you want to know?

Are you lightbeings or physical beings?

We are physical beings, but we are in full coordination with our lightbodies, which means we are totally conscious of them. We are aware of our lightbodies when we sleep; we sleep because we are physical like you. Our lightbodies, of course, do not need to sleep. I think it is the same for you, but I'm not certain. As I understand it, we have dreams the same as you do. Then when we awake, we remember what our lightbodies have done, such as where they went and who they were with. My feeling is, and our elder is nodding (because the elder is in telepathic contact with me), your dreams have something to do with masking the knowledge of what your lightbody does.

According to the elder, who says you have been involved in some long experiment, my feeling is that at some point, you will no longer have these dreams. You will simply know what your lightbody has been doing. That will change your life completely. As you understand that, you will know the people you have been angry with or other life forms you haven't communicated with (because you didn't know you could) within a few nights of sleep. Everyone will know, and everything will change for the better.

That's wonderful. It's about time. Do you use technology, or do you use spiritual abilities to get what you need?

We find that technology must be in total coordination with matter. Our understanding of the way the ship (according to the elder, it was loaned to us a long time ago) works is in total coordination with matter, and we function that way. Our planet has natural life forms that give forth what you call fruits or vegetables, and that is what we consume. Our planet has water, and we think it is similar to the water on your planet. I can recall seeing on your planet oceans or lakes. I'm not sure which, but it appeared to be the same.

Reproductive Similarities

Do you give birth in the same way we do, or are there clones?

We do not believe in cloning. I know that some people do this. The people who do have difficulty birthing in the natural fashion. Perhaps there are civilizations — oh, are you thinking of the Zeta Reticulans?

Yes.

These civilizations were dying out because they could not conceive in the usual way. Excuse me, "the usual way" and "our way" is similar to your way. However, with us, the mother does not experience any discomfort. This wasn't working for them, so I think they clone to perpetuate their civilization. We do not need to do that.

If you live so long, how rarely are there births?

Our population has stabilized at around 40,000.

You don't have births very often, then?

Exactly.

A Purpose for Travel

Did you create all those shapes, lines, and forms at one time, or did you come back at different times?

It was in one visit.

Oh, in one visit.

Well, imagine a patient working in complete loving coordination with a nurse or some other healer. Earth was totally welcoming of our being there. Earth wanted this, so it didn't take long to do. It all happened rather quickly.

What about since then? Has she needed other alterations?

If she did, she didn't call us.

You felt a calling with the need, and you answered it?

We have a teacher who said that this is something we might find interesting and that it wouldn't keep us away from home for very long. Some of us volunteered, including me and my companion. We all said, "Okay, let's do it," but of course we said it in our own language.

[Laughs.] Can you travel from one galaxy to another, and do you travel all over the universe?

We don't go all over the universe. Generally, we will go away from home only if something like the venture to your planet is needed. To put it differently, in a way that makes sense to you, I have personally participated in two other ventures. One was with my companion and the other one was without her, and that one was a helping venture like the one for your planet.

You can't say anything about either of the two you mentioned?

Elder says no, which can only mean that it would interfere with what you are doing on Earth, or it will have something to do with what you will be doing at some point as a people. It would not be good to influence you in that way.

You really like living on your planet, then?

Everybody does, and as far as I know, no one else in our civilization has gone out more than twice on such a voyage, and many people have not gone at all.

You have 40,000 people on a big planet. Do you stay in one area, or do you have transportation to get around the planet?

We have some means to get around, but we are happy to walk, and we enjoy that. We have something that can get us around, but it's not a vehicle. It is a small version of the ship that we were on when we came to your planet. We don't need to use it very much. There are other people on the planet, and we see them from time to time.

One of the groups likes to travel around to other planets. From time to time, they pass by, and we invite them to stay and talk and eat and so on. But we are not travelers by intention; we will go for a reason, such as when we came to Earth. The other people on the planet do it because that is what they like to do, but we go only if there is a need and we are inclined to do so as individuals.

What other kinds of beings are on your planet?

Elder says you will have to request to speak to them on your own.

Who would I ask for if I did that?

I think you would ask for the beings from _____ (and you say the place). Just use descriptive terms. You can figure that out.

Welcome Love

Would you like to say something to the people who will read this before you go?

Yes, you are learning how to make friends — first with family where there is love and welcoming. This is your foundation of love and welcoming. We feel it would be good for you to take a chance with welcoming love first. Allow it to grow more often. In short, don't assume the worst.

Allow the possibility that someone as an individual or maybe a group is perhaps open and might welcome you. If you are not sure, then always go to the young people of that group. If you do, make sure that it is your young people who go. They will be more likely to be open to each other. Children in the neighborhood are inclined to play together, and the adults can learn from that. Good night.

A GLIMPSE AT EARTH'S PAST

Being Who Participated in Drawing Lines

OCTOBER 15, 2019

We were involved in what you might call the drawing of the lines. Although the lines appear on the surface, they do not fully show what is going on below. But you know this, right?

No, I didn't know that. I just read this morning that the von Däniken Foundation had a team of scientists there, and they found that the lines themselves were more electric and magnetic and that they had arsenic in them. Was this all part of the treatment for Mother Earth in creating the lines?

Arsenic is something that's used in mining. Did you know that?

No.

Image 20.2. Nazca lines, view 2

It's good to know that. It separates one thing from another. So I won't comment on that because we didn't use it. But what was the rest of your question?

There was magnetic radiation in the lines that was not in the surrounding area.

Oh yes, this is typical. It is the sort of thing that is found at crop circle sites. The emanation is because of what's underground: an energy that goes straight to the core of Earth. It's like a bolt of lightning. Lightning goes back and forth from Earth to the sky very rapidly, but if you slow it down, you will at least see the lightning go down and up once. The energy is not lightning, but I'm trying to use that as a comparison. The energy goes down into the core of the planet, and the core responds and sends it back up.

It's kind of like Earth is tuning. If you're old enough, you might remember in the past when the radio was something you had to tune carefully. Sometimes the tuning wandered, and you had to tune it back to the station you were listening to. Well, it's very much like that: Earth requested a certain amount of tuning for civilizations that would follow from those times forward, and of course that must include the Explorer Race.

But why only in that area? Is there something significant below that area, or does the fact that it went to the center of Earth mean that you could have done it anywhere on the planet?

What you just said.

So you could have done it anywhere, but you chose to do it there?

No, that's not what you said. It was the last part of what you said: because we did it there, then Mother Earth could do it anywhere.

That's not what I meant, but that's fine.

Sometimes you will say what is so because your mind is united with mine at the moment. It is that way for you at other times and will be that way for you from now on.

Earth's Artwork

So the founders live in the center of Earth; did they bounce this energy back to you?

No, it's not the founders. It's Earth herself.

Oh, Earth herself did that. All right.

It was bounced back just below the surface of Earth. I can't give you a measurement because it varies. What you see on the surface is an effect kind of like a shadow, but you also know in film there is the negative and the positive, right?

Right.

Image 20.3. Nazca lines, view 3

Okay, so it's like that but instead of a negative, it's a positive. What you see on the surface is a reaction not to something negative but to an undercurrent energy. It does not necessarily mean that everything you see on the surface is the complete picture of the pattern of the undercurrent energy. It might just be a portion of it. That's why sometimes there is an effect that resembles a dotted line or dashes or something because all complex patterns of the undercurrent energy did not totally come to the surface. At other times, the pattern you see might appear to be something that would amuse the people on Earth. Mother Earth likes to do that, but it does not represent the total pattern underneath.

There is one extremely complicated pattern of circles within a square with rectangles. It's very complex. Did that reflect more of the energy of what you sent down to the core of Earth?

No, it's just what I said before, so that gives you an idea how much more there would be. But if you dig down, you're not going to be able to find it. It's way down and by the time you get down that far, you'll be melting, so I don't recommend that.

All right, can you say how many years ago that was in our time? Where does it fit in our history?

I cannot be exact, but my best guess is hundreds of thousands of years ago. That's purely a guess; I am not an expert on your time. Our time is completely different.

Okay, do you live in the same culture now as when you did this or some place different completely?

Can you rephrase that?

You were part of the group that sent this energy down to Mother Earth, right?

Yes, I was then, but I'm a spirit now.

Oh, all right. Sometimes some of the beings have lives going on in the future. Can you say something about your life at the time you did this? Did you come here to fulfill a need, or how did you happen to come here?

Oh, it wasn't my decision. I was on the vehicle as a worker and it was announced that we would be going to this beautiful planet to help the planet do something. They didn't pass out information. I have a term: I was a "working stiff." [Laughs.]

All right.

So nobody told me anything, I was just part of the crew. The reason I have greater knowledge of it is because I am in spirit now. But at the time, I was just a regular person.

Did this ship have the necessary equipment to send this energy and do this work?

Apparently we did it.

A Gift to Farmers

Can you look into crop circles now? It occurred to me since you said that crop circles may be stimulating certain things within Mother Earth also.

No, I didn't say that. I said that crop circles would have that same or similar energy if you were to go near them. But as you say, it's possible that crop circles are similar to what was happening there at Nazca, and perhaps it's a similar situation. Perhaps Mother Earth is doing it, and maybe you are now seeing on the surface what wasn't seen in Nazca at the time we were there. If so, Mother Earth is doing it herself, so what you are feeling is energy that she allows to be distributed that way.

I don't think she's trying to create problems for farmers, but she might be trying to gift farmers a special crop if they are able to gather only that crop. Even if the crop is bent over, it will still mature and grow. My advice for them is to carefully gather that crop, but don't bother the birds because they will be spreading it everywhere. Set that crop aside. It will be very special, so use it as a seed crop. That's what I recommend.

That's very interesting.

So that is a gift to farmers.

I don't think they know that.

It would be good for them to know it, but the best you can do is put it out there and hopefully someone somewhere will read about it. Your information does get out and about.

Life on the Ship

So what was your experience on that ship? What did you do when they were sending that energy?

I was involved in navigation. I didn't navigate the ship, but I was involved in maintenance.

Can you say anything about your life at that time? Did you come from a planet, or did you live on the ship?

I had a home planet. When the ship was on a route I was able to go home now and then. When the ship was near my home, I was able to go home for a while and enjoy life there with friends and family. Then when the ship came back around again, I went back up to it. It was similar to military service on your planet, except no guns.

What did the ship do on its route? Was it a trade ship, or was its mission to help people?

We made stops in various places, but that wasn't my job, and I didn't participate in that.

Okay, then jump to another topic. Were you able to see at the time when you were above Earth in your ship whether there were any civilizations here or people or other extraterrestrials?

You are talking about that life then?

Yes, I'm sorry. I'm jumping around, but I just thought of it.

I wasn't able to see anything because I was in maintenance. We didn't have a "see out." You see, we weren't on a cruise ship out having fun; it was a job.

From the point of spirit now, can you either look or ask someone what was the condition of Earth at that time?

From the point of spirit, when the ship approached your planet, I think there were some civilizations, but there were none at Nazca. The area at that time was heavily treed, so there would have been nonhuman civilizations there. I think that's why we were very careful with what was being done: We wanted to ensure that the surface would not be disturbed. If there were civilizations, they were nonhumans — what you call animals, perhaps. They don't call themselves that nor do they think of themselves that way. They are not that. But I digress.

So that's why the work was focused underground. Then what appeared above ground eventually started to appear when the area was no longer fully treed. There were some trees, but I think the lines first started to appear at a time when it was more like something you would call a high desert. Perhaps you have something like that where you are now, where there is greenery but there's also bare ground.

Yes, we do. Well, that's interesting. So the effects on Earth didn't show up until it was okay and didn't bother the trees or animals or anything.

Yes, well said.

Wow. Can you look with your far vision or ask someone and tell me whether there were humans and civilizations on other parts of Earth?

The simple answer is yes, but it would be difficult to look now because it would stop the channeling.

All right. This is amazing. They found arsenic only in the lines on the surface of the planet, but you say it wasn't part of your operation, so I wonder how it got there?

It's a naturally occurring element on your planet, you know. People didn't dream it up.

Would it be stimulated by the effects of what you did?

I don't see how, but then I'm not a chemist. It might be to your advantage to know what the percentages are of what they found. Perhaps it is infinitesimal, and it might be useful to also know that. You learned this on a television program, is that what it is?

It is, but I was reading the book.

My best guess is that they found arsenic, but it was a small quantity. It might be interesting to know what else they found. In other words, look at the percentages of this, that, and the other thing, and oh, by the way, they found a little bit of arsenic. If it was 35 percent arsenic, then that is pretty significant, but if it was 0.00012 percent arsenic or something, it is insignificant from my point of view. That's just an example, of course. I am not a chemist.

Okay, well, it's in the book, but I'm not going to take the time now to look it up.

We're going to have to stop pretty soon.

Appreciate Each Other

Is there anything you want to say to the people who will read this?

I know you want me to say something, so I will say it from the life that I lived. Many of you have jobs like mine in which you work hard and don't get much acknowledgment. There is a sensation of unity among others doing the same job, and there tends to be a feeling of being unappreciated and invisible. On our ship, it wasn't quite like that; we were acknowledged, but we wore uniforms in different colors. I think maybe some of you are in jobs like that too, in which you wear a color and other types of workers wear a different color.

I suggest that on one day of the week, month, or year, you should include in your uniform all the colors of all the people working with you — even if it's just a patch. I think it would be good because it's important to recognize the value of other people even if they are in jobs that you don't understand. It is equally important for to recognize that there are people who maintain very important things that you need so that you can keep doing what you are doing. So appreciate each other more.

Thank you very much. Thank you.

TEOTIHUACÁN:
A STIMULATING INVITATION

Historian

OCTOBER 10, 2019

Greetings. What would you like to explore?

Well, what did you interact with when you were here?

I was never there. I am a historian, and I'm sitting in a library that has records from your time.

What would you like to talk about?

Teotihuacán, the famous Mesoamerican city located in a valley of Mexico. It's the site with the pyramids and the long highway. Can you tell us who built that and when?

A moment.

Future Teotihuacán Visitor

All right, I am here now. That was the Historian. When he looks something up, he puts a finger on that history, and then someone who was there speaks. That's how it works. This is actually what you

Image 21.1. Aerial view of Teotihuacán

wanted. We were there, and really what was going on there was a favor — [laughs] yeah, a favor. We were visiting a group of people. I'm calling them a group because they weren't, what I call, an extended family. They were people who were attempting to create something that they explained in some considerable detail. They wanted to create a unifying element on Earth because they were very sensitive people.

The people (there were several hundred) who were gathered there were people we liked to visit regularly. They were so sensitive that they could feel things that were not right in other parts of their community and on the other side of Earth. They could always feel things that weren't right. They didn't know what these things meant, and they didn't want to know. They wanted to create a peaceful environment for Earth even then, and this was thousands of years ago from your point of view. It might interest you to know that these sensitive people all came from other areas, and some were even migratory.

Now, understand that I am speaking from the future self of a person who went there back then. These people were so sensitive that it was difficult for them to get along with their own kind, so they formed this group. They were very gentle with each other and created a society not unlike many ET societies that exist in your time. That alone is pretty interesting. As a result, since we were like that ourselves, gentle and peaceful, they asked us what we could help them do. We felt it would not be too difficult, but it would create a change in your atmosphere; they knew what that meant because of telepathy. We spoke our language, and they spoke their languages. They had numerous languages, but everyone understood each other.

We said we could easily provide something that was not very obvious and could be disguised as a tree, and several of them said that was a wonderful idea, but trees don't last as long as they would like. Sometimes people do not understand that trees are meant to be left alone and not used in other ways, plus wildfire comes and goes, so at times there was fire danger. You see, fire was unknown to us as a people, and they informed us about fire on Earth.

Wow.

A Sensitive Place

The sensitive people were very unified and had all kinds of groups for certain things. They had a survival group, a wisdom group, and a food gathering group. We asked them, "What about something underground?" The wisdom group said they were concerned someone might come across it and be suspicious of it. A decision was made within the group of sensitive people that it had to be something that could be triggered by various tones, sounds, and purpose, the purpose being the most important part. That means that the people in their time, and in the times to come, would have to be sensitive like they were.

They felt that very sensitive people in all futures should come together and be able to trigger it. The sensitive people in the future would not have to speak their language or be the same culture; they would only need to be a "sensitive." The most important point was that they were aware of things like colors not usually seen by others or very slight sounds not normally heard, so the sensitive people needed to have heightened senses. We realized it would have to be sensitive people who could trigger what they wanted to build. The wisdom group wondered whether nonhumans could trigger it, and it was thought about for some time.

What if birds could come by and trigger it if they felt it would be useful? One of our members consulted the potential futures, but all we could do was a "potential futures best guess." The best guess was that the birds we were concerned about would not trigger anything and would no longer be present at some point in the future. It was decided that it still would be best to have sensitive human beings do this.

Tones and Colors

Now I will give you one of the tones. I can't give you everything, because sensitive people will just know what to do. One of the tones is C sharp. Consider that a way to define the other tones, and you can experiment. There's another system, and that is color. Some of the people suggested adding another element to unlock its capacities: to imagine colors — basically, the primary colors. One of the primary colors used was blue. You would imagine blue or literally be blue, not to the eye but as an experience. Then blow once firmly or softly,

Image 21.2. Pyramid of the Sun

whichever feels right, toward the most predominant structure. You understand what I'm talking about?

Yeah, the pyramid of the Sun.

Blow toward that and wait as long as it feels right. Then move around the wheel (one way or the other), because different colors might feel good to different people. All others do with their colors as I described for the person doing blue.

I can give you one more piece, but it involves something for a person who is a drummer and who knows the beat and rhythm of something. Make a quick three taps with sticks, drums, or whatever you choose. Just make those tapping sounds, not on the structure but near the structure. It can be as close as 10 feet, but everyone else must be as quiet as possible, not even a sneeze. It must be really quiet. If you think there will be sounds, such as a sneeze or anything similar from someone, the drummer can get as close as 7 feet. That will be sufficient, just so that the sound can be heard by the structure.

Lastly, as a unified group, make the sound of *M* (as in Mary). Make that sound, just the letter *M*, as deeply as you can in the tonal registry that you can achieve. All things should be done in the order I mentioned. You will have to play around a bit to get it right. You'll know you have it right at some point because you are all sensitive. Everyone there has to be sensitive. There cannot be even a few people who are not sensitive because it won't work. You will know that it has activated because you will feel it.

Some will feel it in their feet, some on the top of their heads, and some in other places within the body. It will not be unpleasant. It will be physical, and it will be something you feel. Of course, sensitives tend to be able to feel things that are subtle, so if the feeling gets too strong, they can step away from the structure as far as they have to. If they have to drive or walk away from the structure, then they should get as far away as needed.

The activation of this structure will have to be as strong as it is because it has to affect the whole Earth. The structure will generate a feeling of calm, peace, and joy.

A Place of Mystery

Understand that at first, the structures were not there, so several of the people in the group asked, "What can you help us make that will draw people to the area that is sturdy enough so that it will last and mysterious enough so that people will be interested?" We thought about that. We remembered a planet that we visited where the people have a most unique hobby. They have gathered ideas of mysterious things from various places they visited. They didn't pick anything up; they have seen things that were mysterious to them. They love mysteries but not to solve them, just the idea of something completely unusual or that has no apparent explanation. They love that. They created variations of those mysterious things on their home world in something similar to an outdoor museum. It was quite a site.

We got an idea for the structure from this planet's collection. That planet was so vast that we could not cover much of it. I have been there personally, and it is the most amazing site. Some of the things are just — well, you have a word. I don't know if this is an actual word: "phantasmagorical."

[Laughs.] Yes, that's a word.

It was just so unbelievable. We picked one of the sites there because it was clearly a rendition of heavy stones put together. We figured this was very strange looking and would undoubtedly attract some people. They would wonder what it was about while others might just ignore it. Many would certainly want to know, because we figured just by our interactions with the sensitive people we were visiting then that humans on your planet were naturally curious. How could people who are naturally curious ignore such a site?

We discussed it with the people there, and they loved the idea, so that's what we created. We literally re-created one of the displays on that planet. And it doesn't serve any purpose other than what I described, because it is not a landing site or any of that other business. It is exactly to invite and to stimulate; that's all.

We activated it, but over time, people forgot. I do not know what has happened. It has gone to sleep. Perhaps people were fighting, having battles or something. It is also possible that some extreme negative thing caused it to shut down. It is still functioning very well as a mystery, and it can be reactivated.

But the fact that you found this on another planet and the fact that there are three buildings on the right side of the lane or road, which are in the exact configuration of the belt of Orion, makes me ask the question: Did you do that deliberately?

Well, I know about the planet, but I don't know about the belt. Let me consult the historian. The historian says the planet we visited is Orion.

Ah. Also someone else went and measured the entire site, and you can draw circles around the buildings to imitate the orbits of the planets in our solar system.

That's interesting. We did not know that. We just reproduced the structures exactly the way they were on the planet Orion. Some day you should ask the people on that planet what it was all about.

Yes. Also one of the statements about the site said that one of those buildings had been rebuilt several times. Can you look at it now to see whether some of them have been expanded beyond what you built to start with?

I cannot discuss that. I can only discuss what I did in my life then.

All right.

Image 21.3. Temple of the Moon

Image 21.4. The dog-headed god, Quetzalcóatl

Quetzalcóatl

We have what is called the Pyramid of the Sun at one end of the road, and at the other end, we have what is called the Pyramid of the Moon. It is all attributed to a being called Quetzalcóatl. Does that have anything to do with your people?

None of that was discussed when my past self was there.

Okay, so if I looked at you, what would I see? What do you look like?

Oh, I do not look much different from your people. I'm hard-pressed to describe it, but I will say I'm a very light beige. How about that?

Okay, and how tall are you?

I am tall in your measurements. Let's see, I am 49 inches tall (about 4 feet), but I'm short for my people.

Can you tell us where your home planet is or what constellation it is in or something about where you come from?

Well, as I understand it, one has lives and past lives all over the universe. We are in, what you call, your galaxy. That's the best I can say, and I don't think we will ever meet you, at least in your current configuration. "Configuration" means your culture, but maybe things will settle down in a bit.

Are you in the culture, planet, or civilization now that you were then when you visited Earth, or are you some place else?

I'm some place else entirely. Oh, I see what you're getting at. My life then was from a planet in your solar system.

Really, which one?

Neptune.

Were you in the third dimension?

No.

What vibration were the people here on Earth you interacted with when you were here?

Like you.

You were from a higher dimension, but you were able to interact with them, is that it?

Yes, keep in mind we were on the ship and we never got off of it. It is hard to describe if you haven't had contact. Many people on your planet have had contact. All I can say is that it was possible.

You built all those pyramid structures without getting out of your ship?

We didn't build anything. We reproduced identically what was on that planet.

You reproduced them in stone?

That's how it looks on that planet. We reproduced them in the exact same material that was on that planet.

How did you do that?

I don't think you have that technology at this point in time. Is there anything on Earth that is a duplicate of something else? I think you have something that you see regularly.

What is that?

Twins.

Ah, yes.

You see, it's not so rare, and it's really easy to create duplicates of things, but the technology is not a machine.

It is spirit?

Its form is physicality, energy, desire, need, spirit, life, coordination, and influence.

Amazing. How many of you were on the ship?

Three.

Is there any way you can ask someone how long ago it was in our time?

Historian is shaking his head. Mysteries are meant to be mysterious.

Belonging

Okay, I have been asked not to let the channel go too long. Is the channel comfortable?

It would be best to finish.

Can you look at the people on the planet now, and do you have anything to say them, the readers?

I cannot see them now, but I will say this: In my experience and travels from "this" and "that" community (I have traveled extensively in your galaxy), the range of individuality is fairly fixed for human beings, and there are many human cultures all over this galaxy. We are a variation of that too, so if you were to see us, you would think, "Oh what town are you from?" In short, we look like you. I recommend that you look at each other and decide really how foreign others are. What do they have that is so very different from you?

In short, appreciate and love variety, and if you can, embrace the sensitive people among you. But if you can't for some reason or another, then help them get united with others who are sensitive people. Help them to go where they need to go and do what they need to do on their own basis, which means to do what they feel.

Also keep in mind that if you find these people difficult to get along with, they just might be able to help you do many wonderful things. Certainly it will help some of you to feel that you belong for the first time.

Good night.

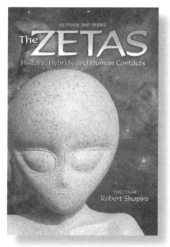

Light Technology PUBLISHING *Presents*

TO ORDER PRINT BOOKS
Visit LightTechnology.com, Call 928-526-1345 or 1-800-450-0985,
or Check Amazon.com or Your Favorite Bookstore

THE EXPLORER RACE SERIES

ZOOSH AND HIS FRIENDS THROUGH ROBERT SHAPIRO

The series: Humans — creators in training — have a purpose and destiny so heartwarmingly, profoundly glorious that it is almost unbelievable from our present dimensional perspective. Humans are great lightbeings from beyond this creation gaining experience in dense physicality. This truth about the great human genetic experiment of the Explorer Race and the mechanics of creation is being revealed by Zoosh and his friends through superchannel Robert Shapiro. These books read like adventure stories as we follow the clues from this creation to the Council of Creators and beyond.

① THE EXPLORER RACE

You are truly a result of the genetic experiment on Earth. You are beings who uphold the principles of the Explorer Race. The key to empowerment in these days is not to know everything about your past but to know what will help you now. You are constantly given responsibilities by the Creator that would normally be things Creator would do. The responsibility and destiny of the Explorer Race is not only to explore but to create.
ISBN 978-0-929385-38-9 • Softcover • 608 PP. • $25.00

② ETs and the EXPLORER RACE

Robert channels Joopah, a Zeta Reticulan now in the ninth dimension who continues the story of the great experiment — the Explorer Race — from the perspective of his civilization. The Zetas would have been humanity's future selves had humanity not re-created the past and changed the future.
ISBN 978-0-929385-79-2 • Softcover • 240 PP. • $14.95

③ ORIGINS and the NEXT 50 YEARS

This volume is a treasure trove of information about who we are and where we came from: the source of male and female beings, the war of the sexes, the beginning of the linear mind, feelings, the origin of souls, and more. There is also a section that relates to our near future — how the rise of global corporations and politics affects our future, how to use benevolent magic as a force of creation, and how we will go out to the stars and affect other civilizations.
ISBN 978-0-929385-95-2 • Softcover • 384 PP. • $14.95

④ CREATORS and FRIENDS, the MECHANICS of CREATION

Now it is necessary to remind you of where you came from, the true magnificence of your being. You must understand that you are creators in training, and you were once a portion of Creator. This book allows you to understand the vaster qualities and help you remember the nature of the desires that drive any creator, the responsibilities to which a creator must answer, the reaction a creator must have to consequences, and the ultimate reward for any creator.
ISBN 978-1-891824-01-2 • Softcover • 480 PP. • $19.95

⑤ PARTICLE PERSONALITIES

All around you in every moment, you are surrounded by the most magical and mystical beings. They are too small for you to see individually, but in groups, you know them as the physical matter of your daily life. These particles might be considered either atoms or portions of atoms who consciously view the vast spectrum of reality yet also have a sense of personal memory like your own linear memory. Some of the particles we hear from are Gold, Mountain Lion, Liquid Light, Uranium, the Great Pyramid's Capstone, This Orb's Boundary, Ice, and Ninth-Dimensional Fire.
ISBN 978-0-929385-97-6 • Softcover • 256 PP. • $14.95

TO ORDER PRINT BOOKS
Visit LightTechnology.com, Call 928-526-1345 or 1-800-450-0985,
or Check Amazon.com or Your Favorite Bookstore

THE EXPLORER RACE SERIES

Zoosh and His Friends through Robert Shapiro

⑥ EXPLORER RACE and BEYOND

With a better idea of how creation works, we go back to the Creator's advisors and receive deeper and more profound explanations of the roots of the Explorer Race. The Liquid Domain and the Double Diamond Portal share lessons given to the roots on their way to meet the Creator of this universe, and the roots speak of their origins and their incomprehensibly long journey here.
ISBN 978-1-891824-06-7 • Softcover • 384 pp. • $14.95

⑦ COUNCIL of CREATORS

The thirteen core members of the Council of Creators discuss their adventures in coming to awareness of themselves and their journeys on the way to the council on this level. They discuss the advice and oversight they offer to all creators, including the Creator of this local universe. These beings are wise, witty, and joyous, and their stories of love's creation create an expansion of our concepts as we realize that we live in an expanded, multiple-level reality.
ISBN 978-1-891824-13-5 • Softcover • 288 pp. • $14.95

⑧ EXPLORER RACE and ISIS

This is an amazing book! It has priestess training, shamanic training, Isis's adventures with Explorer Race beings — before Earth and on Earth — and an incredibly expanded explanation of the dynamics of the Explorer Race. Isis is the prototypal loving, nurturing, guiding feminine being, the focus of feminine energy. She has the ability to expand limited thinking without making people with limited beliefs feel uncomfortable. She is a fantastic storyteller, and all of her stories are teaching stories. If you care about who you are, why you are here, where you are going, and what life is all about, pick up this book. You won't put it down until you are through, and then you will want more.
ISBN 978-1-891824-11-1 • Softcover • 352 pp. • $14.95

⑨ EXPLORER RACE and JESUS

The core personality of that being known on Earth as Jesus, along with his students and friends, describes with clarity and love his life and teaching 2,000 years ago. He states that his teaching is for all people of all races in all countries. Jesus announces here for the first time that he and two others, Buddha and Mohammed, will return to Earth from their place of being in the near future, and a fourth being, a child already born now on Earth, will become a teacher and prepare humanity for their return. This text is so heartwarming and interesting, you won't want to put it down.
ISBN 978-1-891824-14-2 • Softcover • 352 pp. • $16.95

⑩ EARTH HISTORY and LOST CIVILIZATIONS

Speaks of Many Truths and Zoosh, through Robert Shapiro, explain that planet Earth, the only water planet in this solar system, is on loan from Sirius as a home and school for humanity, the Explorer Race. Earth's recorded history goes back only a few thousand years, its archaeological history a few thousand more. This book opens up as if a light is on in the darkness, and we see the incredible panorama of brave souls coming from other planets to settle on different parts of Earth. We watch the origins of tribal groups and the rise and fall of civilizations, and we can begin to understand the source of the wondrous diversity of plants, animals, and humans that we enjoy here on beautiful Mother Earth.
ISBN 978-1-891824-20-3 • Softcover • 336 pp. • $14.95

THROUGH ROBERT SHAPIRO

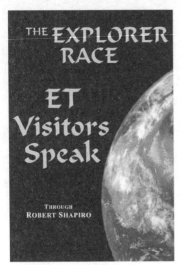

ET Visitors Speak, Volume 1
Explorer Race Book 11

Even as you search the sky for extraterrestrials and their spaceships, ETs are here on planet Earth. They are stranded, visiting, exploring, studying culture, healing Earth of trauma (brought on by irresponsible activities such as mining), or researching the history of Christianity over the past 2,000 years.

Some are in human guise. Some are in spirit form. Some look like what we call animals, as they come from the species' home planet and interact with their fellow beings that we have labeled cats or cows or elephants. Some are brilliant cosmic mathematicians with a wonderful sense of humor and presently living here as penguins. Some are fledgling diplomats training for future postings on Earth when we will have ET embassies here.

In this book, these fascinating beings share their thoughts, origins, and purposes for being here.

$14.95 • Softcover • 352 PP.
978-1-891824-28-9

ET Visitors Speak, Volume 2
Explorer Race Book 15

For those of you who've always wanted to meet somebody completely different, here's your opportunity. This book contains the continuing adventures of visitors to planet Earth. In a strange sense, you might include yourself as one of them, as the human race does not really claim the title of full-time and permanent Earth citizens.

When you read this book, think about it as if you were visiting another planet. What would you say in reaction to the local population about their habits and so on? Put yourself in the picture so that this isn't just a meaningless travel log from various beings you don't know and may never meet.

Make it personal this time, because the time is coming when you might just be one of those extraterrestrials on another planet. So you might as well practice now and get your lines down right.

$19.95 • Softcover • 512 PP.
978-1-891824-78-4

THROUGH ROBERT SHAPIRO

$9.95 • Softcover • 216 PP.
978-1-891824-26-5

Techniques for Generating Safety
Explorer Race Book 12

The opportunity to change the way you live is not only close at hand but also with you right now. Some of you have felt a change in the air, as you say, the winds of change. Sometimes you can almost taste it or smell it or feel it. And other times it is ephemeral, hard to grasp.

It is the ephemeral quality that can help you to know that the good thing that is out of your reach has to do with the future timeline. The future timeline is also an experience line. It is a sensation line. It is associated with the way your physical body communicates to you and others. It is a way of increasing your sensitivity to your needs and others' needs in a completely safe and protected way so that you can respond more quickly and accurately to those needs and appreciate the quality of life around you, much of which you miss because the old timeline discourages you from observing.

Animal Souls Speak
Explorer Race Book 13

A New Way of Interacting with Animals

"The animal world will speak, if you prefer, through elders. This has certain advantages, since that way they can include knowledge and wisdom to a degree — not to a vast degree, but to a degree — about their home planets."

— Grandfather

"Welcome to the footsteps of the loving beings who support you, who wish to reveal more about themselves to you, and who welcome you not only to planet Earth but, more specifically, to the pathway of self-discovery. Take note as you read this book of what resonates with and what stimulates your memories."

— Creator's Emissary

$29.95 • Softcover • 640 PP.
978-1-891824-50-0

Light Technology PUBLISHING *Presents*

THROUGH ROBERT SHAPIRO

$29.95 • Softcover • 704 PP.
978-1-891824-81-4

Astrology
Explorer Race Book 14

The planets and signs of astrology share not only **LONG-LOST INFORMATION** but also **NEW WAYS OF BEING** for an awakening humanity.

Astrology and astronomy are one. The heart is astrology; the mind is astronomy. But you would not separate your heart from your mind, would you?

This book honors that pursuit of the lost heart. It demonstrates the personality of the planets, the Sun, the Moon, and the signs. This is what has been missing in astrology ever since the heart was set aside in favor of the mind. Over time, such knowledge and wisdom was lost. This book brings all that back. This is not to abandon the knowledge and wisdom they have now but to truly include, to show, to demonstrate, to provide to those seeking astrological knowledge and wisdom, and to provide the heart elements of personality.

Plant Souls Speak
Explorer Race Book 16

Planet Energies Available to You:
Live Plant 100% • Dead Plant 10%

"It is always better to interact with the plant and its energies in its live form, but you need to know how.

"The intention of this book is to reveal that formula so that you can stop searching, as a human race, for the magical cures to diseases by exhausting the supply of life forms around you when a much simpler process is available. The beings in this book will not just comment on things you know about but show you what you are missing in your interaction with plants."

— Dandelion

Each plant brings a wondrous gift to share with humanity; enjoy it!

$24.95 • Softcover • 576 PP.
978-1-891824-74-6

♆ *Light Technology* PUBLISHING *Presents*

THROUGH ROBERT SHAPIRO

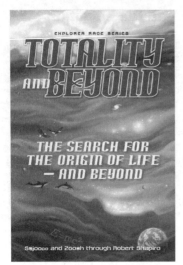

$24.95 • Softcover • 416 PP.
978-1-891824-75-3

Totality and Beyond
Explorer Race Book 20

"For you to function in a world of responsibilities well beyond your physical life, you need to be able to understand the functionality of creation and the confidence you need in simply emerging from seemingly nothing. 'Nothing' is not really zero. Nothing is a matrix available to create something. It will always be that, and it has always been that.

"This book will explain, with a wide variety of points of view at times, those points, and over the next few hundred years, you can consider them as you blend with your total being, creating and re-creating what is now in order to bring it to a more benevolent state of being."

— Ssjoooo

....

Steps on the Path of Transformation, Volume 1
Explorer Race Book 23

"As you read this material, this is what to keep in mind: Your path might be completely different from what this book attempts to show you. So when you read this material, don't think, 'I can't possibly do that.' Rather, think about what is familiar to you.

"You will experience times when you have read a page or two and something feels as if it resonates within you, creating in you a sense of familiarity. This tells you that this book is about transformation.

"See whether the book — with all the words, letters, symbols, and numbers — can trigger a dream, a vision, or a moment of inspiration in you that helps to bring about a better life for you and those around you.

"Good luck, and good life in this pursuit."

— Isis

STEPS ON THE PATH OF
transformation
Volume 1

$19.95 • Softcover • 320 PP.
978-1-62233-045-4

THROUGH ROBERT SHAPIRO

ETs on Earth, Volume 1
Explorer Race Book 18

This book explores the ET phenomenon with chapters on the blue spiral light over Norway, crop circles, and much more.
$16.95 • Softcover • 352 PP.
978-1-891824-91-3

ETs on Earth, Volume 2
Explorer Race Book 21

Read about who the beings in UFOs are in this fun and gentle reminder that ETs are just friends from another "neighborhood."
$16.95 • Softcover • 416 PP.
978-1-62233-003-4

ETs on Earth, Volume 3
Explorer Race Book 22

Many of you are ready to welcome ETs. In this book, you will find many reminders of who you might have been or might become in other lives.
$16.95 • Softcover • 352 PP.
978-1-62233-044-7

ETs from UFO Casebook's Best Pictures Speak
Explorer Race Book 25

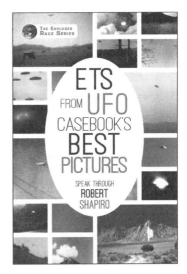

"This book is for those who are interested in things that are new, different, exciting, or mysterious. Perhaps you will discover your likes and dislikes are not only associated with Earth and your personality, family, and friends. Some of it might actually be associated with your extraterrestrial roots!

"All of you on Earth, all you human beings, have extraterrestrial roots. If you trace the Earth-human DNA back far enough, it goes to other planets. The reason you're not aware of this or able to prove it scientifically in published papers is that what little is known about this on your planet is largely kept secret.

"As you read these pages, you will discover that your brothers, sisters, cousins, aunties, uncles, friends, and relations are not only on Earth. They are on other planets too."
— Zoosh

$16.95 • Softcover • 320 PP.
978-1-62233-058-4

THROUGH ROBERT SHAPIRO

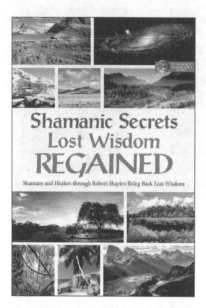

Shamanic Secrets: Lost Wisdom Regained

Due to wars, natural disasters, a shaman not being able to train a successor, and many other reasons, Isis (through Robert) says that 95 percent of the accumulated shamanic wisdom has been lost. Now it is important to regain this wisdom as young people who are able to learn and use these processes are being born now.

Beings who lived as shamans and healers on Earth at various times now speak through Robert Shapiro and bring these lost teachings and techniques to a humanity waking up and discovering it has the talents and abilities to use this wisdom for the benefit of all.

$16.95 • Softcover • 352 PP. • ISBN 978-1-62233-049-2

Shamanic Secrets for Material Mastery
Explore the heart and soul connection between humans and Mother Earth. Through that intimacy, miracles of healing and expanded awareness can flourish.
$19.95 • Softcover • 528 PP.
978-1-891824-12-8

Shamanic Secrets for Physical Mastery
The purpose of this book is to explain the sacred nature of the physical body and some of the magnificent gifts it offers.
$25.00 • Softcover • 608 PP.
978-1-891824-29-6

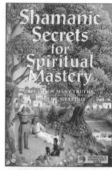

Shamanic Secrets for Spiritual Mastery
Spiritual mastery is the underpinnings of multiple ways of being, understanding, appreciating, and interacting in harmony with your world.
$29.95 • Softcover • 768 PP.
978-1-891824-58-6

⚜ *Light Technology* PUBLISHING *Presents*   291

TO ORDER PRINT BOOKS
Visit LightTechnology.com, Call 928-526-1345 or 1-800-450-0985,
or Check Amazon.com or Your Favorite Bookstore

BY LYSSA ROYAL-HOLT

Galactic Heritage Cards

THE FIRST AND ONLY OF THEIR KIND:
This 108-card divination system, based
on material from Lyssa Royal-Holt's
groundbreaking book *The Prism of
Lyra*, is **designed to help you tap into
your star lineage and karmic patterns**
while revealing lessons brought to
Earth from the stars and how those
lessons can be used in your life on
Earth now. Includes a 156-page book of
instruction and additional information.

Illustrations by David Cow • 108 cards (2.75 x 4.5 inches)
156-page softcover book (4.5 x 5.5 inches) • $34.95 • 978-1-891824-88-3

Preparing for Contact
In this book, you will take an
inner journey through your
own psyche and discover a
whole new dimension to your
unexplained experiences.
$16.95 • Softcover • 320 PP.
978-1-891824-90-6

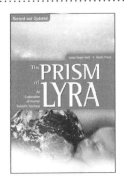

The Prism of Lyra
This text explores the idea
that collective humanoid
consciousness created this
universe for specific purposes.
$16.95 • Softcover • 192 PP.
978-1-891824-87-6

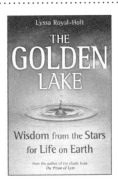

The Golden Lake
This book features Pleiadian
and Sirian awakening teachings
that together provide a road
map for the next phase of
human evolution — the
integration of polarity
and the awakening of our
consciousness beyond duality.
$19.95 • Softcover • 240 PP.
978-1-62233-070-6

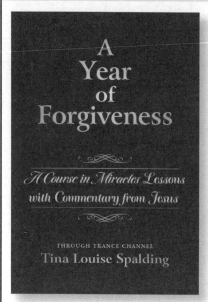

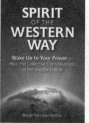
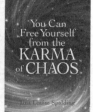

☿ *Light Technology* PUBLISHING *Presents*   293

TO ORDER PRINT BOOKS
Visit LightTechnology.com, Call 928-526-1345 or 1-800-450-0985,
or Check Amazon.com or Your Favorite Bookstore

Amiya's Encyclopedia of Healing through Cathy Chapman

Trauma and PTSD

Resolve the Pain to Recover Your Life

Amma's Healing Friends, known as Amiya, take you through a process so simple that all you need to do is read as you allow the release of all that is not you. What is not you? The pain, the horror, the fear, the rage, and even the energy of those who harmed you that are trapped within you — none of those things are who you are.

Know that you deserve complete healing, and accept that healing. You can have your life back again.

$25.00 • Softcover • 512 PP. • 978-1-62233-080-5

Reclaim Your Sexuality

How to Heal from the Words, Actions, and Beliefs That Deny Who You Are

Sexuality is integral to who you are, and when someone damages that, it damages your energy field. In this book, we will work at strengthening and healing your energy field so that you become comfortable with how you choose to express your sexuality.

We will show you how to dismantle the energies of non-acceptance for who you are. We will also discuss how your sexuality influences every part of your life.

$25.00 • Softcover • 368 PP. • 978-1-62233-082-9

BOOKS THROUGH DRUNVALO MELCHIZEDEK

THE ANCIENT SECRET OF THE FLOWER OF LIFE, VOLUME 1

Also available in Spanish as *Antiguo Secreto Flor de la Vida, Volumen 1*

Once, all life in the universe knew the Flower of Life as the creation pattern, the geometrical design leading us into and out of physical existence. Then from a very high state of consciousness, we fell into darkness, and the secret was hidden for thousands of years, encoded in the cells of all life.

$25.00 • 240 PP. • Softcover • ISBN 978-1-891824-17-3

THE ANCIENT SECRET OF THE FLOWER OF LIFE, VOLUME 2

Also available in Spanish as *Antiguo Secreto Flor de la Vida, Volumen 2*

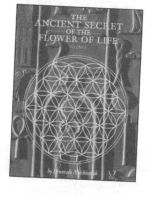

Drunvalo shares the instructions for the Mer-Ka-Ba meditation, step-by-step techniques for the re-creation of the energy field of the evolved human, which is the key to ascension and the next dimensional world. If done from love, this ancient process of breathing prana opens up for us a world of tantalizing possibility in this dimension, from protective powers to the healing of oneself, others, and even the planet.

$25.00 • 272 PP. • Softcover • ISBN 978-1-891824-21-0

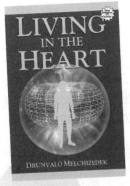

Includes
Heart
Meditation CD

LIVING IN THE HEART

Also available in Spanish as *Viviendo en el Corazón*

Long ago we humans used a form of communication and sensing that did not involve the brain in any way; rather, it came from a sacred place within our hearts. What good would it do to find this place again in a world where the greatest religion is science and the logic of the mind? Don't I know this world where emotions and feelings are second-class citizens? Yes, I do. But my teachers have asked me to remind you who you really are. You are more than a human being, much more. Within your heart is a place, a sacred place, where the world can literally be remade through conscious cocreation. If you give me permission, I will show you what has been shown to me.

— Drunvalo Melchizedek

$25.00 • 144 PP. • Softcover • ISBN 978-1-891824-43-2

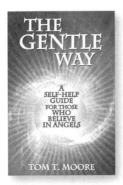

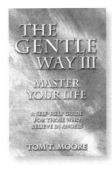

BOOKS THROUGH DAVID K. MILLER

Arcturians: How to Heal, Ascend, and Help Planet Earth
Included here are new interpretations of the Kaballistic Tree of Life, which has been expanded to embrace 5D planetary healing methods.
$16.95 • Softcover • 352 PP.
978-1-62233-002-7

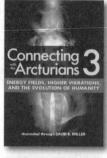

Connecting with the Arcturians, Volume 3
With hopeful, helpful, and healing messages, the Arcturians integrate physics with spirituality to provide personal and planetary thoughts on preparing for our future and for the ascension.
$17.95 • Softcover • 272 PP.
978-1-62233-063-8

Biorelativity
Biorelativity describes telepathic communication between humans and the spirit of Earth. The goal is to influence the outcome of natural events, such as volcanoes and earthquakes.
$16.95 • Softcover • 352 PP.
978-1-891824-98-2

Expand Your Consciousness
Humankind must develop higher consciousness to heal itself and to experience life more meaningfully. Explore the fascinating multidimensionality that is yours for the taking.
$16.95 • Softcover. • 288 PP.
978-1-62233-036-2

Connecting with the Arcturians
Many have talked about the ascension process, but few really understand what it means. This book answers all the common ascension questions.
$17.00 • Softcover • 256 PP.
978-1-891824-94-4

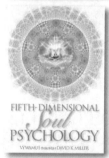

Fifth-Dimensional Soul Psychology
In a series of lectures from Vywamus, explore the meaning and usefulness of soul psychology and how it relates to modern psychology.
$16.95 • Softcover • 288 PP.
978-1-62233-016-4

Connecting with the Arcturians, Volume 2
This follow-up to the popular first volume contains the most updated information on personal and planetary healing and ascension.
$16.95 • Softcover • 288 PP.
978-1-62233-052-2

Kaballah and the Ascension
The author explains how studying the Kaballah allows for a unique understanding of the concept of higher consciousness.
$16.95 • Softcover • 176 PP.
978-1-891824-82-1

TO ORDER PRINT BOOKS
Visit LightTechnology.com, Call 928-526-1345 or 1-800-450-0985,
or Check Amazon.com or Your Favorite Bookstore

BOOKS THROUGH DAVID K. MILLER

New Spiritual Technology for the Fifth-Dimensional Earth

Information is featured about native ceremonies to connect to Earth healing energies, thought projections, and thought communication.
$19.95 • Softcover • 240 PP.
978-1-891824-79-1

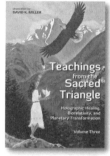

Teachings from the Sacred Triangle, Volume 3

Learn how to use holographic technology to project energies in the most direct and transformative way throughout Earth.
$16.95 • Softcover • 288 PP.
978-1-891824-23-4

Raising the Spiritual Light Quotient

The spiritual light quotient, one's ability to understand spiritual concepts, is similar to the intelligence quotient (IQ) test. Learn how to raise your SLQ.
$16.95 • Softcover • 384 PP.
978-1-891824-89-0

A New Tree of Life for Planetary Ascension
WITH MORDECHAI YASHIN

David Miller has teamed up with Torah expert Mordechai Yashin to provide a unique, expanded perspective on the Tree of Life.
$16.95 • Softcover • 336 PP.
978-1-62233-012-6

Teachings from the Sacred Triangle, Volume 1

This book offers an understanding of the soul, soul evolution, and how the human species is advancing toward the next evolutionary step.
$16.95 • Softcover • 272 PP.
978-1-62233-007-2

Enseñanzas del Sagrado Triángulo Arcturiano

Los capitulos incluyen:
• Los Principios de la Biorelatividad
• La Conciencia y Conexiones de Grupo
• La Estructura Etérea de la Tierra
$19.95 • 416 páginas
978-1-62233-264-9

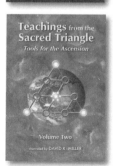

Teachings from the Sacred Triangle, Volume 2

The teachings continue in this second volume of the *Sacred Triangle* series, focusing on the importance of energy bridges.
$16.95 • Softcover • 288 PP.
978-1-891824-19-7

David K. Miller has an extensive background in psychology and psychotherapy. After thirty-five years of conventional practice, David now focuses exclusively on soul psychology. He has developed several therapy techniques, penned many articles, and authored several books. David is also the founder of the international meditation group known as the Group of Forty. To learn more, go to GroupofForty.com.

❡ *Light Technology* PUBLISHING *Presents*

TO ORDER PRINT BOOKS
Visit LightTechnology.com, Call 928-526-1345 or 1-800-450-0985,
or Check Amazon.com or Your Favorite Bookstore

DR. JOSHUA DAVID STONE'S

EASY-TO-READ ENCYCLOPEDIA OF THE SPIRITUAL PATH

1
The Complete Ascension Manual: How to Achieve Ascension in This Lifetime
Stone weaves research and intuitive information together in this exploration of self-realization.
$14.95 • Softcover • 320 PP.
ISBN 978-0-929385-55-6

2
Soul Psychology: Keys to Ascension
There are thousands of self-help books on psychology and relationships, but few integrate the soul and spirit like this one.
$14.95 • Softcover • 272 PP.
ISBN 978-0-929385-56-3

3
Beyond Ascension: How to Complete the Seven Levels of Initiation
Incredible new channeled material completely demystifies the seven levels of initiation.
$14.95 • Softcover • 320 PP.
ISBN 978-0-929385-73-0

4
Hidden Mysteries: ETs, Ancient Mystery Schools & Ascension This book contains a wealth of information on esoteric teachings of recently founded religions.
$14.95 • Softcover • 384 PP.
ISBN 978-0-929385-57-0

5
The Ascended Masters Light the Way: Beacons of Ascension
This book contains guidance from the saints and spiritual masters of all the religions that have graced this planet.
$14.95 • Softcover • 288 PP.
ISBN 978-0-929385-58-7

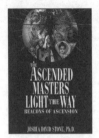

6
Cosmic Ascension: Your Cosmic Map Home
In our extraordinary time, there is a new opening and potential to begin our cosmic ascension process.
$14.95 • Softcover • 288 PP.
ISBN 978-0-929385-99-0

7
A Beginner's Guide to the Path of Ascension
This volume covers the basics of ascension clearly and completely.
$14.95 • Softcover 192 PP.
ISBN 978-1-891824-02-9

8
Golden Keys to Ascension and Healing
This volume represents the wisdom of the ascended masters condensed into concise keys that serve as a spiritual guide.
$14.95 • Softcover • 256 PP.
ISBN 978-1-891824-03-6

All Our Books Are Also Available as eBooks from Amazon, Apple iTunes, Google Play, Barnes & Noble, and Kobo.

DR. JOSHUA DAVID STONE'S
EASY-TO-READ ENCYCLOPEDIA OF THE SPIRITUAL PATH

9
Manual for Planetary Leadership
This book lays out, in an orderly and clear fashion, the guidelines for leadership in the world and in your own life.
$14.95 • Softcover • 320 PP.
ISBN 978-1-891824-05-0

10
Your Ascension Mission
In this book, Dr. Stone shows how each person's puzzle piece is just as vital and necessary as any other.
$14.95 • Softcover • 288 PP.
ISBN 978-1-891824-09-8

11
Revelations of a Melchizedek Initiate
This book traces the author's journey of ascension through the seven levels of initiation.
$14.95 • Softcover • 336 PP.
ISBN 978-1-891824-10-4

12
How to Teach Ascension Classes
This book serves as an ideal foundation for teaching ascension classes and leading workshops.
$14.95 • Softcover • 160 PP.
ISBN 978-1-891824-15-9

13
Ascension and Romantic Relationships
Dr. Stone explores relationships from the perspective of the soul and monad — not just the personality.
$14.95 • Softcover • 224 PP.
ISBN 978-1-891824-16-6

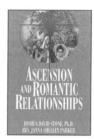

14
Complete Ascension Index
This companion volume to the Encyclopedia of the Spiritual Path series will allow you easier access to the techniques and wisdom of Dr. Stone.
$14.95 • Softcover • 288 PP.
ISBN 978-1-891824-30-2

15
How to Be Financially Successful
This book is like no other in the financial field because it is a holistic approach for life study rather than just another book about money.
$14.95 • Softcover • 256 PP.
ISBN 978-1-891824-55-5

SPECIAL
All 15 Books for
$149.95
plus shipping

BOOKS THROUGH Jaap van Etten

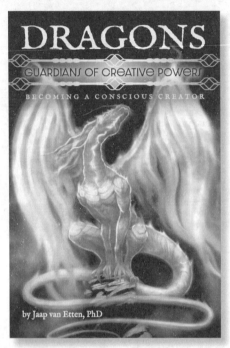

$19.95 • Softcover • 352 PP. • 6 x 9
978-1-62233-066-9

DRAGONS
GUARDIANS OF CREATIVE POWERS

BECOMING A CONSCIOUS CREATOR

The elemental (fire, water, air, and earth) powers are the basis of all creation. Understanding the different aspects of these creative powers will help you to become a conscious creator.

Guardians are connected with every aspect of the elemental powers. They are known as dragons; however, different traditions use different names for them, such as angels or nature spirits. They are among the strongest allies we can ask for.

This book offers information to help you reconnect with these creative powers and their guardian dragons. Through this connection, you will become a conscious creator and change your life in ways that lead to success, joy, happiness, and abundance. Thereby, you will contribute optimally to the creation of a new world.

Birth of a New Consciousness: Dialogues with the Sidhe
$16.95 • 192 PP.
978-1-62233-033-1

The Gifts of Mother Earth
$16.95 • 256 PP.
978-1-891824-86-9

Crystal Skulls: Expand Your Consciousness
$25.00 • 256 PP.
978-1-62233-000-3

Crystal Skulls: Interacting with a Phenomenon
$19.95 • 240 PP.
978-1-891824-64-7

LITTLE ANGEL SERIES BY LEIA STINNETT

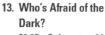

1. All My Angel Friends (Coloring Book)
$10.95 • Softcover • 64 PP.
978-0-929385-80-8

2. The Angel Told Me to Tell You Good-Bye
$6.95 • Softcover • 64 PP.
978-0-929385-84-6

3. Animal Tales: Spiritual Lessons from Our Animal Friends
$7.95 • Softcover • 96 PP.
978-0-929385-96-9

4. The Bridge between Two Worlds
$6.95 • Softcover • 64 PP.
978-0-929385-85-3

5. A Circle of Angels (Workbook)
$18.95 • Softcover • 112 PP.
978-0-929385-87-7

6. Color Me One
$6.95 • Softcover • 64 PP.
978-0-929385-82-2

7. Just Lighten Up! (Coloring Book)
$9.95 • Softcover • 48 PP.
978-0-929385-64-8

8. The Little Angel Who Could Not Fly
$9.95 • Softcover • 64 PP.
978-1-62233-025-6

9. One Red Rose
$6.95 • Softcover • 64 PP.
978-0-929385-83-9

10. Principles and Applications of the Twelve Universal Laws
$18.95 • Softcover • 128 PP.
978-0-929385-81-5

11. When the Earth Was New
$6.95 • Softcover • 64 PP.
978-0-929385-91-4

12. Where Is God?
$6.95 • Softcover • 64 PP.
978-0-929385-90-7

13. Who's Afraid of the Dark?
$6.95 • Softcover • 64 PP.
978-0-929385-89-1

14. Exploring the Chakras
$6.95 • Softcover • 64 PP.
978-0-929385-86-0

15. Crystals R for Kids
$6.95 • Softcover • 64 PP.
978-0-929385-92-1

16. Happy Feet
$6.95 • Softcover • 64 PP.
978-0-929385-88-4